America's Dilemma in Asia:
The Case of South Korea

About the author

Harold Hakwon Sunoo is the Eugene M. Frank Professor of Political Science and Chairman of the Department of History and Political Science at Central Methodist College in Fayette, Missouri. He has been editor-in-chief of the *Korea Herald* in Seoul, visiting professor of Asian Studies at New York University, City College, and editor of the *Korean Christian Scholars Journal* published in the United States. He is the author of *Japanese Militarism: Past and Present* (Nelson-Hall, 1976), *Repressive State and Resisting Church: The Politics of the CIA in South Korea* (Korean-American Cultural Association, 1976), *Korea: A Political History in Modern Times* (Kunkook University Press, 1970), and *A Korean Grammar* (Oriental Institute of Czechoslovakia, 1952). He served from 1976-1978 as president of the Association of Korean Christian Scholars in North America.

Other Books by Harold Hakwon Sunoo

America's Dilemma in Asia:

The Case of South Korea

Harold
Hakwon Sunoo

Nelson-Hall nh Chicago

This book is dedicated to those friends and associates who are committed to bringing about democracy and a peaceful unification of Korea.

Library of Congress Cataloging in Publication Data

Sŏnu, Hak-wŏn.
  America's dilemma in Asia.

  Bibliography: p.
  Includes index.
    1. Korea—Politics and government—1948-
  2. Korea—Relations (general) with the United
  ,States. 3. United States—Relations (general) with
  Korea. I. Title.
  DS917.35.S66   309.1'519'04   78-24029
  ISBN 0-88229-357-5

Manufactured in the United States of America

10 9 8 7 6 5 4 3 2 1

contents

preface

This book is designed to present existing contradictions of political stability and social tensions of South Korea, and the role the United States played in Korea during the past thirty years. Since the liberation of South Korea from Japan in 1945, she has been supported by the United States. Even with a new direction of the Carter administration, the United States' policy to support President Park Chung Hee's dictatorial regime has not been changed.

U.S. policy in Asia seeks political stability. Political stability requires a modernization of society that brings changes in man's social outlook, attitude, and lifestyle. U.S. policy seeks to influence Asian people by seeking economic development; clearly, a significant factor in national development. However, it is not the only factor which dominates the life of a people. U.S. policy, in seeking to influence the Asian people through economic development, paid minimum attention to political and social development. Therefore, rather than stabilizing the transitional societies in Asia, U.S. policy has resulted in weakening these societies.

Let us take South Korea as an example. U.S. policy in Korea seeks political stability. Korea will not be a stable society unless it is modernized. Korea will be neither a democratic society nor a modernized one without becoming a unified nation. There will be no stability without a government which governs fairly and democratically. There will be no peace in East Asia without a unified Korea. These are simple factors we must not forget when we talk about stability in Asia.

President Park Chung Hee's dictatorial regime in South Korea is protected by both internal and external elements. Internally, a traditional political culture, involving authoritarian Confucian values, and a legitimacy rooted in the landowning class supports the dictatorial regime. Externally the United States and Japan support these traditional authoritarian values and systems. They apparently found something in common with the dictatorial regimes of Syngman Rhee and Park Chung Hee. The values explain common aspects of the American, Japanese, Rhee, and Park regimes; the structure of legitimacy explains the persistence of these values across the transitions between regimes, i.e. the interests served by the various regimes have been the same.

U.S. policy, in supporting regimes that serve traditional economic interests, has supported not only traditional political values over modern democratic values, but also prevented balanced and equitable economic development. The result has been the persistence of traditional political and economic structures, as well as traditional values.

This has resulted in socio-political and cultural conflicts, evidenced by indigenous movements for independence, unification and democracy, and economic instability exemplified by rising debt, an expanding vagrant class, stagnant agricultural productivity, and increased dependence on foreign support.

The United Nations, under the leadership of the United States, was to have achieved democratization, modernization, and unification of Korea when the U.N. entered the Korean War in 1950. President Park Chung Hee promised to achieve three main objectives when he took over the government through a military coup on May 16, 1961: modernization, democratization, and unification of the country. It has now become obvious to the world that none of the three goals can be achieved through his regime.

President Park claimed that the Armed Forces was the only stable organization which retained the people's respect, and that the military services only were capable and cohesive enough to take remedial action for the welfare of the nation. They were self-claimed patriots who promised to bring about democracy and freedom for the people. The military regime stressed the temporary nature of their rule. The temporary suspension of democratic government in the Republic of Korea was not to imply the permanent destruction of democratic principles. The leaders of Park's military regime pledged that they would establish a constitutional government as soon as possible. They have mouthed similar promises three times and revised the constitution three times during the sixteen years of rule by President Park and his associates. None of these pledges has been fulfilled. The government of the United States, from Harry S.

Truman to Jimmy Carter, has given almost unconditional support to the dictatorial regime. South Korea is still under martial law. No Korean is allowed to speak to any foreigner under Presidential Decree Nine.

U.S. policy seeks stability in Korea, but has created an unstable condition; it endorses democratic principles, but has supported dictatorial regimes for thirty years; it promotes unification of the nation, but supports a two-Korea policy at the U.N.; it promises modernization, but finances a few selected monopolists.

The American government policy is that any anti-communist political leader is worth supporting as long as he is in power to control that nation. Under such policy, President Park's best possible maneuver to receive support from the United States is to be that strong anti-communist leader. As we are witnessing today, President Park's consistent anti-communist policy has been rewarded and supported by U.S. military and economic support.

President Jimmy Carter, according to his statement at a press conference on June 30, 1977, made a decision to have full diplomatic relations with China. He expressed the hope that the governments of China and Taiwan "can work out the differences between them." Why can't the Carter administration follow a similar pattern in regard to the Korean problem? SEATO (Southeast Asia Treaty Organization) has been recently disbanded, stating that its existence is meaningless as an anti-communist organization. Supporting President Park as an anti-communist leader of South Korea is equally anachronistic.

This book is an attempt to present these contradictory phenomena in South Korea and how the United States is involved in the situation. The author's single purpose in this book is to start a new dialogue with an open mind with the Korean people. Korea should not be omitted from the new direction of the U.S. policy in Asia under the leadership of President Jimmy Carter.

I want to thank my children: Jan and his wife, Brenda, Cooke and his wife, Elaine, for their inspiration and help. Jan read the chapters on the Korean War and Unification, and has given me many insightful comments. I thank my wife, Sonia, for her tireless support of my works and constant companionship in our journey into the search for truth.

I also would like to thank the staff members, particularly the editorial department, of Nelson-Hall Company for their invaluable assistance in preparing this book for publication, just as they have helped me in my previous book, *Japanese Militarism*.

For errors of fact or interpretation, I assume full responsibility.

1 Introduction

In the spring of 1975, with the end of United States involvement in Indochina and the withdrawal of most of the U.S. forces from Thailand, American attention switched to Korea. Meanwhile, President Park Chung Hee of South Korea has taken this opportunity to prolong his power indefinitely with the expectation of continued support from the U.S. government.

South Korea, the only country where American military forces are stationed in the Asian mainland since the collapse of the South Vietnamese government, has suddenly become "more important to the United States than South Vietnam."[1] This view is, indeed, somewhat perplexing in view of the past American official position including the historical remark by Secretary of State Dean Acheson and the Joint Chiefs of Staff prior to the Korean action.[2]

The Korean and Vietnam military actions proved conclusively that the American public will not support involvement in a land war on the Asian mainland. Yet, much opposition was expressed when President Jimmy Carter announced the eventual withdrawal of American ground troops from South Korea. The withdrawal, however, does not include all American troops. The U.S. Army will retain Honest Johns and other weapons capable of firing either conventional or nuclear warheads, and the U.S. Air Force also retains its nuclear capability.[3]

The withdrawal of ground troops alone actually does not reduce American involvement in South Korea,[4] in spite of continuous debate on the issue among the members of the U.S. Congress.[5]

On March 29, 1977, the Department of Defense submitted to Congress a military construction authorization bill for FY1978 totaling $3.6 billion, including $27,518,000 in South Korea. The Pentagon requested $13.6 million for military construction in South Korea for the current fiscal year. At the same time, it announced that the objective of the proposed new construction is to strengthen and improve the combat readiness capabilities of land, sea, and air forces, wherever they may be stationed, and provide them with the modern facilities required to support our personnel and the advanced weapons with which they are equipped.[6]

The global strategy of American militarism is not dead. It grows together with the dictatorial powers abroad, whose survival depends on U.S. support. The Pentagon spends much of its $110 billion-a-year budget in direct procurement at home. As the military budget has climbed, the Pentagon has had greater and greater influence upon U.S. foreign policy, upon domestic policy, and upon the educational, health, and environmental institutions of the U.S. It has become, perhaps, the strongest independent power in world affairs. The military-industrial complex is, indeed, here to stay.

When President Carter announced his decision not to continue with the deployment of the B-1 bomber, congressional leaders of the Republican party and many supporters of the B-1 bomber pronounced their opposition to the decision.[7] Each B-1 bomber would cost about $100 million, and it is understandable why President Carter hesitates to engage in such an expensive project at this time. The Sentinel defense system of ballistic missiles has been an expensive one, probably costing $100 billion, but essentially the nation is no better defended than before.

Not counting the Korean and Vietnam wars, the United States has deployed its military forces for political purposes abroad in at least 215 incidents since the end of World War II, according to a recent study by the Brookings Institution.[8] Among them, we have had what we called the "Berlin Blockade" and in Cuba the catastrophe of the Bay of Pigs and the "Cuban missile crisis" of October, 1962. Comparing these incidents with the Korean and Vietnam wars, which were matters of fairly free choices by the U.S. and thus avoidable, we can easily conclude that both the "Berlin Blockade" and the Cuban missile crisis of 1962 helped to improve the two superpowers' relationships. If so, there may be in these contrasting events a lesson in how and where the United States and the USSR can best compete for military domination.

In view of the dominating influence upon foreign dictators like President Park Chung Hee by American generals, and their influences upon American domestic policies, we wonder whether the traditional system of checks and balances will be strong enough to assure continued civilian control over the ever-expanding influence of the military in American society and government.

The Carter administration, in an action designed to dramatize its commitment to human rights, has recommended cuts in foreign military aid to Argentina, Uruguay, and Ethiopia because of concern that those nations are abusing their citizens' rights. The treatment of political prisoners is an issue in all three countries, whose governments are military-dominated. The South Korean situation is no different from these countries. Yet, Secretary of State Cyrus Vance told a Senate Appropriations Subcommittee that the Carter administration has decided not to cut aid to South Korea. Vance said, "We believe it would be a mistake to cut the required economic assistance, despite the fact that we have a deep concern regarding the human rights situation in South Korea."[9]

It is difficult to follow American logic. As it stands now, it seems all right for a dictatorial regime to violate human rights in a country which the U.S. government considers strategically important for U.S. national interests, but it is not all right to violate human rights in places like Ethiopia. It is also difficult to distinguish between President Carter's new morals-based foreign policy and the previous administration's national-security-oriented foreign policy. For instance, Secretary of State Henry Kissinger of the Ford administration testifying before a Senate Appropriations Subcommittee was asked by Senator Edward W. Brooke on July 24, 1974, how the administration justified continual aid to countries like South Korea, which is a police state. Secretary Kissinger replied that the administration "decided to authorize economic and military assistance even when we would not recommend the action of the government of South Korea."[10] He made it very clear that the American government is willing to support the South Korean regime because of South Korea's strategic position.[11] He deliberately avoided mention of either the welfare of the people or the security of Korea itself. "Where we believe the national interest is at stake we proceed even when we don't approve of a country's policies," said Secretary Kissinger at the hearing.

Taking advantage of America's unconditional support of the regime, President Park has continued his oppressive policy against Korean democratic forces in South Korea. A representative of Amnesty International, who visited Seoul to investigate conditions, reported that South Korea holds approximately 1,100 political prisoners charged with or convicted of "political crimes" as a result of President Park's desire for total autocratic and totalitarian power. The report states that prisoners have been tortured, held incommunicado for long periods and denied the right to call witnesses on their behalf.[12]

Professor Edwin O. Reischauer of Harvard University, former U.S. Ambassador to Japan, stated that the American government should cut back on aid to South Korea and withdraw troops because of continuing repressive policies of President Park. At a joint meeting of the two House Foreign Affairs Subcommittees, Professor Reischauer argued that he had always supported continued presence of American troops and aid in Korea because it was more strategically located than South Vietnam, for instance. But the professor argued that recent events had eroded popular will in South Korea and alienated the important intellectual community from the government.

Referring to the acts of President Park during the first six months of 1974, which systematically sought to eradicate all criticism or protest against his dictatorial regime, more than forty American church leaders and educators stated, "The injustice and inhumanity of these sentences against students, intellectuals, and religious leaders, and the detention of outstanding democratic political leaders calls for international protests in the name of humanity and human rights. We call on the United States to distance itself promptly from the oppressive acts against the people of Korea which the government of President Park has carried out (supported by U.S. arms) and to use its influence for the restoration of participatory government in Korea."[13]

It became evident to many that the American government has now violated earlier policies of the Truman administration in 1950. Secretary of State Dean Acheson said: "United States aid, both military and economic, to the Republic of Korea has been predicated upon the existence and growth of democratic institutions within the Republic."[14]

The Park regime of South Korea does not even remotely resemble such a state. On December 6, 1971, President Park declared a "State of National Emergency" in response to the changing situation in Asia, particularly, the admission of the People's Republic of China into the United Nations. The proclamation stated, "All social unrest that risks the national security will not be tolerated and every citizen must be prepared to concede some freedoms he enjoys for the sake of national security." This concept of an artificially created "national emergency" and national security is much like the idea advocated by Dr. Henry Kissinger. President Park has claimed that the deprivation of freedom and democracy is necessary because of the threat from North Korea. Were there any visible threats recently from North Korea? Contrary to Park's claims, according to the Department of Defense in Washington, incursions into the DMZ in 1971 and 1972, during the period before the declaration of martial law by President Park, numbered but one incident in 1972, as compared with 829 incidents in 1967.[15]

Secretary of Defense James Schlesinger, knowing of all these events, advised the Senate Appropriations Subcommittee on Foreign Operations that military aid to the Republic of Korea was urgent "for the prevention of war" and was an "indispensable condition for the North-South dialogue." The Ford administration had asked a total of $24.5 million for security assistance to the Republic of Korea for the current fiscal year of 1975. Such military and economic aid for South Korea continues even under the Carter administration.

Present U.S. policy in South Korea is not only a violation of the spirit of the Truman-Acheson administration's commitment, but also violates the U.S. Foreign Aid Act. Section 32 of the current U.S. Foreign Aid Act states: "It is the sense of Congress that the President should deny any economic and military assistance to the government of any foreign country which practices the internment or imprisonment of that country's citizens for political purpose."[16]

The United States at this time in history should at least determine not to continue as a cold war warrior in world affairs. It is an anachronistic policy. Can the United States afford to have generals dictate U.S. policy in South Korea as they did in the past?[17] Professor Hans Morgenthau suggests that a nuclear war would destroy the meaning of life even for the survivors.[18] Today the danger of the use of nuclear weapons by the U.S. may be greater in Korea than anywhere else in the world. James Schlesinger, when he was Secretary of Defense in the Ford administration, declared the possibility of such a nuclear war while he was visiting South Korea and shocked the world. Armed with hundreds of nuclear weapons and poised at the DMZ in Korea, U.S. troops constitute a potential tripwire for nuclear war, even without a threat from the American Secretary of Defense.

American policy-makers should never forget the dimension of moral horror and the resentment that white men should think again of Asians as targets for the testing of the latest nuclear weapons. To use these weapons on helpless people, as was done with non-nuclear weapons in Vietnam, might bring about some immediate military victories, but it would be a moral and political disaster, as we have already experienced in Indochina.

American historical claims as defenders of freedom and democracy could not be sustained in such a catastrophe; the United States would be condemned as the world's most hated power.

The desire of the Korean people for independence has been denied.[19] The U.S. government is still supporting the dictatorial regime which denies economic justice and modernization, social justice and human dignity. The Park regime creates an economy completely dependent upon foreign capital and based on the heavy sacrifices of underpaid workers.[20] The American government has spent more than $37 billion of American taxpayers' money, and continues military and economic aid to the Korean dictator, yet the stability that the U.S. seeks and the democracy the Korean people desire are farther away from them than ever. The U.S. must find ways to reduce tensions and to limit the danger of nuclear war under the existing conditions. It also must seek radical disarmament and other alternatives to violence in Asia, particularly in Korea.

2 Korea Under Japan's Domination

Japan annexed Korea in 1910 after two major wars: one against China, 1894–95; the other against Russia, 1904–05. Japan's domination of Korea ended when she surrendered to the Allied powers in September, 1945. The Korean people experienced much agony and suffering during those thirty-six years under Japanese imperialism.

There are about 50 million people who inhabit an area of 220,845 square kilometers, comparable to the size of South Carolina and Georgia combined. Korea is one of those rare countries that may be called homogenous in the sense that it possesses a common language and a cultural background which dates back to 2000 B.C. The language, a branch of the Ural-altaic family, is one of the most systematic and scientific phonetic languages in the world today. To be sure, however, it is as different from Chinese and Japanese as English is from German or French. The Koreans are from Mongoloid stock; many of them are tall and robust and have a lighter and fairer complexion and more regular features than other members of the Mongol family.

The mountainous peninsula of Korea juts out like the handle of a pot from the Asian continent and lies in the straits between Japan and China. To the north on the mainland it is separated from Manchuria by the Yalu River and the White Head Mountain, and a small northeastern tip of the border lies adjacent to the Maritime Province of the Soviet Union. The Yalu River is economically important as a source of hydroelectric power. It was in the Manchurian hills across from this river that Kim Il-sung, at the age of nineteen in 1931, started a "Korean Patriots' Band" with eighty men and eventually organized the "Autonomous Korean government" of five counties. There are still more than a million Koreans living in the Manchurian area of new China.

Geographically, Korea is in about the same latitude as South Carolina and Georgia, and has a humid subtropical climate. It has a temperature range of 12 degrees below zero to 32 degrees above zero centigrade.

During the Japanese occupation, Korea was predominantly a land of farmers. Agriculture comprised slightly less than half of the total value of production while forestry, fishing, mining, and industry made up the remainder. The farm lands were concentrated in the south while industries were in the north, close to the natural resources of coal and iron ore and other rich mineral deposits.

Relatively little was known of this tiny country, once called the "Hermit Kingdom of the Far East," until the latter part of the past century. Its natural resources and strategic position as springboard to the continent were to provide keen interest to the imperialist Czarist Russia, Japan, China, and Western powers. Korea became a primary factor in the Sino-Japanese War of 1894 and the Russo-Japanese War of 1904. From the very first conflict, Korea was catapulted into the arena of intra-imperialist intrigues and struggles, and fell a victim to imperialism's inevitable and insatiable drive for markets and cheap resources. The Russo-Japanese War definitely established Japan as the sole power in the Far East and, flush with victory, she then proceeded without moral qualms to annex Korea formally as a colony. All these imperialistic activities of Japan were fully supported by the United States through the Taft-Katsura Agreement.

In 1945, after thirty-six years of Japanese rule—rule not altogether without sporadic uprisings and harassments, especially on the border regions—Korea was liberated by the entrance of the Soviet Army from the north and American troops from the south. The days of slave servitude to Japanese imperialism had ended.

Japanese imperialism began in Korea with the treaty of 1876, the first which Korea ever negotiated with a modern power. According to this treaty, Korea was recognized as an independent and sovereign state, and Japan received the right of extra-territoriality which in turn gave her the first impetus for territorial ambitions on the Asian continent. In 1894-95, the Sino-Japanese War was fought in which Japan defeated China and simultaneously exerted increasing influence in Korea.

The year after this war, Japan found another rival force interested in Korea, namely, Czarist Russia. The Japanese government suggested that Russia should have special interests in Manchuria and she in Korea; however, Czarist Russia refused to accept these propositions, insisting that she should enjoy privileges in Manchuria and Japan in South Korea with North Korea as a neutral zone. No agreement was reached and war finally broke out in 1904 between the two nations.

Japan fought the war with British and American backing while Russia had French backing. President Theodore Roosevelt cooperated as much as possible in forcing Russia out of Manchuria where American financiers had some commercial interests.

Meanwhile, the British government revived the Anglo-Japanese Alliance in which she recognized Japan's "paramount political, military and economic interests in Korea" and further, granted "the right of Japan as she may deem proper and necessary to safeguard and advance those interests always." The United States was the unsigned partner to this revised treaty when President Theodore Roosevelt sent his secretary of war, William Howard Taft, to Tokyo to negotiate a secret agreement with Japan. The result was that the United States approved of Japan's "suzerainty over Korea," while Japan promised not to take any aggressive action against the Philippines. It became quite obvious that both Great Britain and the United States betrayed Korea and violated the Anglo-Korean and the American-Korean treaties.

As a result of her defeat, Russia was forced to recognize Japan's sphere of influence in Korea through the Portsmouth Treaty which stated "The Imperial Russian Government . . . engages neither to obstruct nor interfere with the measures of guidance, protection and control which the imperial government of Japan may find necessary to take in Korea."

Therefore, the road to Korea was thrown open to Japan, abetted by the major world powers. At that time the Korean government was not aware of the situation nor of the threat of domination by Japan. In March, 1904, Marquis Ito, chairman of the Japanese privy council, arrived in Korea to hold a conference with the emperor. Marquis Ito emphasized to higher officers of the government that the Koreans must learn from the Japanese, the pioneer of the new civilization in the Far East, and advocated the promotion of cooperation between the two nations. After Ito returned, the emperor of Korea dispatched a special envoy, Yi-Siyong, to Japan on behalf of good relations. However, the Japanese had a different plan for Korea.

A few months later, in the agreements of July and August, 1904, the Korean government was forced "to accept a Japanese financial adviser and to consult the Japanese government on all matters affecting foreign affairs." Japanese advisers on police, judicial and military matters followed shortly. In April, 1905, the Korean postal, telegraph and telephone services were taken over by Japan.

The conclusion of the Portsmouth Treaty further enhanced Japan's position in Korea. In November, 1905, Marquis Ito arrived at the Korean capital to present new demands which amounted to the virtual establishment of a Japanese protectorate over Korea. The Korean emperor and ministers refused to sign the new treaty at first, but when Japanese soldiers were placed around the palace with machine guns and the Korean Prime Minister was dragged out of the conference hall by Japanese officers, the government was forced to accept the terms. The protectorate was established and Marquis Ito assumed the post of Resident-General of Korea in February 1906.

The Korean emperor sent a secret mission to the President of the United States, requesting aid on the basis of the American-Korean Treaty. The result was a foregone conclusion: President Theodore Roosevelt ignored the appeal and tacitly approved of Japan's actions.[1]

Japan's imperialist designs on Korea culminated in 1910 when she annexed Korea as a territory of the Japanese Empire. The pretext was the assassination of Prince Ito (promoted from Marquis) in 1909. According to the Japanese, ungrateful Koreans killed Ito in Harbin (Manchuria) and Japan did not really desire annexation but was forced to take this measure because of Korean opposition to the reforms instituted by Japan.

Prior to Japanese annexation in 1910, Korean society was based on an "Asiatic" mode of production in the agricultural slavery system. There were no such groups as the European medieval handicraftsmen in Korea, and the isolated families and tribes-people still had remnants of the feudal domestic handicraft which provided them the necessary and semi-primitive articles. Consequently, there was no real source for the accumulation of capital. The transformation from feudalism into capitalism accelerated when the Japanese capitalists invaded Korea.

Japanese capitalism emerged at the end of the Tokugawa period as the "Meiji Restoration" which was characterized, in contrast to the development in Europe, by a compromise of feudal elements with the rising mercantile class. Industries underwent rapid development, while agriculture remained basically semi-feudal. Characteristic of Japanese capitalism was the strong influence of militarism, which was necessitated by Japan's late entrance into the field of world competition when the other major powers were already entrenched in their colonies and markets.

Korea, one of the backward nations in Asia at that time, was an object of envious interest to Japanese capitalists, but the matter was not so simple because of the close relationship between Korea and China; moreover, other nations had set their eyes on Korea. Consequently, Japan followed the technique of the Western powers in insisting upon opening trade in Korea.

In January, 1874, the militaristic Meiji government had commissioned Count Okubo to investigate the "Korean problem" and secretly planned to pursue a policy of eventually conquering Korea. The treaty of 1876 was the opening wedge for the penetration of Japanese capital into Korea. The Japanese "colonial system" in Korea provided good profits in rice, soy beans and agricultural grains, so much so that capital investments in Korea were given priority because of the decided advantage in exploiting colonial people.

The economy of Korea, as of China and most of the other countries of Asia, is founded on land and agriculture; for this reason, Japan's control over Korean land, especially farm land, meant control over Korea's economic livelihood. Likewise, it also meant economic chaos for the Korean peasants who comprised nearly 85 to 90 percent of the population in 1910.

Because of this fact, the Japanese tried to control the cultivated land through the government, semi-governmental organizations and through individuals. In 1942, of the 4,600,000 jungbo (one jungbo equals 2.45 acres) of cultivated Korean farming land, about 424,000 jungbo were owned by Japanese, excluding the big companies. In addition, about 80 percent of the cultivated land was owned through semi-governmental agencies, especially by the Water Utilization Association, the Village Monetary Association, the Oriental Development Company and the Bank of Korean Colonization.

Under Japanese administration, Korean farmers were forced to submit to the demands of Japanese imperialism without the benefit of any aid or protection from the Japanese government. Korean landlords, on the other hand, received encouragement and support, and they became the co-workers and appeasers of Japanese aggression in Korea. Thus, Korea's rural economy was placed wholly at the disposal of the Japanese, leaving the farmers in a tragic economic condition. In fact, since the Japanese annexation of Korea, the agrarian economy was in such a chaotic state that about 10,000 middle-class Korean farmers were forced into bankruptcy, while tenant farming increased by 15,000 families a year.

In 1945, at the time of the Allied occupation in Korea, the class composition of the rural population was as follows:[2]

Class	No. of Households	Percentage
Landlord	87,026	3.0
Self-farming	442,621	15.4
Semi-tenant	729,431	25.1
Tenant	1,641,702	56.5
Total	2,900,780	100.0

More than two and a half million (2,572,229) or 60 percent of the total cultivated acreage of the 4,475,326 acres was tenant land, and the remaining 40 percent was self-farmed.

Japanese landlords concentrated more in the southern part of Korea than the northern area since there were more rice fields in the south. For instance, by 1931, Japanese landlords held about 90 percent of rice fields in North Jolla Province, while they held about 70 percent of the same in South Jolla.

The following table gives a bird's eye view of Japanese concentration on land purchasing at different parts of Korea during the ten-year period from 1922 to 1931.[3]

Starting with fifty landlords in 1910, the number increased to about 7,000 in 1915, bringing the average acres down to about thirty jungbo. The majority of them were medium-sized farmers. The big landlords, having more than one thousand jungbo, numbered thirty-seven,[4] outnumbering the number of big landlords in Japan proper. There were only twenty-two big landlords in Japan who had more than one thousand jungbo. As a whole, Japanese landlords held about 80 percent of the cultivated land in Korea, and about 70 percent of them were in fertile rice fields.

How did the Japanese manage to own so much in such a short time? There have been no disputes among scholars as far as the number of Japanese holding Korean land. All these statistics were published by the Japanese government. There have been disputes, however, among the scholars on the method used by the Japanese for acquiring land.

The apologists of Japanese imperialism explained that Korea had been waiting for the "enlightened" policy of Japanese imperialism. Sending Japanese citizens to Korea, therefore, was supposed to be good for the Korean as well as for the Japanese.

A leading Japanese economist, Fukuda Tokujo, wrote a series in the Japanese periodical *Naikai Roncho* for three consecutive months beginning in November, 1904, after his brief visit to Korea in 1902. In his articles, Professor Fukuda observed that Korea was about a thousand years behind Japan. He compared the 19th century Korea with the Fujiwara Era (the 8th century to 11th century) in Japan. As a learned scholar, he should have known that the characteristics of the Fujiwara Era were not present in Korea. Korea was a feudalistic society, unlike the Fujiwara Era which was ruled by one family. There were intrigues and conflicts for leadership of the family, but the Fujiwara never needed a united front with another family to rule Japan.

Distribution of Japanese Possessions of Land in Korea

Area	1922		1925		1929		1931	
	No. of Landlords	Jungbo	No. of Landlords	Jungbo	No. of Landlords	Jungbo	No. of Landlords	Jungbo
1. Kyonggi	19	8,107.8	35	7,527.0	33	8,282.8	29	8,368
2. No. Tsung-tsong	2	525.3	3	320.2	2	375.9	3	475
3. So. Tsung-tsong	23	6,616.2	65	7,909.4	30	5,889.3	24	7,812
4. No. Jolla	30	20,617.9	66	26,566.1	98	32,027.4	64	32,439
5. So. Jolla	24	18,871.0	182	33,308.7	158	34,967.4	73	30,560
6. No. Kyong-sang	4	1,698.6	30	3,896.2	4	1,887.8	11	2,747
7. So. Kyong-sang	11	4,212.9	34	9,207.1	33	5,669.3	27	9,463
8. Whang-hae	12	17,434.7	41	19,432.7	48	29,111.0	30	23,613
9. Kang-won	6	3,912.0	8	2,432.0	27	7,804.8	10	6,908
10. So. Pyong-an	7	2,973.2	5	1,255.9	15	1,744.9	8	1,962
11. No. Pyong-an	3	1,507.9	6	5,692.1	6	5,140.7	10	6,420
12. So. Ham-gyong	1	32.9	3	106.6	15	762.1	5	622
13. No. Ham-gyong	1	270.0	—	—	1	58:3	4	642
TOTAL	143	86,780.4	478	117,654.0	470	133,721.7	298	132,031

Another characteristic of Japan society under the Fujiwara was the rise of feudalism with its *shoen* system. Privately owned lands which were not subjected to periodical redistribution constituted *shoen*. These were similar to the manors of European feudalism. Small farmers in the country did not receive proper protection from the imperial government as the central government was weak. They saw little advantage in paying taxes to a government which could not protect them. The large tax-exempt estates held by powerful nobles or warrior chiefs provided the answer to their problem; a small farmer could put his land under the warrior chief's estate and escape the payment of heavy taxes. The farmer, of course, worked the land as before, paying a fee which was less than the tax for this privilege. As a result, the farmer gained a powerful protector, and the warrior chiefs expanded their powers in their regions. The practice required military power and from it came the development of a military class. All this happened before Kamakura Bakufu. None of these features existed in 19th century Korea.

Professor Fukuda claimed that in Korea there was no sense of land ownership by the people. In fact, there were no owners of land. The only landowners were the royal family. The people merely entertained a vague sense of common ownership of land.

Although the majority of the people did not own land, it did not mean they had no sense of ownership. Nor were the landowners necessarily of the royal family; many were feudalistic landlords. Professor Fukuda misunderstood the Korean system. His theme was that Korea, being a pre-feudalistic society, was incapable of developing by itself and Japan, therefore, should develop Korea for her.

Professor Fukuda and his successors were more than willing to cooperate with the Japanese government to promote the chauvinistic interpretation of history in order to support Japanese imperialism. His theory was supported by many Japanese scholars, including Yokada Hiroshi, Sujuki Takeo, Moritani Katsume and others.[5]

A recent study reveals that there were several basic methods of acquiring land that Japanese landlords employed in Korea. Asada, in his *Japanese Imperialism and Old Colonial Landlord System*, listed four methods: 1. Japanese used Korean names or bribed Korean officials who made it possible to register land in their names; 2. lending base as a semi-permanent lease type; 3. making official contact without having the buyer's name appear in the contracting papers; 4. double entry of selling papers and mortgage papers, and many similar underhanded schemes.[6]

Evidently the Japanese had no difficulty in buying Korean farmlands even before Japan annexed Korea, in spite of the law prohibiting such action. The purpose of buying Korean farmland was not all for the farming. Many Japanese landlords rarely operated the farms directly. They leased the farmlands to Korean tenants, usually to those Koreans who helped them to buy the land.

As soon as Japan annexed Korea, tricks and bribery were no longer needed. Now the Japanese government-general openly promoted Japanese acquisition of Korean land. Although the attractions were there, most Japanese farmers were not about to leave their homes to go to a strange land to start a new life.

Two groups of people were most attracted: the big landlords and the merchants. The low price of Korean farmland attracted big Japanese landlords while the opportunity to earn high profits in a short time attracted merchant groups.

The choice land near the Kunsan area cost no more than fifteen to twenty yen per jungbo, the second choice between ten to fifteen yen, third choice was ten yen or less. Of course, dry fields were much cheaper. These prices as compared to the Japanese rice lands were less than one-tenth to one-thirteenth.[7] It became evident to the big Japanese landlords that acquiring Korean farmland made good business sense to them; besides, all their investments were well protected by the Japanese government.

Three private groups, a well-known Mitsibishi Zaibatsu, Okura, and Shibuzawa, were active participants in purchasing Korean farmland. Mitsubishi's Higashiyama farm and Shibuzawa's Chosen Kogyo Company were outstanding examples. Shibuzawa, for example, held 16,000 jungbo in 1936, employing 20,000 tenants. As far as the Japanese government was concerned, Japanese immigration to Korea was too slow in spite of all the activities of the big landlords.

The majority of Japanese immigrant farmers owned less than ten jungbo, and their investments were a little over one thousand yen just prior to the annexation in 1910. The following table indicates the situation in Korea at that time.[8]

In order to speed up mass immigration to Korea from Japan, the government-general needed further attractions for Japanese immigrants. The government-general undertook the most infamous land-grabbing project ever witnessed in any colonial policy in history.

During Terauchi and Hasegawa's administration from 1910 to 1919, the government-general of Korea set up the notorious "Bureau of Temporary Land Investigation" which surveyed all the lands and made a definite

Japanese Landlords in Korea, Dec. 1909

Amount invested	No.	Total owned acreage (Jungbo)	Acreage per individual	Total amount invested	Investment per individual
100,000 or more	21	28,964	1,379	4,881,415	232,448
50,000 or more	27	14,033	519	1,810,935	67,072
10,000 or more	90	11,754	130	1,874,240	20,825
5,000 or more	67	2,435	36	473,143	7,062
Less than 5,000	545	5,076	9	630,177	1,156
Total	750	62,262	83	9,669,910	12,893

land demarcation in Korea. The government spent a large sum for the project. The survey classified land into either state-owned or private-owned, the state-owned land being public land, uncultivated fields or private land for which no claim was established at the time of land registration. Through this project the government became the biggest landlord.[9] This act proved unreasonable because a large majority of the farmers who did not understand the Japanese language failed to register their land and land which was not registered in a given period could not be claimed by them. In this way, many farmers lost much of their land.

In addition to this survey, the establishment of the Oriental Development Company brought another tragedy to Korean farmers. This semi-official company became the second largest landlord next to the government. With the government's support, the company successfully confiscated in 1926 the richest land in Korea, amounting to more than ninety thousand jungbo. Most of the land was used to support Japanese immigrants in Korea. In other words, the government financed the company to acquire the land from Koreans so it could turn it over to Japanese immigrants. This basic policy, using Korea as the rice bowl of Japan, was essential to Japanese imperialism.

The following statistics show the progress of the company's land grabbing in Korea.[10]

1910	11,035	jungbo
1912	48,037	"
1913	64,860	"
1916	73,382	"
1921	85,554	"
1926	90,462	"
1927	89,450	"

Thus, the Oriental Development Company played an important role in Japanese Colonial Policy in Korea.

Korean farmers were attacked on two sides. On one side was the colonial policy, such as the land survey and the Oriental Development Company; the other attack came from Japanese merchants. They were ordinary merchants. They were out to snatch Korean purses as quickly as possible. The most effective way to achieve this goal was to engage in the pawnshop business. Through the pawnshops, much of the land was stolen indirectly as compared with the direct methods described above.

The usual interest rate was between 6 to 10 percent per month, and most of the borrowers used the money for emergencies, such as arranging parents' funerals or children's weddings. There was no way they could return the borrowed funds on time. In some cases, when the borrowers returned the principal, the lender made excuses to refuse it.[11] Although land was cheap as discussed earlier, Japanese lenders knew that they could grab it at one-third the normal price if they used pawnshops, and they did.

Most farmers needed cash to buy grains to sustain themselves between May and September. While working their farms, they could not sell their labor for extra cash. Especially when the farmers needed to buy tools and fertilizers, there was no way they could get money, except at pawnshops. They mortgaged their farmland and borrowed cash to buy necessities to maintain their farming. Among borrowers, 80 to 90 percent were never able to return their borrowed money. Thus, they lost their farm land.[12]

It was no wonder then that there were so many Japanese pawnshops in Korea. In 1905, fifty-nine out of seventy-four Japanese residents in Kaesong City engaged in the pawnshop business, while there were forty-three in Seoul and twelve in Intsun.

Thus, the Japanese used many tricks to acquire land from Korean farmers, and the exploitation intensified with time.

It was never the intention of the imperialists to improve the lot of the natives. Their job was to exploit the people. Many students of Korean history attempt to bring to the fore the improvements Japan made in Korea. They claim that the infamous land survey was to distinguish the private and public properties. It is true that the private property system of modern capitalism was introduced through the land survey. They claim that farmland has been improved, irrigation systems have been initiated, cultivated land acreage has increased, domestic cattle encouraged, and the silkworm industry promoted, etc.

What they don't tell us, however, is that the Japanese imperialists destroyed the existing irrigation system and set up a new system for big landlords. There were 3,735 lakes and 9,386 ponds throughout the country before the irrigation system was introduced in 1917. As soon as the irrigation system was introduced by the government, farmers suffered directly and indirectly.[13] The production of rice increased, but Koreans consumed less rice than before because of the official price controls. Rice was needed in Japan. Ever since the famous rice riot in Japan in 1919, the Japanese government has had to import about five million bushels of rice a year. The Japanese population, increasing by nearly a million, did not help the situation.

The following table indicates the comparative situation of rice production and rice consumption in Korea.[14] As rice production increased, the Korean consumption decreased since rice was being exported to Japan.

Date	Rice Production Average Per Year	Export to Japan	Korean Consumption Per Person
1916 1920	14,101,000	2,196,000	0.6858
1921 1925	14,501,000	4,342,000	0.6858
1926 1930	15,799,000	6,607,000	0.4963
1931 1934	16,782,000	8,456,000	0.4059

Increasing rice production was not meant to improve the economic situation of the Korean farmer, but rather to supply Japan. Korean farmers who submitted to the policy of the Japanese and changed the dry fields to paddy fields were put to great expense and labor; furthermore they were not protected by the government.

As soon as Governor-General Saito took office in 1919, he announced great plans and hopes for increasing rice production in Korea for Japan. His "enlightened policy" is the story behind this rice production. His plan was to improve existing rice fields, to change dry fields to rice fields, and to cultivate more new lands, amounting to 800,000 jungbo in thirty years. Thus, he established a new "land improvement section" in the Bureau of Colonization under his direction to carry out his policy.

The policy was destined to fail because it hurt the people. When Japan increased its own rice production, as in the period 1930–1931 Korean farmers had good crops also and the price declined automatically. Korean farmers were in no position to pay land taxes, irrigation fees, and many other obligations even when they sold their entire crops. When the government-general faced the reality of this price crisis, he simply dissolved the newly created "Land Improvement Section." It had been simply a symbolic means to answer the crisis and not a plan to rescue the farmers. What was the result?

In 1931, there were 1,393,424 households classified as tenants which increased to 1,546,500 such households in 1932. Tenant households in-

creased more than 140,000, and tenants represented then 53.8 percent of
the farm population against 48.4 percent in 1931, due to the government-
general's deliberate rice policy which worked against the interests of small
farmers. Incidentally, there was no status change among the large landlords; they remained about 3.6 percent. The government then advised
farmers to convert their rice fields back to dry fields. Again, when Japan
needed more rice, as during the Sino-Japanese war in 1937, the produce-
more-rice policy was readopted.

Meanwhile, the farmers' livelihood went from bad to worse. Japanese
official reports stated that there were 1,147,094 households at starvation
levels and 5,439,446 starving persons—27 percent of the total population. This situation was much improved after good crops during 1930-31.
The situation in the spring and summer of 1930, however, had been a
more normal one as the Japanese official had reported. The following table
tells that story. Nearly half of the Korean people were starving during the
spring and summer seasons in 1930.[15]

We are compelled to note that more Japanese landlords penetrated the
area and more Koreans confronted starvation. For instance, as previously
pointed out, the Japanese arrived first in South Korea in Jolla and Tsungtsong provinces and expanded their penetration there. As a result, these
areas created more starving peasants even though these areas have the
richest rice fields in the country. It was not the shortage of rice that
created starvation among the peasants for the rice which the peasants
produced was placed in government storehouses. When fewer Japanese
landlords penetrated the area, there were fewer starving people. Hamgyung province had only 20.5 percent of the population starving, because
there were only twenty Japanese landlords who owned no more than
thirty jungbo, and none of them was considered a big landlord.

What the government wanted was to create as many landless farmers
as possible in Korea. They were successful in doing that. Close to
1,551,000 families were leaving Korea each year for Manchuria, seeking a
livelihood and thus making room for Japanese poor people to move into
Korea.

To make this policy more systematic, the government established a
company to exclusively handle affairs with the Oriental Development
Company. The sole purpose of the Korean-Manchurian Development
Company was to handle the Korean immigrants who settled in Man-
churia. The Japanese government had more than one reason to have
Koreans migrate to Manchuria. First of all, by moving Koreans out of
Korea, they made room for the Japanese immigrants to settle at desirable

The Starving Peasants in Korea in Spring 1930

Area-Province	Percent Population of Small Landlords	Percent Population of Owner-Tenants	Percent Population of Tenants	Total
So. Tsungtsong	30.9	45.2	89.6	69.7
No. Jolla	28.7	42.6	71.5	62.2
No. Tsungtsong	19.9	40.3	76.3	57.3
So. Jolla	23.2	46.9	81.2	56.4
Kyonggi	13.1	33.3	69.8	54.3
So. Kyongsang	21.2	37.2	63.2	46.5
Hwang-hae	12.2	34.0	63.0	46.5
Kang-won	20.5	37.9	76.9	45.9
No. Kyongsang	20.0	36.1	57.8	42.1
So. Hamgyung	20.7	42.2	72.3	38.1
So. Pyongan	14.3	23.0	58.4	36.6
No. Pyongan	8.8	19.4	42.1	28.6
No. Hamgyung	10.5	35.6	55.2	20.5
Total	18.4	37.5	68.1	48.3

21

locations. There was another significant political reason behind the movement. The Japanese government wanted to build an anti-partisan movement in Manchuria.

It became evident to the Japanese government that to thwart Kim Il-sung and other Korean partisan movements in Manchuria, it was necessary to cultivate the area where the partisans were active and confront the Korean revolutionary groups with well-indoctrinated pro-Japanese immigrants. At the same time, by providing favorable farming conditions, they thought they could prevent the *Hwajonmin*[16] activities in the border area. The government was trying to save the timberlands which the Hwajonmin were supposed to have ruined. What the government was most concerned about were their political activities as allies of partisan groups.

Thus, the Korean-Manchurian Development Company was established and supported by the government-general with an initial capital of twenty million yen in 1936.

The initial investment was divided among the major companies that had prime interests in Korea and Manchuria. The Southern Manchurian Railway company took 100,000 shares. The Oriental Development Company took 99,900; the Bank of Korean Colonization took 60,000; the Bank of Korea, 40,000; Mitsui Busan, 25,000; the Mitsibishi Company, 25,000; and the Sumitomo Company, 16,000. In other words, the Korean-Manchurian Development Company was financed by semi-governmental companies and the major Japanese Zaibatsu groups. Where the profits involved Zaibatsu groups, they worked closely with the government. Their responsibilities in exploiting the people were no less than those of the government officials. Thus the Korean farmers were exploited by the Japanese from the beginning of their arrival until their departure.

As Japanese landlords advanced and occupied major roles as dominating powers on farms, the nature of Korean farm population changed. The surviving Korean landlords were more closely associated with the Japanese, and the alienation between Korean landlords and Korean tenants was similar to that of the Japanese landlords and the Korean tenants.

Through the commercialization of agricultural products by these big landlords, the system depended on the capitalistic mode of production rather than the feudalistic one. This changing system created tensions between landlords and peasants which they had never experienced before. During the time of the feudalistic system, where feudal lords and farmers were the two major classes, their normal relationships were more cordial.

Such a simple social relationship, however, disappeared when the new class, the captialistic landlords, began to emerge as the ruling power.

Japanese agricultural policy changed constantly according to the needs of the empire rather than the needs of the Korean inhabitants. When Japan needed extra rice to supply Japan proper, the government was forced to increase production in Korea. In order to increase the production of rice in Korea, the government had to change dry fields into paddy fields, and establish water utilization systems. This meant that the farmers had to pay heavy water taxes, and gradually turn over their land to the Water Utilization Association for accumulated unpaid debts. In 1929, the association controlled 50 percent of the rice fields in Korea.

The Japanese government's policy regarding rice affected not only the Korean farmer but also the Japanese farmer, because when rice was exported to Japan it affected the production of rice in Japan. Thus, the government had to solve two problems: first, the over-production of rice, and second, the competition between the Japanese rice and that of her colonies. A serious question was raised as to how the Korean government could dispose of the six to eight million bushels of rice formerly used by Japan and now unwanted by them. At this time, the price of rice was higher than that of millet, thus, the Korean peasant could not afford to use his rice instead of millet. A further difficulty was that the rice policy was not constant but changed according to the situation in Japan—if the supply was sufficient in Japan, no imports were needed; if, however, there was famine in Japan, Korea was immediately called upon for rice imports.

For this reason, the Korean government-general changed its policy and advocated a greater consumption of rice at home to dispose of the accumulated rice. But this policy only led to a further dilemma: first, the Manchurian government protested that the million and a half bushels of millet formerly exported to Korea could not be used elsewhere; and second, rice had to be stored in anticipation of famine in Japan. Therefore, while the Japanese stored rice in Korean warehouses for their own consumption, the Korean people, on the point of starvation, were forced to seek roots and grass in the hills to sustain themselves.

In 1933, the Korean government-general under General Ugaki was obliged to change its agricultural policy altogether. General Ugaki advanced his famous slogan: "Cotton in the South, sheep in the North." Could General Ugaki get cotton plants from the paddy fields? It was obviously ridiculous, but General Ugaki insisted that growing rice be replaced by cotton.

There were two reasons for the cotton-sheep policy: first, home industries in Japan needed raw materials; second, Korean cotton and wool did not provide competition with Japan. General Ugaki's cotton-sheep policy had to change again when Japan engaged in war with China, causing a greater demand for rice in Japan. General Minami, who succeeded General Ugaki, decided to increase the production of rice in Korea, and advocated "not to eat rice" instead of Ugaki's "eat more rice."

Imperial Japanese policy regarding the industrial development of Korea likewise showed the classical pattern of imperialist exploitation. Prior to 1920, "the corporation law" made it impossible for a Korean to engage in any industrial enterprise. And even after its repeal, the Japanese government encouraged only those "desirable" small-scale industries using local raw materials, such as mats, lacquers, straw ware, etc., to be produced. A decisive change in policy took place only after Japan had invaded Manchuria. By that time Japanese militarism had already laid plans for future campaigns in Asia, and Korea was to play a strategic role.

However, the so-called "rapid development of Korean industries after 1931" was a relative issue. The subscribed capital in Korea was only 4.4 percent of production in Japan, and of this percentage, "household" industries accounted for a quarter of the output. (A "household" industry is an enterprise conducted at the home of the entrepreneur, by members of his family, usually during their spare time.) This latter figure revealed the undeveloped state of factory industries. Japanese controlled 72 percent of industrial production, while Koreans controlled only 26.5 percent, of which "household" industries were responsible for one-half of the production, indicating the decisive domination by Japan in Korean economy at that time.

The living conditions of the Korean workers were in a pitiful state and were continually aggravated by two factors: first, the Japanese were given preferential treatment and received twice the normal wage given to Koreans; and second, the poverty of the countryside was driving people into the cities, thus adding to the ever-increasing pool of surplus labor.

In conclusion, it is obvious that Japanese imperial policy in Korea brought not one iota of benefit to the Korean people. Rather they were exploited and impoverished. Whatever measures were taken to develop the resources or to increase the production were done only on the basis, and only to the extent, that they aided Japanese imperialism.

3 Korea Against Japanese Imperialism

From the very first day of the Japanese imperialist venture into Korea, the Koreans have shown an undeviating will in their struggle to oust the invaders and regain independence.

The sporadic patriotic movement spread at home and abroad. The major military action against Japan was led by Lee Suk-chun and Hong Pum-do in different areas along the northeast border between Korea and Manchuria, and Lee Tong-hwi in Siberia.

The first famous fighting against Japanese forces occurred in May, 1906 in south Tsungtsong Province where more than two hundred of the "Ewi-pyong" or "Righteous Army" declared their campaign to emancipate their countrymen from Japanese domination. From July, 1907 to the end of 1908, 14,566 Korean rebels were killed and 8,728 captured by the Japanese army. After the annexation in 1910, outbreaks continued consistently, but it was a war of medieval weapons against the modern, mechanized Japanese military forces and gendarmerie. Many Koreans were forced to flee to Manchuria and China and, from points along the northern border, they conducted forays into the frontier districts.

The military actions were not the only means employed to protest Japanese aggression. There were several political-diplomatic movements by Korean patriots abroad: the New Korean Youth Party (Shinhan Tsungnyun-tang) in Shanghai led by Dr. Kimm Kieu-sik and Kim Chul; Young Korea Academy (Hungsadan) in Los Angeles led by Ahn Chang-ho; Comrade Society (Dongji-hoe) in Honolulu led by Dr. Syngman Rhee.

The outstanding event in Korea's resistance struggle was the March First Independence Movement of 1919. On that day, a "Proclamation of Korean Independence" signed by thirty-three representatives was read and half a million Koreans throughout the country held demonstrations. From March first to the end of May, twenty-one cities and two people's militias participated in 1,542 mass meetings.

It was a completely peaceful movement. People ran out into the streets waving the Korean flag and shouting "Mansei" or "Long live Korea." So well organized were the demonstrations and so loyal were the people to their national cause, that the Japanese, despite having a most highly efficient spy system, were completely ignorant of the impending storm until the day it happened. This infuriated the Japanese government, and within two months it ruthlessly suppressed the movement. Seven thousand Koreans were killed, 40,000 wounded, and 50,000 arrested, while hundreds of churches, schools and homes were destroyed.

The national independence movement was started and directed by the leaders of civic and religious organizations and members of the intelligentsia. Ministers of the Presbyterian and Methodist churches were just as active as the Buddhist priests and the leaders of the Tsondokyo, or the Heavenly Way Teachings, an indigenous religion. The bourgeoisie in Korea was greatly influenced by the revolutions in China and Russia and the winning of independence by many small European nations, such as Poland, Finland, and Czechoslovakia. The declarations of independence by small nations and their recognition by world public opinion stimulated the Korean national revolution.

Among Korean leaders responsible for the organizational process were Son Pyonghi of Tsondokyo, Lee Sung-hun of the Christian church, and Han Nyong-un of the Buddhist church. The initial idea of a nation-wide nationalistic movement among the Koreans overseas was conceived in Shanghai by the New Korea Youth Party at its regular monthly meeting on February 1, 1919. The group decided to send a Korean delegation to the world peace conference in Versailles to demand independence. To strengthen the delegation's position at the conference, the group planned nationwide anti-Japanese demonstrations to express the displeasure against Japanese occupation of Korea. The group dispatched delegates to key places: Kim Tsol to Seoul, Lyu Woon-hyung to Siberia, Chang Duk-Su to Tokyo, and Dr. Kimm Kieu-sik to Paris.

The news which Chang Duk-Su brought to Korean students in Tokyo stirred the Young Patriots, and the student associations drafted a

Korean "Declaration of Independence," which Choi Pal-yong, Lee Kwang-su and eight others signed.

While they were preparing the nationwide movement, the former King Kwang-mu of Korea was murdered on January 22, 1919, by the Japanese. The news of the king's death shocked the Korean people. The leaders of the nationalist movement decided that the anniversary of King Kwang-mu's funeral would be the date for the mass demonstration.

The 1919 independence movement's demonstrations took place on March first and continued for several months in Korea. Two hundred eleven cities and about two million people, about 20 percent of the national population, participated in the demonstrations. More than fifteen hundred meetings were held between March first and the end of May. Seven thousand five hundred Koreans were killed, nearly sixteen thousand were wounded, and about forty-seven thousand were imprisoned. Besides these casualties, forty-nine churches and mission schools were burned to the ground and more than seven hundred private dwellings were demolished.

There was such diversity in the leaders' individual backgrounds that some internecine violence was highly possible. Some of the groups approximated what Professor Karl W. Deutsch has called "pluralistic security communities," since they preserved interunit harmony in the absence of political amalgamation.

In spite of the failure of its immediate goal—national independence from Japan—the nationalist movement attracted worldwide attention and laid the spiritual groundwork for the future nationalist movement in Korea.

What were the significant features of the 1919 patriotic movement? First, the movement was led by religious leaders who advocated non-violence. No one was to harm the Japanese or Japanese property. The movement's intention was to convince Japanese leaders on the basis of the spirit of justice and goodwill. Their beliefs and behaviors were in the spirit of martyrs. They believed that their physical pains and hardships were necessary parts of the process of the spiritual freedom they sought.

For instance, on the night before the demonstration, twenty-nine of the thirty-three signators of the Declaration of Independence gathered in Myongwol-gwan, a Korean restaurant in Seoul, for a final meeting before the big event. Being fully aware of Japanese militaristic harshness, all of them expected capital punishment, but upon concluding their meeting, they officially informed the Japanese police of their plan for the next day.

One of the signators, having arrived too late to participate in the ritual meeting, went to the police station and voluntarily surrendered to the Japanese police. Their spirit is expressed in the following statement:

> Our part is to influence the Japanese government, dominated as it is by the old idea of brute force which is opposed to reason and universal law, so that it will change and act honestly and in accord with the principles of right and truth.[1]

The statement is quoted from the *Declaration of Independence*. It indicated the non-violent character of the movement.

Second, the nature of the movement was inevitably a humanistic one. The Declaration did not state any hatred of the Japanese, but rather, a desire to live peacefully as a neighbor nation. It said:

> . . . we tell it to the world in witness of the equality of all nations and we pass it on to our posterity as their inherent right . . . if the defects of the past are to be rectified, if the wrongs of the present are to be righted, if future oppression is to be avoided, if thought is to be set free, if right of action is to be given a place, if we are to deliver our children from the painful heritage of shame, if we are to leave blessing and happiness intact for those who succeed us, the first of all necessary things is the complete independence of our people.. . . .[2]

The document explains the conditions and the reasons of subjugated people's motives for self-determination. The thirty-three signators pledged and advised the people to follow three terms of agreement:

> This work of ours is in behalf of truth, justice, and life, undertaken at the request of our people, in order to make known their desire for liberty . . . [Then, it concluded] . . . 1. Let no violence be done to anyone; 2. Let those who follow us show every hour with gladness the same spirit; 3. Let all things be done with singleness of purpose, so that our behavior to the very end may be honorable and upright.[3]

Third, the movement had democratic ideals. Korean guerrilla movements continued along the border in the north while various patriotic movements continued abroad. The two major revolutions in Russia and China had stimulated these patriotic movements. It was, however, none other than the Wilsonian idealism expressed in his Fourteen Points that excited the Korean leaders. Wilson announced his policy in a speech to the Senate in 1917. He declared:

> . . . henceforth, inviolable security of life, of worship, and of industrial and social development should be guaranteed to all peoples who have lived hitherto under the power of governments devoted to a faith and purpose hostile to their own. . . .[4]

President Wilson thus became the champion of "self-determination." "Every territorial settlement must be made in the interest and for the benefit of the populations concerned," said President Wilson. This message found lodging in the mind of every subjugated man; it became the basic thought and desire for millions of Korean people who did not know that they were words in a vacuum.

Japanese police and gendarmes used their weapons indiscriminately against the peaceful demonstrators besides arresting the Koreans. Soon the jails were filled to overflowing; the Japanese set up temporary jails, but their efforts to stop the demonstrations were futile. The demonstrators probably believed that the Korean government in exile would soon return and establish a republican regime. By now, nearly 200 American missionaries had gained the confidence of Koreans who regarded them as reliable and friendly, although some of the missionaries were openly sympathetic to the Japanese government.[5] The Korean people had no reason to distrust Wilson's "self-determination" concept. Here is a clear case of a false political promise that brought premature chaos and tragedy, as the world witnessed more recently in Hungary in 1956.

It is interesting to note here that none of the national leaders advocated a revival of the monarchical system in Korea. The democratic republican form of government was their unanimous choice. An editorial entitled "The Dignity of Life" appeared in the *Los Angeles Times* concerning the Korean Declaration of Independence. "In our opinion this proclamation will stand on a plane of exaltation with our own Declaration of Independence."[6]

So far, we have mentioned three characteristics of the early Korean nationalism of 1919. Now we should add two elements which do not appear in the Declaration of Independence.

What the signers did not stress in the Declaration is as important as those points which they did. The Declaration did not stress such important conditions of self-determination as the homogeneity of the Korean language and the economic exploitation of the nation by the Japanese.

First of all, the Japanese had already invaded the Korean market and dominated Korea's natural resources. The newly organized Oriental Development Company took control of the land and the water systems. In other words, economic exploitation had been initiated, although it was still in its infant stage. Korean national leaders, however, did not stress the economic issue as a major factor of their movement.

Early German nationalists like Johann Gottlieb Fichte and Ernest Moritz Arndt stressed the superiority of the German language over the French, Italian, Spanish, English and Slavic languages as a major factor making the German nation superior. Fichte insisted that among the Euro-

peans, the Germans alone spoke an original, not derived, language. Therefore, the Germans alone were destined to provide world leadership. The
Korean language is one of the most advanced among modern languages,
but Korean national leaders did not even mention the language as a
condition of independence. We do find German nationalism as expressed
by Fichte or Arndt in Korean nationalists' writings,[7] but there is no
hatred of the Japanese as Arndt advocated hatred of the French.

One American reporter, Professor Nathaniel Peiffer of Columbia
University, said of the demonstrations of 1919:

> The first line was cut down and ridden down by mounted men, the second
> came on shouting, "Mansei," or "long live Korea." Every man and woman in
> the line knew what was before him, every man and woman had seen the
> penalty paid; it meant brutal beatings, arrests, torture and even death. They
> did not quiver. When one procession was broken up, another formed and
> marched straight at the waiting troops, only cheering, waving their flags and
> cheering.[8]

The eyewitness here reveals the physical pain the people endured and
the brutality to which they were subjected. Many American missionaries
reported similar stories to the mission boards of the Methodist and Presbyterian churches in the United States. The importance of the national
movement, in spite of these most brutal and painful physical phenomena,
was in its spiritual aspect.

The leaders of the movement mixed political self-determination with
religious concepts. In the Declaration of Independence and subsequent
mass demonstrations throughout the country, the entire movement reveals
a politico-religious tendency, not only because the leaders of three religious groups led the movement, but because of the context in which the
people endured the mass physical suffering and left an immortal spirit of
pride and honor to the Korean people. They were more inclined to be free
spiritually and have inner liberty than political liberty. "We wish to
inspire the government of Japan," was their declaration. The essential
nature of their whole action was primarily dominated by spiritual motivation. From the standpoint of political liberation, it was a failure and
negative, but from the standpoint of a spiritual movement, it was a success
and positive.

It was successful because of what the leaders felt in their hearts: the
existence of liberty and morality preserved by the people. The document
expressively accepts the morality, which is not a product of human knowledge, but is the outcome of obedience to a universal law. It states that
". . . it will change and act honestly and in accordance with the principles

of right and truth." Here we detect that the leaders of the movement refer to "transcendental sense" of Kantian freedom, of which they had little or no knowledge.

Morality, they believed, was independent from consequences, and impermeable to rewards. They volunteered to be imprisoned and expected worse, but they believed themselves to be free if their will was free; and their will was free when their actions were in accordance with their inner-directiveness.

Their ethico-religious teachings and attitudes expressed and propagated among the people a new attitude to political questions. They made a new political temper popular among the young intelligentsia. Moral vigor became the hallmark of virtue; political action could not be good unless it was the outcome of deep moral conviction. The Korean nationalists asserted themselves against a world which paid no attention to them, but they had no choice, they felt, their conviction could move mountains and their heads were bloody but unbowed.

The spirit of the March First Movement is now one of the dominating traditions of Korean national culture. The spiritual and inner movement has continued, even though the physical part of the movement ceased under severe pressures by the Japanese. It may sound strange, but the Korean Communist Party was dissolved and the members were forced to join the Japanese Communist Party, at one time under the direction of the Comintern. Such paradoxical actions of the international communist movement have been revealed more than once in the history of Korean nationalism.

After experiencing the complete failure of the 1919 nationalist movement, leaders and youths alike began to reorganize their respective groups to pursue the patriotic movement. Since the youth, especially college students, had taken the leading roles in the demonstrations, they were more disappointed than the older generation with the outcome of the movement. The young generation understood now that future movements must not rely upon support from the West, for it had failed them. The intention of the older generation was, as it is expressed in the Declaration, to let the world know of the desire of the Korean people and expose Japanese imperialistic rule, rather than to achieve immediate independence. They knew that non-violent protest would not bring about national independence, but that only world opinion and approval would help the Korean cause. The pressure of world opinion, especially from the United States, changed the Japanese policy in Korea from military rule to cultural rule, although the latter policy did more damage to the national conscience in the long run. The Korean people did gain some freedom in the area of publication.

The older generation was satisfied, at least temporarily, with the change of atmosphere and the new regime's political leniency. Among the older generation there were two distinct groups. One was known as "Young Korea Academy" or "hungsadan," under the leadership of Ahn Chang-ho, and the other was "Comrade Society" or "Dongji-hoe," under the leadership of Syngman Rhee. The two groups emerged at about the same time and though rooted in the United States, nevertheless they had considerable influence in Korea proper. Ahn's group advocated national independence through strengthening individuals and becoming an organized group. Thus, his group emphasized self-discipline and education. Mr. Ahn knew the shortcomings of the nation, and he wanted very much to teach the group to prepare to be future citizens of an independent Korea. Therefore he and his followers disapproved of the immediate action that General Lee Tong-hwi's military took in Manchuria against Japan. He was afraid that terroristic and military actions would bring about harsh policies against Koreans within Korea, and would jeopardize the educational programs and the cultural activities which had been gained after the March First Movement.

Rhee's group went one step further, by submitting Korea as a possible mandate of the League of Nations. The implication was clear that Korea was not ready for independence in the view of Dr. Rhee. Eventually, this advocacy caused the Korean provisional government in Shanghai to dismiss Dr. Rhee as president of the government in exile.

The failure of this bourgeois revolution immediately raised the problem of the future leadership of the independence movement. The people recognized that the civic and religious leaders were no longer capable of giving adequate guidance to the independence movement. The people waited for a vanguard force which could pursue a consistent revolutionary line and overthrow Japanese imperialism. The young generation lost its confidence in the leadership of the older groups. They were impatient with both Ahn and Rhee. Their groups lacked the action and the dynamic movement which youth found in communism.

The communist movement gradually developed and took over the revolutionary leadership although the party was still young and small in numbers. The failure of the 1919 revolution and subsequent events led to two significant results: first, the bourgeois nationalists as a group began to collaborate with the Japanese—even such outstanding leaders as Ts'oe Rin, Ts'oe Nam-sun, Yi Kwang-su and many others; second, the Communist Party, following a policy of no compromise with the Japanese and consequently suffering the most, was able to demonstrate its sincerity and organizational ability to the people.

There is no doubt that the economic policy of the Japanese was a major factor in the transfer of political hegemony from the nationalists to the communists, for the latter were able to explain the economic issues and economic foundations of Japanese imperialism to the people, whereas the nationalists, basing their fight against Japan on self-interest and emotion, were unable to do so.

The communist movement in Korea came about as a result of several factors: first, the most significant was the economic exploitation by Japanese colonial policy; second, the colonial people's movement throughout the world contributed to the cause of the national liberation movement; third, the numerous proletariat movements in Japan encouraged the Korean labor movement; fourth, the split in the schools of thought within the nationalist groups, especially in the Tsondokyo which had provided such great national leadership and influence. One of the Tsondokyo groups held to an opportunistic tendency in the political movement and leaned towards a compromise with the Japanese administration, which caused the group to lose popular support.

The beginning of the Korean communist movement can be traced back as far as 1918. General Lee Tong-hwi organized that Korean Socialist Party at Khabarovsk in June 1918. This was the first communist group organized in the Far East, antedating even the Comintern. General Lee was a recognized leader through his military activities against the Japanese in Manchuria and was highly respected among his compatriots. When the Bolsheviks engaged the White Russians militarily and the Japanese intervened in Siberia, the Koreans became their natural ally in the struggle, although for different reasons. Disappointed Koreans living in Manchuria and China were glad to join the Bolshevik force, and fought against the Japanese. General Lee Tong-hwi proceeded to Shanghai from Siberia and joined the Korean provisional government in September, 1919 and became premier within a short time. Meanwhile Lee, utilizing his prestige as premier, began to recruit his Korean compatriots for the purpose of organizing the Koryo Communist Party in January 1920. The Korean Socialist Party at Khabarovsk now had virtually moved to Shanghai with him, and recruited such important nationalists as Kim Rip, Lyu Woon-hyung, Ahn Pyung-tsan.

While Lee Tong-hwi was organizing the Koryo Communist Party in Shanghai, another Korean Communist Party had been organized in Ir-

kutsk under the guidance of Boris Shumiatsky who was the head of the
Far Eastern Secretariat of the Comintern and served as commander of the
Fifth Army of the Russian Revolutionary Forces in Siberia. To strengthen
the Bolshevik military forces in the Far East, Shumiatsky contacted the
nationalist leaders of the Congress of Korean People and organized "The
Korean Communist Party in Russia" on September, 1919. Ahn Pyung-
tsan, who attended the conference, returned to Shanghai, named the
Koryo Communist Party as the Shanghai branch of the Korean Communist Party and was assigned to establish a branch in Korea. The
committee which was assigned for this task included Lyu Woon-hyung,
Kim Man-gyom, Cho Tong-u, and Park Heun-Young was appointed
functionary of the Communist Youth Group.

Thus, the Irkutsk group, under the domination of the Soviet agent,
challenged the nationalistically oriented Lee Tong-hwi's Shanghai group.
Meanwhile, Lee sent Park Chin-sun, his private envoy, to Lenin in
Moscow and convinced Lenin that he should support Lee's group; he
received one million rubles of the promised two million rubles as aid to the
Korean communist movement. Lee's group was, thus, well financed while
the Irkutsk group was suffering financially. Lenin either neglected to
check with his agent, Boris Shumiatsky, or was anxious to add General
Lee to his camp, probably for military purposes. It appears that the latter
group, however, had increased its membership to one thousand in the area
of the Maritime Province by 1922. Learning of this situation, Lenin
dismissed both the Irkutsk and the Shanghai groups by December, 1922,
and organized the Korean Bureau in the Comintern to control the Korean
communist movement.

In February, 1923, the Korean Bureau was transferred to Vladivostok
with Vishinsky as its chief, and Katayama Sen, Han Myung-sun of the
Irkutsk group, General Lee of Shanghai group as the members of the
Bureau, and Chung Chai-dal was sent to Korea as a secret agent. Thus,
the Korean communist movement, once organized by nationalists and
communists alike, was short lived, and officially became an integrated part
of the international communist movement.

The radical elements of the nationalist group and the communists
realized that the working class had to be mobilized and organized. Several
organizations emerged. Among the more outstanding groups were the
North Wind Association, the Seoul Youth Association, and the Tuesday
Club. The North Wind Association was formulated in 1922 by a group of
progressive Korean intellectuals headed by Kim Yak-su. Probably the
most active group in the radical movement was originally known as the

North Star Association, most of whose members were educated in Tokyo. The second organization, Seoul Youth Association, was formed in 1922 under the leadership of Kim Sa-kuk and Lee Yong and consisted of four hundred different organizations and represented approximately fifty thousand members. The third group was the Tuesday Club. It was composed of 500 organizations and represented 60,000 members. The Tuesday Club was under the leadership of Park Heun-Young, Kim Tan-tsi. Of the three groups, the North Wind Association was the strongest and exercised the most influence in the labor movement.

In 1924, the League of the Korean Labor and Farmers was organized with some 180 organizations; and the League of Korean Youth was established with some 220 youth organizations, and so the labor and the farmer movements became unified under radical elements. It was the first successful nationwide unified effort since the 1919 movement and also the first time radical elements were able to get together.

With such a prelude, the Korean Communist Party was officially organized on April 17, 1925, in Seoul. Fourteen leaders of the radical movements assembled at a restaurant at one in the afternoon and discussed organizing the Korean Communist Party and officially announced the purposes of the party. Their goals were: first, Korean independence, and second, abolition of the private property system. Eight of the organizers were selected to form the Central Executive Committee and three were selected for the inspection committee. The Central Executive Committee was to draft the party constitution and also to complete the organization. After several meetings, the committee set up a secretariat, departments of organization, and propaganda. As soon as the Central Committee drew up a party constitution, the group immediately applied for affiliation with the Comintern. The committee members then spread throughout the country to recruit members. They had enrolled fifty-three new members mostly from among the intelligentsia within a year. From then on the party's influence spread throughout the country, focusing especially in the cities.

In May, 1926, the Korean Communist Party sent a group of agitators to Manchuria under the leadership of Cho Bong-am. The group organized the Manchurian branch of the Korean Communist Party in Ningkota. One of their tasks was to aid the families of the professional revolutionaries. Thus the activities of the Korean communists in Manchuria were renewed. The communist activities, however, were soon spotted and about thirty communists were arrested by Japanese police with the cooperation of the Chinese police in December, 1927. These communists were sent to Seoul and imprisoned.

In September, 1928, Kim Tsol-san and forty other communists who had not yet been arrested were also sought out and imprisoned by the Japanese and Chinese police. These two large-scale arrests seriously handicapped the infant communist movement in Manchuria and the result was a complete reorganization of the communist party in Manchuria. The party went underground and organized several front groups, including farmers, students, and intellectuals, along the more popular issues rather than along outright revolutionary lines. The old radical names were abandoned and substituted with League of the Youth of Manchuria, League of East Manchuria Labor, and others. These popular organizations, however, were supervised by special communist representatives from Northern Manchuria and also from Irkutsk, where the Korean communists were still active; these supervisors had close connections with the Korean communist movement under the direction of the Comintern.

The League of East Manchuria Youth included forty-eight organizations with a membership of 100,000. The League of East Manchuria Labor included forty-eight organizations with 2,500 members. Four executive members of the Koryo Youth Association, one of the forty-eight groups in the youth organization, were arrested in Changchun and sent to Sinueju, Korea. The discovery of communist propaganda sheets sent to Korea from Manchuria aroused police suspicions and resulted in the arrests. Later in 1930, police who were assigned to the Japanese consulate-general arrested Kang Sok-jun and 122 others associated with the youth group and sent them to Seoul. Following this incident, the Japanese police dissolved the Korean communist organizations located in Manchuria and prohibited all public meetings there.

Soba, head of the Japanese police of the consulate-general, stated, "We have sent to Seoul eighty persons who were thoroughly investigated, and who proved to be real communists. I was surprised by their courage."[9] Thus the communist movement ceased to exist temporarily in Manchuria, and the focus of the movement was in Shanghai. On March 26, 1926, Korean residents in Shanghai organized the Korean Youth Association under the leadership of Chu Yo-sup. The aims of this organization were: first, Korean independence; second, to weld the organizations into a united front; third, to make an effort to establish, as soon as possible, one national movement party; fourth, to cooperate with the people's liberation groups of the neighboring countries; fifth, to study the practical policies and ideals of the national movement.

It was a time of compromise between nationalists and communists, and a time for formulation of the united front movement, and the youth organization became a front group for the Comintern. The organization immediately branched out to ten cities in China and received support from the Comintern for the purpose of unifying nationalists and communists. The Comintern advocated that Korean communists join the nationalist groups and work with them for common causes, rather than try to compete with each other. It was almost imperative for communists to cooperate with nationalists since they had lost most of their leaders, and besides, the Comintern Far Eastern policy at this time had already been geared toward a united front.

To promote revolutionary activities, the Youth Association organized the central military committee with the cooperation of all the Korean organizations which surfaced again in Manchuria. The first step in this undertaking was to call an official meeting at Tai-sai-chan of all representatives, and twenty-seven revolutionary leaders, who represented various revolutionary armies in Manchuria. The group elected Kim Cha-jin, chairman of the military committee, as he already had been recognized as the leader in military affairs. Kim's military action against the Japanese disturbed the government's policy more than any others at that time. The group also began the publication of the official magazine *Oltsi* in Korean. *Oltsi* and other propaganda materials were smuggled constantly into Korea.

The Comintern followed the united front policy in China, and ordered Korean communists to cooperate with the nationalists as was the case in China, resulting in the organization of Sin-kan-hoe on February 15, 1927. Since both communists and nationalists were not able to carry out an anti-Japanese movement alone, they welcomed the opportunity to organize the united front. Communists were planning to apply a dual policy—Sin-kan-hoe as a front organization while maintaining the communist movement in the underground. This policy was in accord with the Marxian concept of historical materialism. Korea was not ready for a protetarian revolution and a bourgeois revolution had to take place first. It was the time when the Comintern insisted on Chinese communists joining the Kuomintang (Nationalists) Party, and establishing a united front, rather than fighting against the Nationalists. The major enemy of Korea was not the Korean bourgeoisie, but the foreign exploiter— Japanese imperialists. Therefore, the logic was clear to communists in Korea, and they followed the order from Moscow.

The principles of Sin-kan-hoe were: first, promotion of the political, economic, and social awakening of the people; second, promotion of national unity; third, absolute refusal to recognize opportunistic (or pro-

Japanese) groups. Thus, Sin-kan-hoe was the first united political organization to exist in Korea. The organization was composed of some one hundred and forty various branches in all parts of Korea with fifty thousand members, including most of the intelligentsia, nationalists, and communists.

The organization was revolutionary in name only and failed to carry out many activities because of close surveillance of the strict Japanese colonial policy which had become even more restrictive.

The majority of the leaders of Sin-kan-hoe were well-known nationalists since many of the communists had been arrested, especially during the third communist roundup in 1926. Nationalist leaders of Sin-kan-hoe included Lee Sang-jae, a well-known patriot, first chairman; Kwon Tong-jin, a leader of the Tsondokyo, second chairman; Ho Hyun, a renowned lawyer, third chairman. It was under the leadership of Ho Hyun that the organization attempted a mass demonstration for the first time. It failed as the police arrested the leaders before the plan for the demonstration materialized. The plan was connected with the 1929 student movement.

Sin-kan-hoe was soon dissolved by Japanese police. Communists actively carried out strikes in factories and sabotaged farms. They organized the "Association of the Reconstruction of the Korean Communist Party," and the "League of Young Communists." On the other hand, the nationalists organized "The League of Christianity and Tsondokyo." Thus each group established its own league and undertook activities separately. The communist group led strikes which extended nationwide, involving approximately 250,000 people in the movement. In 1931, Yong-hing Farmer's Union with a total membership of 18,000 sponsored a big demonstration, and approximately 150 farmers were arrested by police in connection with the strikes in the Hong-won area alone.

Nong-tson Tenant Union with a membership of about two thousand six hundred led a starvation sit-down strike, and Jong-pyong Farmers Union conducted a strike which ended with two hundred members being arrested in Yong-hing county during October, 1931. The modern peasant movement began in Yong-hing county. The peasants became the major force, not the intellectuals and certainly not the middle class, in the struggle against Japanese imperialism in Korea from then on. Why this change in leadership in Korea at this particular time?

The peasant class, the landless group but the real producers, was confronted with one major aim as the new stage developed. Subsistence was the chief concern of the peasant. The goal of the peasant class was, thus, simple and direct, while their target, capitalistic landlords, characteristically was more complicated. The dominating landlord elements were not only capitalistic and profit motivated, but also harsh and severe. They had been the biggest landlords in Japan before they came to Korea and they were experienced in dealing with tenants. Their lands were their capital, and they established severe rules and regulations to control their ·Korean tenants. Japanese landlords were violent, merciless, and not given to humanistic handling of Korean tenants.

To illustrate the treatment of Korean tenants, we cite the case of the Higashiyama Farm which belonged to Mitsubishi Zaibatsu. The following conditions appeared in a Higashiyama tenant contract. First of all, the landlord reserved the right to demand that farmland be returned whenever he so desired; second, the contract could be revised according to the desires of the landlord; third, all damages and expenses were to be paid by the tenants. Under such conditions, the landlord was able to evict any tenant who was not in the landowner's favor.

Conditions which could result in the tenant's dismissal from his land included: delay of the payment of rent; damaged land regardless of whose fault it might have been; changing the farming system, etc. Under these conditions, the landlord could, with validity, boast that he was able to get his land back any time he desired. He merely revoked the tenant's rights and confiscated the land.

In order to keep up his tenancy, the tenant had to spend a great amount of his income for repairs and improvements which only profited the landlord. The Shimadani Farm, another big Japanese farm, had an even more unscrupulous contract. The reasons for dismissal of tenants were: first, damage to the landlord's prestige; second, complaints about the rental situation. In other words, tenants were not allowed to talk about their present contract or about the landlords. Freedom of speech had been prohibited by the contract.

In the contract of the Oriental Development Company, when a tenant violated a good custom, the standard of a good custom being set by the landlord, he could be dismissed. These clauses could obviously be interpreted by the landlord in any way he pleased, and the unfairness of the contract was clear.

Other peculiar clauses appeared in the Kumamoto, Nakashira, Ishikawa Farms' contract: first, tenants had to post signs on the premises designating the owner and the amount of land for which the tenant was responsible; tenants had to deliver the entire crop to the place designated by the landlords; the landlords would subtract from the total crop the amount coming to them for rent, interest, dues, etc., and the remainder to be hauled back by the tenant to his home. In most cases, the vast majority of the crop went to the landlord, leaving only a minute part of the harvest to the tenant.

Since landlords held the power of dismissing tenants at any complaint, intimidated tenants registered few or no complaints against their landlords. These conditions existed for these tenants who had written contracts, but the majority of tenant contracts were oral ones. In 1930, 73 percent of all tenant contracts were oral agreements. In Kyonggi Province, 89 percent of the contracts were oral while in North Hamgyung Province 99 percent were oral.[10] The risks tenants took with oral agreements were very obvious. The Japanese official report listed twenty-eight reasons which landlords could use against their tenants. For instance, the landlord could dismiss the tenant when he felt that the tenant was not working hard to raise additional crops; dismissal could result when the landlord thought that the tenant's behavior was undesirable, such as joining an undesirable association; landlords could dismiss tenants who instigated other tenants and disturbed their work. Under such conditions, the dismissals of tenants were frequent occurrences, and it was the landlords' main weapon in intimidating the peasants. In Kyonggi Province, 27 percent of the entire cultivated land's tenantship changed hands in 1930. Similar situations existed in other parts of the country: 25 percent in North Jolla, 20 percent in South Jolla, 35 percent in North Kyongsang, 10 percent in South Kyongsang, 30 percent in North Tsungtsong, 20 percent in South Tsungtsong, etc.[11]

Those who lost their tenancies either left for Manchuria or became Hwajonmin (illegal farmers of the "firefield"). The landless tenants accepted the situation as a natural occurrence of human life. They complained but did not organize themselves to protect their natural right—the right to live. They were not conscious of their personal rights. This situation was not to continue long.

Korean farmers were divided in two classes: one group, although small in number, stayed with the Japanese landlords, while the vast majority became poor tenants. In other words, the capitalistic land system coupled with primitive agriculture methods created these two extreme classes. As the landlords expanded their possessions more and the numbers of the tenants increased, the competition of getting land tenancy became acute. Meanwhile, the landlords made their rules and regulations even more crude. As the landlords' exploitations increased, the peasants' resistance increased. This was an inevitable result. The peasants had nothing to lose. They lost their lands, and now their livelihood had been threatened. Even from a pure economic sense, there were enough reasons to anticipate the class struggle between the two extreme classes.

The political and national conditions of the time were cause enough for rebellion. However, as exploited as they were, the peasants were unable to resist the landlords until they were organized by progressive students returning from Japan. These college students had been impressed by the October Revolution and witnessed the peasant movement in Japan. They returned to Korea to organize the tenants. The Tenants' Association and the League of Peasants became the pioneering organizations against the landlord class. A early as 1920, there were fifteen tenant strikes against landlords with 4,000 tenants participating. These were new experiences for them and they created a new situation in Korea. The government-general dissolved these peasant organizations immediately to protect the landlords, but the peasant strikes increased in spite of the suppression.

Following is a table that shows the number of peasant strikes during the years from 1920 to 1932 in Korea.

Year	Number of strikes	Number of people[12] participating–
1920	15	4,140
1921	27	2,967
1922	124	2,539
1923	176	9,060
1924	164	6,929
1925	204	4,002
1926	198	2,745
1927	275	3,973
1928	1,590	4,863
1929	422	5,319
1930	726	13,012
1931	667	10,282
1932	323	416

Not all the tenants' strikes were violent in nature. Some of them were rather moderate and the tenants hoped to settle the matter peacefully. The tenants' prime concern was economic. In 1931, when strikes numbered 667 with more than 10,000 tenants participating, 42 percent of the causes of the strikes were classified as dismissal or increase of tenant fees by landlords. The other reasons for strikes were also closely related with the fees, rent payments, etc. According to official Japanese reports, there was no mention of political and national feeling among the rank and file members of the tenant group. Yet, the Japanese government arrested and imprisoned leaders of the peasant movement saying they were "undesirable elements." This rigid control increased when Japanese militarism expanded to China in 1931.

A similar situation existed in Japan. As the military adventure in China expanded, monopoly capitalism in Japan collaborated with the military adventurists. Landlords had government support to enforce their semi-feudalistic methods on tenants. This system did not help to increase agricultural products. Furthermore, the low-price system of agricultural products was maintained while an inflationary economy continued in the country. The gap between the prices of agriculture products and industrial products was so great that farmers suffered unbearably. The fertilizer price contracted by the monopoly trust forced farmers to borrow cash to pay for the fertilizer, which had been inflated, thus the farmers' debt increased. All these conditions òccurred on Japanese farms, as the tenants' struggle against landlords intensified during the '30s.

The main causes of the tenants' struggle were the tenant rent, improving tenant conditions, etc. They were purely economic factors. Lowering the rent, the price of fertilizer, and loan interest rates were economic issues. In 1934, there were 5,828 strikes with more than 100,000 participating in them, but the major grievance remained economics. The nature of the tenant strikes in Tsungtsong and Jolla Provinces were very similar to the tenant strikes in Japan during the '30s. One characteristic of Korean tenant strikes was that the vast majority occurred in the South; including South Tsungtsong, North and South Jolla, and North and South Kyongsang, Kyong, and Kyonggi Provinces.[13] It is clear that those places where the most Japanese landlords penetrated, the most strikes occurred, and the main cause of the strikes was economic, in spite of the biracial situation which existed. The tension between Japanese landlords and Korean tenants was caused by immediate problems rather than long-term political reasons. The peasant movement was, therefore, based on the struggle between capitalist landlords and poor farmers, leaving out the middle-class farmers. It was a revisionistic type of economic struggle.

Due to the nature of the movement, the peasant effort in the south at this time was regional rather than national in scope. This situation reveals a significant factor in the Korean peasant movement. In spite of wide-spread tenant strikes year after year from 1920 to 1932 in South Tsungtsong and the North and South Jolla areas, there were no major political movements among the peasants. In comparing these areas with North and South

Hamgyung Provinces, we find some of the major political movements among the peasants, although there were not as many strikes during the same period.

The strike in Yonghing in 1931 is an example. The Yonghing Farmers' Union with a membership of eighteen thousand staged a big demonstration which resulted in the arrest of 150 strikers. After this initiation, the Nong-tson Tenant Union with a membership of two thousand six hundred conducted a starvation-sit-down strike. The Janpyong Farmers Union joined the strike. As a result, about two hundred members were arrested by police during the month of October in Yonghing County alone. The strike had nothing to do with tenant fees or rents or any economic issue. The cause of the strike was the refusal by police to permit the opening of the village night school.

On the night of October 21, 1931, eight union members organized four separate groups which attacked the county office, police station, railroad station, and homes of landlords where the rioters destroyed official documents and other important papers. They beat up the head of the county and the landlords. Police headquarters of South Hamgyung Province received the news with surprise and sent out armed police forces to Yonghing County. The fight between armed police and farmers continued with heavy casualties and ended with five hundred union members being arrested. This was one of the significant peasant movement events in Korean history.

Why was it that a political movement initiated by peasants occurred at Hamgyung Province, where fewer exploitations had taken place by Japanese landlords, and why did it not happen at Tsungtsong Province or even in Jolla where more severe exploitations took place? Was this simple accident? We can speculate that such a significant movement came about in the north, rather than in the south, because of the degree of exploitation. When tenants were exploited with such extreme harshness as we have witnessed in the south, they were physically exhausted and too busy with eking out their livelihoods to think beyond their immediate needs. While the farmers in the north still remained small self-farmers, the majority of them at least had some leisure time to think and organize themselves to enhance their livelihood as a group. Organizing a village night school was such an example.

Another reason was an external one. Being closely connected geographically with Manchuria and Siberia where the Korean revolutionary movement was active, the people of the north were constantly reminded of the anti-Japanese movement as a necessary ingredient of their total struggle for decent living. In other words, the peasants in the north did not separate the economic issue and the political issue while their brothers in the south did.

Japanese imperialist policy in Korea exploited not only the Korean farmers but also produced problems for the Japanese farmers. Japanese landlords were not kind to their people when it became a matter of profits. They had no humanitarian concern over either Koreans or Japanese.

Japanese capitalism destroyed not only the agricultural economy but also small-scale handicraft industries in Korea as well and thereby destroyed the self-sufficient basis of Korean economic independence. By monopoly control of all machinery, tools, fertilizer, and other supplies, two changes were immediately brought about. First, daily living expenses rose and debts were incurred to meet the immediate economic crisis. Secondly, the home industries, which usually kept the peasant employed during slack seasons, were abolished under Japanese control. Thus, with higher farm rent, water taxes, debt interest, and farm supply costs, the peasant did not earn enough for his livelihood after his debts were paid, unless he borrowed more money—only to become more immersed in debts, which, as they gradually accumulated, led inevitably to bankruptcy.

In conclusion, we are able to make the following observation about Japanese imperialism in Korea. First of all, the greater penetration of Japanese imperialism, particularly by landlords in early occupation days, the greater the number of tenant protests occurred, primarily for economic reasons. The political protests, on the other hand, came from the less penetrated areas. Secondly, the number of starving people were in direct proportion to the exploitation of Japanese imperialism and penetration of Japanese landlords into the region. Thirdly, the more the peasant increased his production and produced more rice, the less he became worthy and the less rice was available to him. He actually became devaluated as a commodity, which brought him misery. As a matter of fact, he was alienated from his own creation. He was not only totally dehumanized but eventually left his land and his home, looking for a new place and a new hope to live.

4 Liberation and After

Independence for Korea was decided upon at the Cairo conference of October, 1943, by the leaders of the Allied powers prosecuting the war against Japan, President Franklin D. Roosevelt, Prime Minister Winston Churchill, Generalissimo Chiang Kai-shek. Here they declared "in due course Korea shall become free and independent." The words "in due course" were the brake that provided the dilemma. Many leading patriots abroad worked hard to convince the Allied leaders that the Korean people were qualified to govern themselves.

President Harry S. Truman, Britain's Winston Churchill, and the Soviet Union's Joseph Stalin reaffirmed Korean independence in the Potsdam Declaration of July 26, 1945, with China later agreeing to it. On August 8, 1945, one week before the termination of hostilities, Soviet armed forces marched into North Korea. On September 2, after the Japanese surrender, the Supreme Commander of the Allied Forces announced that the U. S. and the Soviet armed forces would share in the occupation of Korea. The Soviets were already in their northern zone of occupation; the Americans landed on September 8, and took over the area south of the 38th parallel. This convenient arrangement was for the sake of the military occupation of enemy-held territory. No one, however, foresaw that such a temporary division of the land would bring tragedy to the nation later.

Korea was, like any other enemy-held territory, subjected to government by the Allied forces, and the problem of governing a country like Korea was no simple matter.

World War II produced about the same problems for non-self-govern-

ing peoples as did World War I. Colonial problems have been some of the
prolonged causes of international conflicts and wars. The big powers had
already mentioned their trusteeship problems at the Dumbarton Oaks
Conference. However, the subject was not resolved and this matter was
carried over to the Crimean Conference where President Roosevelt and
Prime Minister Churchill discussed a possible addition to the Dumbarton
Oaks proposals. A final decision on territorial trusteeships again was
deferred.

The matter of trusteeships was raised at the United Nations Organization conference in San Francisco. At this conference the task of drafting
a plan for a new trusteeship system was turned over to Committee Four of
the General Assembly. Three main conceptions of the trusteeship plan
were represented at the conference. The American principles concerning
dependent territories had already been submitted by Secretary of State
Cordell Hull to President Roosevelt, who endorsed them in March of
1943. These principles set forth that all people who aspire to independence should get the cooperation of the United Nations. Specifically, the
trustees section of the U.N. was to help the people of such territories
unify in preparation for independent national status. The proposal was
approved by President Roosevelt two days before his death.[1]

The basic aims of the international trusteeship system, according to
the charter of the U.N., are international peace and security and to
promote the political, economic, social and educational advancement of
the inhabitants of the trust territories and their progressive development
towards self-government or independence, depending on the particular
circumstances of each territory and its people and their freely expressed
wishes. Special circumstances were to be stated by the terms of each
trusteeship agreement. These common principles finally were agreed
upon and the plan was accepted by fifty-one nations.

The case of Korea came under Article 77, which stated that territories
may be detached from enemy states as a result of the Second World War,
and a five-year trusteeship system was announced in Moscow by the
foreign ministers of the United States, Great Britain and the Soviet Union
in December, 1945.

Prior to the Japanese surrender, the Korean underground movement
had established the Korean People's Republic under the chairmanship of
Lyu Woon-hyung, an old patriot and hero. Immediately after this, and
shortly before the arrival of Allied troops, General Abe, then governor-
general of Korea, asked Lyu Woon-hyung to protect Japanese citizens
and insure peace and order. Lyu accepted the proposals with certain

reservations. It is curious to note that General Abe, representative of the Imperial Japanese Government, should approach the recently formed de facto government of his subjects with such supplication. One can only surmise that the People's Government had the unanimous support of the population and consequently had the only authority that might restrain the wrath and anger of the Korean people toward the Japanese in their midst.

Soviet military forces arriving in North Korea immediately recognized the People's Government and cooperated with it in establishing the North Korea People's Interim Committee on a much wider political and social basis than the initial body. Moreover, the Russians gave wholehearted support to the Koreans' initiative in removing Japanese-appointed puppets, dividing the large estates and nationalizing former Japanese industries as the property of the Korean people. With Soviet encouragement, farmers' unions, labor unions, women's associations, and unions of youth began to appear quickly and to participate in the national life of the country.

To the south of the 38th parallel, Lt. Gen. John R. Hodge, commander of the American forces, maintained the People's Republic to be illegal and retained the hated Japanese in administrative capacities. Korean delegates waiting to greet American troops at the port of Inchon were fired upon—by the Japanese. A protest to the American Military Government (AMG) was ignored with the claim that these Japanese soldiers "had the legal right" to maintain law and order! General Hodge then proceeded to create the Korean Advisory Council, consisting of eleven members, to aid the AMG. The chairman of this body was Kim Seung-soo, one of the biggest landlords in South Korea. During the war he had been an active member of the central council of the Japanese government. He was also chairman of the Korean Democratic Party, an organization of landowners and big business men. It was from this party that the members of the American Advisory Council were chosen, although there were numerous more representative political and social groups which were more than willing to help the AMG. An amazing and rapid metamorphosis took place: The pro-Japanese became pro-American.

Within six months the Korean people, who once welcomed the American liberators, were demanding to know how soon they would leave Korea. An editorial in *Chosun Ilbo*, a conservative Korean daily in Seoul, characterized the American occupation "as worse than under the Japanese."

In spite of the Cairo Declaration of December 1, 1943 promising

Korea independence, there was no precise formulation of a plan to govern Korea until December, 1945 when representatives of the Soviet Union, the United States and Great Britain met in Moscow. It was agreed there that Korea was to endure military occupation for one year, followed by five years of civilian trusteeship. To assist in the formation of a provisional government, the Soviet and American military commands in Korea were instructed to establish a joint commission which, in consultation with democratic Korean organizations, was to make recommendations to the Four Powers. The joint commission, in cooperation with a proposed provisional government, was to promote the economic and social progress of the Korean people in developing democratic self-government.

The conservatives, Kim Koo, Syngman Rhee and Kim Seung-soo, violently opposed the decision. Rhee and Kim Koo were in exile for the greater part of their lives and, returning home, they sought to capitalize on the anticipated unfavorable mass reaction to the proposed trusteeship of Korea. Kim Koo started his "fight to death campaigns," calling for national strikes and demonstrations. The supporters of Kim Koo launched a wave of terrorism and intimidation: offices of newspapers supporting the decision were stoned and vandalized; members of democratic organizations were kidnapped and beaten, and oftentimes murdered. These terrorists openly declared they intended to kill Park Heun-Young, secretary of the Communist Party in the South, and Lyuh Woon-heung, a leader of the People's Republic. The handful of conservatives who were anti-Soviet became now also anti-American and anti-United Nations; however, the American Military Government continued to tolerate their activities and recognized them as representatives of the Korean people.

On the other hand, democratic organizations and the vast majority of the population accepted the decision on trusteeship. They thought that Korea, emerging as a weak and relatively backward nation, would again be easy prey for imperialism. They felt that the only way to insure her future independence was to have collective action of the major powers in helping Korea to her feet. In its message of January 2, 1946, to the major powers, the Central Committee of the People's Republic declared that the three ministers' conference was a progressive one and their decision would result in a democratic Korea. They said the gradual fulfillment of Korean independence had been advanced and they pledged to support this progressive agreement.

On January 3, 1946, more than two hundred thousand people gathered in Seoul to "support the Moscow Agreement," while in Pyongyang, one hundred thousand participated in a similar meeting. During this period demonstrations were held throughout the south and north.

Among the organizations involved were the Korean Federation of Trade Unions with a membership of three million, and the Youth and Women's Federations, each representing one million members. These massive demonstrations indicated decisively the overwhelming sentiments of the Korean people who were not to be mistaken for political opportunists.

In the midst of this enthusiastic atmosphere, the American-Soviet Joint Commission met for the first time on January 5, 1946. This conference dealt only with the most urgent problems regarding interzonal mail service, allocation of radio frequencies and movement of persons and goods from one zone to the other. The sessions on major questions of policy took place on March 20 between the two military commandants. On the crucial issue of the formation of the provisional government, the growing rift in the overall Soviet-American relations became evident—the cold war freeze was taking hold.

In these discussions, Soviet authorities maintained that consultation on the provisional government should be only with genuinely democratic Korean organizations and not with national traitors and collaborators who aided Japanese militarists during the Japanese occupation. The Soviet position was a reiteration of the Moscow Agreement.

But American authorities held that "all groups should be entitled to state their views," and that the Soviet viewpoint was a violation of freedom of speech and of the Moscow Agreement as it wished to restrict the participation of the Korean people. By this time American authorities sought to justify their already adopted policy of supporting the groups of collaborators and conservatives who would be certain to protect the gradual penetration of American economic and political interests in South Korea. As the Soviet's Molotov showed a year later in a memorandum to the American Secretary of State George Marshall, of the organizations recommended by the American Military Government for consultation, seventeen were opposed to the Moscow decision and a token three supported it. Stated in another way, the American position in the Joint Commission was tantamount to saying that General Tojo should be consulted in the creation of a democratic Japan. The conference reached no satisfactory solution.

In April, 1947 Foreign Minister Molotov submitted a three-point proposal to the U.S. Department of State as a basis for resuming Joint Commission discussions.[2] The Joint Commission reconvened in May only to adjourn once again without any agreement. The point of departure was still the major question regarding the kinds of organizations to be consulted in the formulation of a Korean provisional government.

From these two conferences it became clear to the Korean people that their independence was still in the distant future. The Koreans were forced to conclude that the United States was in principle fundamentally opposed to the international agreement and was using and aiding the conservatives. It seemed to be the American intention to have this articulate group create the impression that the anti-Moscow decision was the true and popular wish of Korea. The United States hoped that the situation would provide the moral justification to abandon in toto the international agreement, making it possible to push through her own economic and political interests in South Korea, as happened in later days. Although the American Military Government in the beginning attempted to maneuver within the framework of the Moscow decision, it soon dropped all pretensions and facades and openly followed its unilateral policy in South Korea.

Failure of American Military Government Policy

The postwar situation in Korea offered ample opportunity for the United States to demonstrate goodwill and friendship by tangibly aiding Koreans in recovering from the oppressive Japanese rule. When American troops landed in South Korea, they were joyously welcomed by the Korean people as liberators. Despite this advantage, the American Military Government from the very outset taxed to the extreme any feeling of friendship the Koreans had for the American occupation troops.

During the first few days after liberation the American Military Government declared a policy of "non-fraternization," forbidding American soldiers to acquaint themselves with the Korean people. It could hardly be argued that health consideration was the sole reason for the measure. And still less could it be thought that Korea was an occupied enemy state where a non-fraternization policy would be appropriate. Soon, American soldiers were engaged in "gook" hunting. "Gook" is an American derogatory term referring to Koreans. It originally came from the word "mi-gook," or "America," which the Americans interpreted as "me-gook" or "I am a gook" when Koreans welcomed the Americans. The episode was an unfortunate affair which American authorities condoned at the time.

Immediately after the end of the war, Dr. Syngman Rhee, aged conservative political leader who spent thirty-three years of exile in the United States, was flown to Korea under State Department instruction. He had at one time participated in the anti-Japanese struggle and was president of the Korean provisional government in exile. Consequently, the American Military Government sought to use him as "the Korean leader." He was, to be sure, thoroughly oriented towards American interests. As a matter of fact, prior to his departure, Dr. Rhee had committed himself to secret transactions with financiers concerning Korean mining industries worth two million dollars. Thus, the man who was destined to play an important role in Korean politics already had tied himself to the American business world before he got to Korea.

In regard to probably the most crucial economic question in the South, the AMG confiscated 353,000 jungbo of Japanese owned land, which accounted for 83 percent of the total cultivated land. It declared these lands for sale, a maximum of ten jungbo to a person, thus putting the buyer in the landlord category. According to this plan, there would have been created 35,000 more small holders. In practice, however, this theoretical figure was considerably reduced and the position of the large landlords was enhanced. Consider who had money to purchase the properties:

1. Present landlords and big business interests who bought directly and also through black market deals, providing the money and acquiring land under other names;

2. Those able to borrow money from landlords and wealthy people, generally through blood relationships and marriages.

This reconcentration of farm lands had its subsequent effect on the rice policy in the early part of 1946. Despite an extremely good rice harvest the previous year in the South, a 60 percent increase, and the fact that compulsory export of rice to Japan had stopped, the American Military Government's "principle of free enterprise in matters of trade and commerce" virtually choked off the supply of rice to the population. Landlords and merchants hoarded the harvest in warehouses and attempted to raise the price of rice through this artificial scarcity. Consequently, while during the war the people were able to obtain 2.3 "hops" of rice per person a day from the Japanese, in 1946 there was barely one "hop" available. In the midst of plenty, starvation was still rampant.

Similar disastrous practices guided disposition of Japanese industrial enterprises. The American Military Government took over all these establishments and created the "New Korea Company." Shares and interests were sold to individuals and corporations, purportedly to encourage the development of native economic resources and capital. However, this plan was rendered meaningless by the pouring in of war surplus goods which were rusting in the South Pacific, and finished commodities which were either of no practical value or stifled native industries. To illustrate this point, let us take the dispute which arose in May, 1948. Hydroelectric plants in North Korea had been supplying power to the whole of the South, and in payment, which was already two years in arrears, the North Korean government asked the AMG for electrical equipment. There were shortages of such equipment to meet the urgent demands created by the developing economy. The American authority refused and, instead, offered "nylon stockings, tobacco, and Hollywood films." The North simply shut off the electricity and waited.

This American policy of dumping ravaged the economy in the South. Figures for 1948 show the textile industry, largest in that part of the country, declined by 67 percent compared to the previous year; heavy industry and farm machinery suffered losses of 50 percent. Moreover, the AMG, shortly after arrival, completely dismantled six large factories of key importance, either burying the equipment or throwing it into the sea.

In 1948, there were more than 1 million unemployed out of a rough total of 16 million people. Due to inflationary prices, real wages of workers were about one-fifth of that before liberation. The lives of farm-tenants were no better. The attempts of the workers to solve these pressing economic problems were met with rebuff by the American authority. The American Military Government stressed that there would be no jobs if there were no business; therefore, business must be protected first. With the "business first" concept, any agitation from workers was not tolerated. Leaders of the Korean Federation of Trade Union were imprisoned, and members intimidated by mass arrests. Finally, the workers' committees, which were formed in factories after the liberation, were dissolved and replaced by collaborators. Not only the workers but the whole population were angered.

The American Military Government was quick to sense the seriousness of the situation and forthwith promulgated Ordinance 55 regulating the activities of political organizations. Under its dictum, any group of three or more persons constituted an organization and, to conduct any form of political activity, had to be registered as a political party. Furthermore, it required that complete membership lists and addresses, plus financial records be submitted to the American authority. Persons not members of the organization were forbidden to make financial contributions. Violators of this regulation were to be subject to civil or criminal prosecution. The measure was clearly aimed at the resistance of democratic forces in South Korea. The trade union groups denounced this repressive act and described it as "more vicious and severe than the peace preservation law of the Japanese."

The path of political suppression centered first in eliminating the communists. Accordingly, on May 18, 1946, the American authority indefinitely suspended publication of *Haibang Ilbo* or *The Emancipation Daily*, organ of the Workers' (communist) Party of South Korea. The official pretext was that the building in which the newspaper was located, formerly Japanese property, was under the control of the American Military Government. All former Japanese properties were under the control of the American authority at that time. Besides, the American authority claimed that it found that the Chikasawa Printing Shop which was also located in the same building had printed fraudulent currency.

The Korean Democratic National Front, a broad coalition which developed from the People's Republic, made a statement which denounced as irrelevant the accusation of the currency fraud incident and defended the Workers' Party and its organ, *Haibang Ilbo*.[3]

The AMG was unable to offer the least evidence to substantiate its charges against the communists but, nonetheless, continued the persecution, eventually driving the organization underground and declaring a reward for the apprehension of its general secretary, Park Heun-Young. Three more newspapers were soon closed up: *Inminbo* or *People's News*, *Hyundai Ilbo* or *Modern Daily News*, and *Chungang Ilbo*, or *Central Daily News*. Editors critical of the American Military Government were imprisoned. The Americans were now outdoing their Japanese predecessors in filling the prisons with Korean patriots. In American-occupied South Korea, the number of those jailed was twice the number during the Japanese regime for both North and South Korea.

The disastrous chain of events in postwar Korea pivoted around three conservative political figures: Syngman Rhee, Kim Koo, and Kim Seung-soo. Consequently, some have regarded the failure of American policy in South Korea as a simple unfortunate mistake on the part of the AMG in having relied on the advice of these three leaders. The claim has been advanced that the United States was not well acquainted with Korean affairs and badly prepared to undertake the occupation of that country, and therefore, the mistakes were inevitable but not deliberate. There has been a consistency and cohesiveness to American policy in South Korea which raises very serious doubt whether the American authority had any real intention of building a democratic Korea.

In one year after liberation, the Korean people had suffered enough, had experienced bitter disillusionment enough, that outbreaks occurred throughout South Korea in the proportions of a mass, popular revolt. It started in September, 1946 when the Railway Worker's Union submitted a list of grievances to be negotiated with the AMG. The following is a part of the strike diary issued by the Korean Federation of Trade Unions.

On September 15, 1946, the South Korean Railway Workers' Union, a member of the KFTU, submitted its demands to the Transportation and Railway Bureau of the American Military Government and requested an answer within a week. The demands were: (1) Four "hops" of rice per worker per day, three "hops" per day for each dependent; (2) Increase of living cost differential to 2,000 won (Korean currency) and 600 won for family allowance; (3) Abolition of the daily pay system; (4) Withdrawal of the planned cut in the number of employees; (5) Continuation of lunch service; (6) Institution of democratic labor laws, freedom of press, speech and assembly, the right to organize, bargain collectively and right of labor to strike.[4]

On September 21, 1946, the American Military Government ignored the union's demands. Having received no reply within seven days, the union requested KFTU to intercede in its behalf. Two delegates from KFTU called on General Hodge, the American commanding office in Seoul, and requested his mediation. The general denied the request.

On September 23, 1946, 7,000 railway workers in Pusan, largest port in South Korea, went out on strike, followed by the entire membership of eighteen locals of the Railway Workers' Union. There were about 36,000 workers on strike.

On September 24, General Learch, American Military Governor, made a special radio broadcast in which he declared the strike illegal and said all strikers were liable to arrest. He explained that since the AMG was the legal owner of the railway, all railroad workers were government employees and that it was illegal for them to strike against the government.

This summary declaration by General Learch was reinforced by General Hodge who, discarding all pretences, urged the Korean people "to exterminate the elements who organize strikes and provoke discontent."

Sensing the threat to the entire Korean labor movement, workers in all major industries joined the strike which quickly developed into a general strike, involving about 330,000 workers in communications, electrical, metal, chemical, printing, transportation, food, textile, and shipping trades. The strike demands of all unions were essentially the same as those of the railway workers unions. All unions demanded an adequate rice ration and all unions stressed their demand for democratic labor laws. The only variations in demands pertained to local situations where the release of arrested leaders and strikers was sought.

Thus, for the first time in Korean history, a general strike affected all areas throughout South Korea, completely tying up transportation and communication and shutting down all plants and factories. In Pusan, seventy armed policemen, seven detectives and three American MPs attacked the strikers in attempts to arrest the union leaders.

On September 26, in Seoul, police launched a systematic attack on all local strike headquarters, arresting union leaders and strikers. The next day, police intensified attacks on workers in all provinces of South Korea and mass arrests took place in all towns and districts. On September 28, armed police surrounded and attacked the workers' dormitories in Taigu City, slaying several workers.

On September 30, more than two thousand armed policemen and American MPs in Seoul attacked the strikers, injuring about forty of them, killing one, and arresting seventeen hundred strikers.

The violence used against the workers only strengthened their determination and solidarity and raised the wrath of the entire population to white heat. By the first part of October, workers, peasants and students of the eight provinces of South Korea were clashing with the Korean constabulary and American troops which were sent under a declaration of martial law to quell the uprisings. An estimated 100,000 students of universities and high schools participated in sympathy strikes.

The case of the students in the city of Taigu will provide an insight into the nature of this movement. On October 2, 1946, the students of the Taigu Medical School, the Teacher's College, and Agricultural College, as well as those from high and middle schools, were having an orderly demonstration through the city, carrying the bodies of several slain workers. The procession was halted in front of the police station where two machine guns were installed and more than a hundred policemen waited, ready to fire a deadly volley into the crowd. The chief of police ordered the demonstrators to disperse. Three more truckloads of police arrived at the scene. The nervous excitement heightened, but the students maintained their ranks solidly and demanded the police force be withdrawn. The police disregarded the appeal, whereupon the students rushed into the police station in waves and occupied it before anyone was injured. They were successful, for the police were uneasy and reluctant to shoot, facing thousands of courageous young people. In fact, many of the policemen threw away their weapons and joined the students. The students quickly made full use of this opportune situation by forcing police to concede to three points: (1) Release of all democrats from jail; (2) No retaliatory action by the police; (3) Police duties to be performed without arms.[5]

Meanwhile, American tanks and motorized units were mobilized in the city and attacked the demonstrators in the afternoon, leaving a wake of mutilated and murdered youths. This was on October second. An International News Service report of October 4 stated twenty-four hours of bloody rioting occurred with thirty-eight police officers and an undetermined number of civilians killed; the city looked like a veritable battlefield.[6] Radio Moscow reported severe fighting even up to October 20.

In the port city of Inchon the workers "arrested" local officials and took over municipal buildings. In Kyonggi Province 10,000 people participated in a virtual armed insurrection. So tremendous was this upheaval in South Korea that in one instance on October 14 the AMG found it necessary to send the Sixth Infantry Division in full battle order to Kyongsang Province, where some 36,000 railway workers were putting the local police to route. The National Chief of Police described the situation as "worse than the 1919 anti-Japanese revolution."

The spontaneous uprising, despite its vigor and popular support, was still a disorganized expression of anger and dissatisfaction. The democratic forces, despite their potential, were not yet congealed into a solid fighting front. Moreover, effective leadership and guidance of the movement were quickly lost through brutal suppression waged by the AMG. For example, by the end of October, the last person in the central leadership of the KFTU was arrested. Within two months from the beginning of the general strike, the uprising, for the most part, was crushed.

Contrary to what General Hodge alluded to be the precipitating factors, "elements who . . . provoke discontentment," the summary by the Korean Democratic National Front laid the full responsibility on the American Military Government.

Why the revolts? There are a few suggestions which could be considered as indirect causes of the revolts. First of all, owing to the scarcity of food, the people were in a state of starvation. Notwithstanding this, the foodstuffs collected to date had not as yet been distributed to the people. Second, without any definite policy to promote the welfare of the people, the American Military Government had employed after liberation the same vicious officials of the Japanese regime. As a result, oppression of the people by these militarists and national traitors was intensified. Third,

American Military Government ordinances changed so rapidly, and corrupt officials violated the laws so frequently, that the people simply had no faith in the American Military authority. Fourth, the American Military Government policy in denying fundamental liberties was considered by many worse than that of former Japanese masters.

Against this background, there were two important immediate reasons which caused the revolts. First, despite the reasonableness of the demands of strikers, who reflected the desires of all working people, strikers were illegally shot to death on numerous occasions by police forces. Second, in the summer grain collection, the American Military Government disregarded entirely the welfare of the peasants and, in addition, used unfair and illegal methods in extorting the grain.

5 The Cold War Begins

The American-Soviet Joint Commission held its forty-second meeting on July 14, 1947 in Seoul. This session, as was also true with the previous ones, was concerned with seeking agreement on the list of Korean organizations to be consulted preliminary to the formation of a central provisional government.

The American authorities insisted "all groups" be eligible for consultation, especially those opposed to the Moscow Decision, namely, Syngman Rhee and Kim Koo. Although the American authority insisted "all groups" be available for consultation, Americans significantly excluded the bulk of the democratic organizations, including the Korean Federation of Trade Unions, the Korean Women's Association, the Korean Youth Alliance and the Korean Peasants' Union, which alone had a membership of three million.

The Soviet delegation, on the other hand, insisted on including these organizations. The disagreement was a serious one. It was not purely coincidence that anti-trusteeship elements were also the landlords, big businessmen, and the collaborators who had associated with Japanese interests in the past and were so unprincipled as not to hesitate one minute in doing so again. It would have been very difficult to expect any of these elements to fulfill the wishes, the overwhelmingly popular wishes of the Korean people for a free and independent Korea.

The American Military Government remained adamant, and thus an apparent "impasse" was created. Then, on September 17, 1947, General George Marshall presented a prepared address in the U.N., calling upon the General Assembly to deliberate on the Korean question. This was a unilateral action entirely unjustified. First, it was outside the jurisdiction of the United Nations Organization, and secondly, the problem was far from being as incapable of solution or deadlocked as the United States insisted. Possibilities for a successful outcome of negotiations had not been exhausted. The reason for the maneuver was that in the U.N. the United States could wield its influence effectively over a large number of members of the world body. In short, the United States hoped to achieve in the U.N. what it could not achieve in direct discussion with the U.S.S.R.

The U.N. General Assembly voted to place the Korean question on the agenda and referred it to the First Committee for initial discussion and report.

A few days later in Seoul, the Soviet delegate on the U.S. and Soviet Joint Commission proposed both American and Soviet occupation troops withdraw simultaneously from Korea at the beginning of 1948 and allow the Korean people to organize their own government without outside interference. This suggestion was also submitted to Secretary of State Marshall in October.

The U.S. proposed to the U.N. General Assembly that elections be held in the Soviet and American zones before March 31, 1948, and these elections be under U.N. supervision as a first step toward establishment of a national government. To supervise the elections and to help in the subsequent steps of establishing security forces and organizing a government, the United States proposed establishment of a U.N. Temporary Commission on Korea. The General Assembly approved the American resolution on November 13, 1947.[1]

Andrei Gromyko, debating the resolution before the General Assembly, characterized the American plan as "putting everything upside down." He insisted that the evacuation of foreign troops must precede the election of representative organs and the establishment of a democratic government in Korea, but the evacuation would be considered as the concluding measure in the chain of events proposed in the U.S. plan. He complained that the U.S. proposal contained a formula which did not obligate anybody to do anything. He stated that the elections had to take place while foreign troops were still present in Korea under the United States plan. Naturally the foreign troops would interfere in the elections, he said.

Already enough Korean patriots were imprisoned and enough democratic organizations persecuted, made illegal and driven underground to render meaningless any election as projected by the United States. It was akin to gagging a man and then telling him he had all the freedom of speech he wanted. Also, the experiences of various U.N. commissions, specifically the Balkan Commission, had provided ample evidence to judge the action of this new body a foregone conclusion.

The Soviet Union boycotted further proceedings of the Temporary Commission on Korea which, the U.S.S.R. delegation contended, was set up without the participation of the Korean people. Earlier the Soviet Union had submitted a draft resolution to invite elected representatives from both North and South Korea to take part in the discussion of the question. The Americans disagreed, insisting that the elective character of these representatives be first assured through a United Nations-sponsored election. In other words, the U.N. should decide the fate of fifty million Korean people and then ask them what they thought of it. The logic of this plan was "to put everything upside down." Consequently, with the Soviet Union boycott in effect, any U.N. election had to be confined to the South, and the resulting government would be a separatist regime, not a national one. That was not the end Korean people wished for, but they were not allowed to express their desires.

The Korean people reacted quickly and indignantly to this new American proposal. All shades of political opinion were united in opposition and refused cooperation with the U.N. Commission. Even before the American proposals were formally acted upon by the General Assembly, twelve major political parties in South Korea assembled to form a Joint Committee based on (1) a demand for immediate recall of occupation troops and (2) calling of a national election for the formation of a united central government. The committee also proposed a meeting to be convened in the near future of representatives from both sections of the country—a significant step to national unity.

The Korean Public Opinion Institute in Seoul showed 71 percent of the people in the South definitely against the U.N. election and only 11 percent supporting it. Press dispatches in February of the following year reported widespread sabotage of rail traffic and telegraph communication lines in protest to the election. AMG authorities announced the death of eighteen civilians and four policemen and the arrest of one hundred fifty in violent demonstrations.

After conducting an initial investigation, Krisna P. S. Menon of India, chairman of the U.N. Commission on Korea, and Victor Hoo, secretary, flew back to Lake Success from Seoul to report to the Little Assembly. They stated the commission was "all but unanimous" in thinking a separate government elected and set up in the American zone "cannot be a national government." Whereupon Dr. Phillip Jessup, American delegate, served notice the United States would press for the establishment of a government in the South which would be recognized as a representative national body.

On February 26, 1948, the Little Assembly by a vote of 31 to 8 instructed the Commission on Korea to proceed with preparations for a separate election in South Korea, which was to be conducted not later than May 10 of that year.

During the debate in the Little Assembly, Ralph Harry of Australia, a member nation of the commission, expressed scepticism as to the advisability of the proposed action. He was fearful of the danger in creating "rival authorities in North and South Korea." Lester Pearson, Canadian Under-Secretary of External Affairs, warned the Little Assembly his government might consider withdrawing from the commission should it follow a course which he considered "unconstitutional and incorrect."

Meanwhile, important developments were taking place in Korea. During February the Central People's Council, which as the result of the November, 1946 elections in North Korea assumed the functions of the previous Interim Committee, drafted a constitution to be distributed through both zones of Korea and discussed by the people. The charter called for a popularly elected assembly which would choose a fifteen-member presidium as the central administrative organ, provided for government ownership of all mines, forests, utilities and major industries, and abolished absentee landlordism. It was adopted on May 1, 1948, by the Central Council and approved by the Korean Unity Conference.

A few days before, on April 22, 545 delegates from fifty-six political and social organizations of both zones, with a combined representation of ten million Koreans, met in Pyongyang to hold the Korean Unity Conference. This event occurred in the midst of preparations for a separate election in the South and was a tremendous blow to the AMG machinations. Among the many representatives from South Korea, there were none other than Kim Koo, regarded as the second most powerful rightist leader, and Dr. Kimm Kieu-sik, hand-picked president of the AMG Interim Legislative Assembly. The AMG, by way of rather blunt reasoning, branded the Unity Conference as a "strictly communist run and dominated affair" since the meeting was held in Pyongyang. The presence of Kim Koo and Kimm Kieu-sik, two avowed anti-communists, however, contradicted the claims of American authorities.

The Unity Conference denounced the coming election in the South, and advocated national unity, a common appeal strong enough to overcome certain of the existing political differences. The resolution adopted by the conference castigated the U.S. for refusing to accept the proposal of simultaneous withdrawal of troops from Korea and demanded the unlawful, coercive and unreasonable election in South Korea be stopped and that the U.N. commission leave immediately.

After three weeks of full discussion, the Unity Conference proposed: establishment of a unified government for all Korea through a general election in both parts of the country, establishment of a democratic government by rejecting any form of dictatorship, recognition of private property rights and rejection of monopoly capitalism, rejection of military bases for any foreign nation in Korea, and other matters of national concern. The conference was, indeed, an important step toward national unification.

Politics with Terror

On March 1, 1948, Lt. General John R. Hodge, American commander in South Korea, issued a proclamation in which he announced May 9, subsequently postponed a day, as the date of national elections in South Korea. Twelve days later in Seoul preparations for the event began. Cho Byong-ok, chief of the national police, called the heads of the district police forces to brief them on instructions which explicitly stated that the police were to deal severely with anyone opposing the election and support in every way those individuals and organizations which supported it. To implement this policy, the chief established "Police Election Committees" consisting of the local chief of police, the local chief investigator, and the local chief of public safety on all district levels.

The constabulary was mobilized and equipped with the latest American weapons. In April, Major General William F. Dean ordered the formation of "Hyangbo-dan" or community protective corps, which were to function as auxiliary agencies to the local police force during the election. On the 30th of April, Cho Byong-ok circulated instructions to all police stations to shoot down anyone obstructing the election. The following day, the AMG issued Order 21 totally prohibiting any assemblage and demonstrations until after the election.

Korean right wing terrorists now went to work. Their special task was to call on every house and see to it that people were registered to vote and that they cast their ballots on election day. These hoodlums, carrying clubs and baseball bats, played havoc—sadistically beating innocent people and threatening them with imprisonment unless they voted.

American troops also cooperated in this campaign by carrying the unconscious victims in their jeeps and trucks to the election booths.

These, then, were the elaborate preparations to insure "a free and fair election," to insure an "atmosphere conducive to a proper and unhampered expression of the people's desires."

On May 10, election day, American warships—employed in a similar manner as in the Greek plebiscite—ominously cruised up and down the southern coastline. American fighter planes roared endlessly overhead. In the city streets, heavily armed MPs drove about in their jeeps.

In Seoul, for example, the newspaper *Jayu Shinmoon* or *Free Press* reported "several thousands of police and specially hired civilians in cooperation with the United States occupation forces erected barricades on main roads and intersections of the city, and at every entrance to a back alley of the city were stationed armed police."[2]

At every booth in the city were placed twenty policemen and two detectives, and also the Election Committees were there to supervise the voters. Members of the Hyangbo-dan were seen everywhere, herding the more reluctant citizens to the polls with their menacing clubs.

Despite all the precautions taken by the AMG and the reactionaries, the people resisted. Cho Byung-ok later reported that between February 7 and May 25 more than eight thousand instances of resistance took place, including 44 strikes and 244 demonstrations. Students were particularly active in this movement. The Korean Federation of Trade Unions called two general work stoppages: one in February on the arrival of the U.N. Commission, and the other on May 8, two days before the election.

The most outstanding incident during this period was the outbreak on the island of Cheju, off the southern tip of the mainland. Koreans call it the "Paradise of the South Sea" since there are no beggars, no thieves, no disorders which might disrupt the peaceful life of the island. The inhabitants were hard working and not quickly prone to take to violence. But on April 3, the series of outrages committed by the corrupt officials and gangs of terrorists followed by the announcement of the separate election culminated in an armed uprising by the people. On that day alone, police stations at thirteen points on the island were attacked. Although the AMG hastily dispatched the constabulary, the fighters effectively continued the struggle for months after, until the establishment of a People's Committee in full control of the island.

In all, nearly five hundred people were murdered in South Korea and scores upon scores were beaten and imprisoned.

The newspaper *Jayu Shinmoon* commented: "Although the election day was a holiday, the city was surrounded by an atmosphere of being under martial law. Korean women used to put on yellow- or green-colored smart dresses on Sundays and holidays, but on this particular day they put on yellow-whitish dull dresses or slacks. They were seen looking around them as they cautiously went to the election booths. . . . Throughout the city of Seoul none but children laughed."[3] The conservative Catholic newspaper, *Kyung-hyang Shinmun*, also made a similar statement.[4]

By whatever criterion of democratic procedure, the South Korean election was a far cry from any semblance of a free election. The election regulations were drawn up in such a way as to guarantee the results in favor of the rightist candidates. The Department of State declared that the election received public approval and enthusiasm. If there were any "enthusiasm and public approval," it was the perverted enthusiasm of the Hyangbo-dan and the police; it was the approval of the handful of reactionary politicians.[5]

On June 25, the U.N. Temporary Commission on Korea reported to the General Assembly that a reasonable degree of free atmosphere characterized the election. Despite the dominant and decisive voice of the American government, the unconcealed violations of basic civil rights could not be ignored, and three member nations of the U.N. Commission dissented, refusing to give their full endorsement to this mockery of democracy. James Roper, United Press correspondent, described how in one instance he witnessed members of a U.N. observers team reprimand inspectors at three election booths for illegally searching voters within the designated area of the polls. As an illustration of the mockery of fairness, anyone running unopposed in a particular election district was automatically assured office even if all the votes were cast against him. Consequently, Syngman Rhee was elected even before the ballots were counted since his terrorist supporters succeeded in persuading his opponent to withdraw.

The rightists won the election. Of those elected representatives who formed the National Assembly, forty-eight were landlords and thirty-two were capitalists; not a single worker or peasant was elected. At its first session, the assembly chose Syngman Rhee president of this newly created regime, and he then proceeded to select his cabinet or State Council from the ranks of his faithful followers.

The Americans called them "men of experience in government and politics."

However, in five months a split occurred between these worthy gentlemen of the Assembly and Rhee. The forty-eighth meeting of the assembly charged him with including collaborators in his cabinet, specifically:

Lim Moon Wha, assistant in the Ministry of Commerce and Industry, who had served the Japanese as head of a county and was a high official in the Department of Mining and Industry;

Yoo Jin Oh, assistant in the Ministry of Law, who had participated in the Japanese-sponsored Great Asia Cultural Conference; and

Min Heu-sik, Minister of Communication, who held a high position in a Japanese public high school.

As soon as Rhee took office, as election rewards he began to appoint incompetent individuals to lucrative government positions, especially in the diplomatic service, which was absorbing a great part of the budget. The charges against these three individuals are undoubtedly true, but for that matter all the leaders of the government were implicated in one way or another with the Japanese, or were presently supporting collaborators.

The complete inability of the administration to meet the real and immediate needs of the people began to wear thin the cloak of legality so precariously acquired through the U.N. election. Living conditions had not improved, political suppression had gone unabated, rampant corruption of government officials was tolerated—how could it be reasonably argued that this government represented the Korean people?

On October 20, 1948, members of the 14th Regiment of the National Army of South Korea stationed in Yosu mutinied. The previous day this particular unit received orders to proceed to the island of Cheju, about 170 kilometers off the coast, in a punitive expedition against the population, which was continuing its armed resistance started in the spring in connection with the election.

The soldiers and officers rallied together the people of Yosu and captured all strategic points and buildings. A mass meeting was called. The entire population of Yosu, more than forty thousand people, responded enthusiastically and declared their loyalty to the Korean Democratic People's Republic, which was formed two months before and had its provisional capital in Pyongyang. From October 20 to 26 the elected People's Committee administered and defended the city against the troops.[6]

The strategy of the mutiny was not to hold Yosu but to go to the nearby Chiri Mountains and surrounding districts and establish bases for extended guerrilla warfare. The insurgents left the city as quickly as possible and joined forces with others who had gone ahead and captured

Sunchon, a neighboring town, and had enlisted more volunteers. Together—now numbering more than four thousand—they succeeded in arriving safely at their destinations and laid the basis for the national liberation movement which then covered more than half of South Korea.[7]

The people of Sunchon and Yosu, for the most part youths armed with old Japanese rifles, were to hold the towns as long as possible to cover the retreat of the partisans.[8]

Realizing fully that this event might very well kindle the whole South in open rebellion, the government launched a desperate attack to crush the uprising. No longer could Syngman Rhee indulge in wishful thinking that it was merely a sporadic and isolated outbreak. The existence of the People's Republic in the North made a powerful rallying point for the people.

Government troops, equipped with modern American weapons, tanks, armored cars and ten times stronger numerically, attacked Yosu on October 24. They were supported by shell fire from American warships lying off shore. Despite this military superiority, it took the 3rd, 5th, 12th, and reformed 14th Regiments two days of fierce fighting to overcome the rebellious forces of Yosu. The defenders fought to the last man. Not one surrendered.[9]

The retaliation that followed was an orgy of cruel and inhuman massacre. The *Noryukja* or Toiler, an underground newspaper in Seoul, wrote, "Many tens of thousands of innocent people were arrested and stripped naked on the playgrounds of the schools, and then, the enemy took out before the firing squad any person he pleased. Thus, many thousands of innocent people were executed. . . ."[10]

North Korea

On August 25, 1948, elections called by the People's Council in Pyongyang were held in both zones of Korea. In the North, according to Pyongyang, 99 percent of eligible voters cast their ballots, while in the South, 77 percent of the people defied violent opposition to vote through underground election committees.[11]

The Supreme People's Assembly of the gathered representatives was to be the highest body of the republic, and Pyongyang, the provisional capital city. The constitution, drafted in February of the same year and tentatively adopted by the People's Council of the North, was discussed and ratified by the assembly as the basic charter of the state.

In compliance with the request of the new government, the Soviet Union began to withdraw her troops amidst tumultuous manifestations of friendship and gratitude by the Korean people. Evacuation was completed before the December 31 deadline. The same note requesting troop renewal submitted to the United States was ignored on grounds the southern regime asked for prolongation of occupation.

At the second plenary session of the People's Assembly on January 28, 1949, Premier Kim Il-sung stated: "The democratic foundation of the Korean People's Democratic Republic has been firmly consolidated; the most important economic basis for the development of our state laid; the standard of the people's material and cultural life elevated day by day; and the conditions created in which many daily necessaries of the people can be manufactured."[12]

The task now was to defend and strengthen the republic and carry out the unification of the divided nation, he believed. Kim Il-sung further stated: "The Two Year Plan will raise the living standard of the people by strengthening all the more firmly the economic foundation for the northern half of the Korean People's Democratic Republic. Not only that. When our fatherland is unified, this Plan will create basic conditions for a rapid restoration of those factories and places of enterprise as well as the railway transportation services in the southern half of the Republic which have been destroyed. And also it will create conditions in which the living standard of our compatriots in the South, who are groaning under the suppression and terrorism and who are suffering from starvation, can be rapidly elevated."[13]

The plan, for example, envisaged an increase by 143.2 percent in 1949 in industrial production as compared to 1948 and projected another 194.1 percent increase in 1950. In this connection, it should be borne in mind that the mountainous regions of the North afford little opportunity to raise production by the extension of lands under cultivation. Consequently, the problem would have to be solved in the main by improved scientific methods of agriculture and rational utilization of the soil. In education, the plan called for an overall expansion of facilities in 1949 to provide for compulsory education to go into effect in 1950 for the first time in the history of Korea. Also, a goal of 77,700 additional staff members and technicians was set for the end of the plan. This is merely a glimpse into the ambitious program the Korean people set for themselves, imbued now with greater zeal to build a strong and prosperous homeland.

Another historic step forward during this period was the Korea-Soviet Agreement for Economic and Cultural Assistance signed on March

17, 1949, in Moscow. The Korean delegation, headed by Premier Kim Il-sung and Park Heun-Young, Vice-Premier and Foreign Minister, met with Premier Stalin and Vice-Premier Molotov during the first week of March.

"In an atmosphere of friendship, with a spirit of understanding and aid, and on an equal footing," Kim said later in his report, "we carried on our discussion with the Soviet delegation."

The result was a treaty valid for ten years, whereby the two contracting countries, on the basis of assistance, equality and mutual interests, vowed to leave no stone unturned in strengthening and developing their commercial relations as well as relations in the fields of culture, science and the arts. A satisfactory arrangement on the list of commodities and raw materials to be exchanged was promised. Because Korean imports from the Soviet Union would exceed her exports, the Soviet government established a credit of 212 million rubles for Korea, starting from July 1949 and extending until July 1952. The Soviet Union also agreed to lend technical assistance in the reconstruction of Korea, and moreover, to train Korean students in various sciences. A provision was made for common exchanges of experiences in agriculture, industry and culture. The agreement was equitable and no party derived any special advantage from it to the detriment of the other. This was an extension of the basic Soviet policy that "The dependent countries should be enabled as soon as possible to take the path of independence."

Compare this treaty with that concluded by the southern regime with the United States in the fall of 1948. As it was, even prior to the agreement, the Americans had gradually crippled the South Korean economy by predatory policies. In the agreement, Americans gained an unchallenged monopoly, for example, over the mining, fuel and transportation industries. Among the strands of the tight network of American interests, the Standard and Texas Oil Companies controlled jointly the entire liquid fuel industry through their Daihan (Korean) Petroleum Company. Further, the United States insured its position by stipulating that private investment by foreigners in Korea as well as entry of private traders of all countries be facilitated. This was simply one of the many clauses making South Korea subject to foreign control again.

The events of the past were not without meaning to the people of Korea. Especially in the South, bitter lessons of experience were deeply ingrained. The artificial division of the country—the very condition which kept Syngman Rhee's dictatorship in power—had to go. Toward this end, the Democratic Front for the Unification of the Fatherland was created in

Pyongyang on June 25, 1949, by delegates of nineteen organizations from the North and forty-nine from the South. This body was a loose coalition centered on the premise that for any further progress toward independence, Korea first had to be unified. The main points agreed upon were:

1. Immediate withdrawal of American troops from the South, which is the basis of the puppet regime, the force that maintains it.

2. Recognition of and support to the People's Democratic Republic of Korea as the legally and democratically instituted government.

3. Mobilization of the people in a struggle against traitors who are hindering unification.

4. Struggle to carry out in the South land reform, nationalization of basic industries and the guarantee of the elementary rights of a citizen in a democratic state.

The Democratic Front called for a peaceful unification. It realized fully the entire population was in complete accord with the demand of unification. Indeed, the points raised by the Democratic Front were the crystallized expressions of the masses. Consequently, unification was not a conspiracy that had to be imposed by force.

In its efforts to arrive at a solution, the Democratic Front was even willing to concede its recognition of the People's Republic as the legitimate government. Instead, it proposed an immediate general election in both parts of Korea to decide the issue in a democratic manner. Rhee declined the offer. He was quite aware of his precarious position.

The whole South Korean regime was beginning to shake to its very foundations. The despotism that it was creating by violent force would have to generate its motion of existence. Up to July 1949, 93,000 Koreans were massacred, and 154,000 imprisoned in South Korea. The worst incident occurred on Cheju Island where 30,000 people were slaughtered in one month in the spring of 1948. Demagogic appeals to "patriotism," and "a fight to death against Communism," were used to whip up and bolster the morale of the South Korean troops. The officers were boasting everywhere that they were ready to invade the North at the moment President Syngman Rhee gave the order.

The only "invasions" to the North were sporadic forays into the border regions. They were not military expeditions but simply attempts to harass and spread terror among farmers in small villages. The Democratic Front, investigating the series of border incidents, reported some 432 armed attacks were made by the South Korean Army in 1949. The most shameful atrocities were committed by these brigands; no one was spared in the debauchery. Special service squads trained by the Americans were sent to the North to carry out specific assignments of assassinations of leading figures, to destroy railways and factories, to poison drinking water.[14]

While the South Korean army seemed to be effective in its own back yard, the whole front had flared up in rebellion. The partisan movement which started on the mainland with four thousand men after the Yosu uprising in October 1948 had gained strength. News dispatches in the fall of 1949 reported the number of guerrillas had increased by twenty-five thousand. The total figure, however, is unknown.

The fighters were now militarily and politically well trained, moving in solid groups under a unified command. Even Shin Sung Mo, Minister of Internal Affairs in the South, admitted, "Six hundred of them could withstand six thousand experienced regular troops." Most important, they had the support of the people, without which no guerrilla movement can exist. When the units attacked a car or train, they never touched the innocent passengers and their belongings. When they came down to a village from their mountain hideouts, they helped the farmers in tilling or harvesting. And at places where the guerrillas were established, land reform was immediately instituted together with all the democratic reforms so eagerly awaited for by the people.

Thus, the partisans of South Korea in the fall of 1949 were working in an area of 81 counties, including three cities, out of the total of 130 counties—or more than two-thirds of the South. Their bases controlled the spine of mountains, going from the eastern tip of the 38th parallel—the division between the North and South—running diagonally across to the south-western tip of the mainland. Consequently, this north-east and south-west diagonal completely sliced South Korea into two. People's Committees were established at three points in the Chiri Mountain area— the southern part of the diagonal—and in the Halla Mountain on Cheju Island off the southern coast. The forces of resistance were spreading quickly throughout South Korea.[15] It required a quick decision for the Seoul regime to defend its life. A war between North and South was inevitable under such conditions.

6 The Korean War: An Interpretation

Korea had been divided by occupation zones, and no one expected the transition from such zones to a joint American-Soviet administration and eventual independence to be quick or easy. The United States and the Soviet Union had made much effort to secure some sort of cooperation in the establishment of a unified Korea, but the two powers were not able to achieve the promises of the Moscow decision of 1945.

In his address to the Oversea Press Club on March 1, 1946, Secretary of State James F. Byrnes declared that the United States intended to prevent aggression, by force if necessary. He tempered his remarks with the assertion that he was "convinced that there is no reason for war between any of the great powers," and added that only an "inexcusable tragedy of errors could cause serious conflict between this country and Russia."

Byrnes suggested a list of "must nots" for the world's nations. As his first point, he said: "We will not, and we cannot, stand aloof if force or the threat of force is used contrary to the purpose of the United Nations Charter."[1] Regarding America's role, Secretary Byrnes declared: "The Charter forbids and we cannot allow aggression to be accomplished by coercion or pressure or by subterfuges such as political infiltration." Then, the American Secretary of State continued, "We must make it clear in advance that we do intend to act to prevent aggression, making it clear at the same time that we will not use force for any other purpose."

Four years later, the American government's attitude in the Far East, particularly with regard to Korea, changed somewhat without any clear indication of a major policy shift. Secretary of State Dean Acheson in addressing the National Press Club on January 12, 1950, on Far Eastern Policy said, "In Korea, we have taken great steps which have ended our military occupation and in cooperation with the United Nations have established an independent and sovereign country recognized by nearly all the rest of the world. We have given that nation great help in getting itself established. We are asking the Congress to continue that help until it is firmly established." Following this sympathetic introduction, Acheson drew a U.S. defense perimeter running from the Aleutians to Japan, to the Ryukyu Islands and then to the Philippines. This put Korea on the outside of the American defense orbit. But Acheson said: "We have a direct responsibility in Japan and we have a direct opportunity to act." As some authorities pointed out [2], Acheson's statement reflected the views of the Joint Chiefs of Staff, who evidently felt that in case of a global war in the Far East, Korea would not be a main theatre of operations and was therefore of little strategic importance. It can be stated that, without political ideological considerations, modern war strategy cannot be understood. Purely military strategic concepts do not explain it.

President Truman asked Congress for a grant of as much as $150 million for economic assistance to South Korea while endorsing fully Acheson's now famous view of the Far East Defense Line. Acheson wrote a letter to the President on January 20, 1950, saying: "The Republic of Korea owes its existence in large measure to the United States, which freed the country from Japanese control. The peoples of the Republic of Korea, the other peoples of Asia, and the members of the United Nations under whose observation a government of the Republic of Korea was freely elected, alike look to our conduct in Korea as a measure of the seriousness of our concern, with the freedom and welfare of peoples maintaining their independence in the face of great obstacles." He added, "It is our considered judgment that if our limited assistance is continued, the Republic will have a good chance of survival as a free nation. Should such further aid be denied, that chance may well be lost and all our previous efforts perhaps prove to have been in vain." Of this letter, President Truman said: "I entirely concur in the Secretary's views as to the seriousness of this action and the necessity for its speedy rectification. I shall take up this matter with congressional leaders and urge upon them the need for immediate action, in order that important foreign policy interests of this country may be properly safeguarded."[3]

Congress reluctantly approved $60 million in aid for South Korea up to June 30, 1950. It previously authorized the same amount for an earlier period. The grant represented a reduction of $30 million from the sum originally requested by the State Department. It is interesting to note a statement in the Korean Aid Bill, "Not withstanding the provisions of any other law, the administrator shall immediately terminate aid under this section in the event of the formation in the Republic of Korea of a coalition government which includes one or more members of the Communist Party or of the party now in control of the government of northern Korea."[4]

Evidently, this clause shares no common ground with other U.S. treaties such as the United States-Australia-China and the United States-Australia-China-Philippines draft resolutions which were approved by the U.N. General Assembly on Dec. 12, 1948, and Oct. 21, 1949, respectively. These seek "to bring about the unification of Korea," and call upon "member states to refrain from any acts derogatory to the results achieved and to be achieved by the United Nations in bringing about the complete independence and the unity of Korea." Thus, we notice two major contradictions in the U.S. policy toward Korea: the first, the Acheson view, and second, the provision of the Korean Aid Bill, which tended to harden the division of Korea against the spirit of the U.N. resolution.

Secretary Acheson defended his position regarding aid to Korea when the Korean War began, saying, "The defeat of the Korean Aid bill would 'bulk large' as one of the factors that encouraged the Communist attack upon the Republic of Korea."[5]

Regardless of the hidden desire of Secretary Acheson to support the Republic of Korea, the majority of governments throughout the world were led to believe that the United States was really committed very deeply to saving the Republic of Korea.

The idea that the U.S. was not strongly committed to the survival of South Korea was strengthened when Senator Tom Connally, Chairman of the Senate Foreign Relations Committee, stated in an interview that since Korea was divided by the 38th Parallel with communists in control of the North and since the Soviet Union was close at hand, the North could easily overrun South Korea whenever it wanted to do so. He hinted that the U.S. would probably have to abandon South Korea, and if there were a large-scale military conflict, it was probable that the United States would not intervene.

On the other hand, there were among responsible decision-makers those who advocated war. For instance, Secretary of the Navy Francis Matthews advocated "instituting a war to compel cooperation for peace . . . we would welcome the just aggressions for peace." More than any single man, General Douglas MacArthur had influenced America toward a war atmosphere. He spoke of Taiwan as a part of an island defense chain from which the United States could dominate by air power every Asian port from Vladivostok to Singapore, and Major General Orvil Anderson, Commander of the Air War College, said bluntly: "We are at war. . . . Give me the order to do it and I can break up Russia's fine A-bomb nests in a week."[6]

General MacArthur's changed Japanese policy created more war tension than any single action by others. He had moved in overseeing Japan's occupation from the original goals of democratization, disarmament, and decentralization of occupied Japan toward a return of the old ruling groups of pre-war Japan in 1948. Japanese militarism was ready to come back under MacArthur's protection.

General MacArthur believed, as he advocated consistently during the Pacific War, that the fate of man's civilization would be decided in Asia, not in Europe, and he saw himself as the man who would dictate such destiny by destroying the newly-born Communist China. MacArthur declared that:

> 1000 American bombers and large quantities of surplus U.S. military equipment, if utilized efficiently, could destroy the basic military strength of the Chinese Communists.[7]

Such public statements and a changing policy in Japan to rearm posed a serious threat to the People's Republic of China. It wasn't only MacArthur who followed a hard line, but Secretary of War Henry Stimson also looked forward in 1945 to the creation of a friendly Japan as America displaced the defeated enemy in Japan and Korea.[8]

The hard-line military advocates led by General MacArthur deliberately created the crisis in the Far East, and Korea was to become the battleground of another international war, much like the first Sino-Japanese war of 1894–1895, and the Russo-Japanese War of 1904–1905.

In this tense atmosphere, none other than John Foster Dulles arrived at Seoul, South Korea in June 1950 to give a moral boost to President Syngman Rhee and his government. He gave belated support to Korea in a speech:

> The American people give you their support, both moral and material, consistent with your own self-respect and your primary dependence on your own efforts.
>
> We look on you as, spiritually, a part of the United Nations which has acted with near unanimity to advance your political freedom, which seeks your unity with the North and which, even though you are technically deprived of formal membership, nevertheless requires all nations to refrain from any threat or use of force against your territorial integrity or political independence. . . .

> The free world has no written charter, but it is no less real for that. Membership depends on the conduct of a nation itself; there is no veto. Its compulsion to common actions are powerful, because they flow from a profound sense of common destiny.
>
> You are not alone. You will never be alone so long as you continue to play worthily your part in the great design of human freedom.[9]

Dulles' speech, however, really gave no definite support to the Koreans. He said nothing about American intervention in the case of an attack from the North, nor did Dulles speak of "more active economic and military aid." Dr. Rhee, however, took Dulles' speech as active support of the Republic of Korea in the event of a military conflict. Dulles' appearance in Korea, although his speech was ambiguous, encouraged Dr. Rhee to fulfill his lifetime ambition for the unification of Korea.

North Korea interpreted Dulles' remarks as an American intervention in South Korea in the Greek style. The Chinese certainly saw America applying the Greek solution to Asia. That's what America had tried with Chiang Kai-shek in China. It failed in China, but the hardliners blamed the Truman-Acheson-Marshall soft policy. Senator William Knowland of California favored sending American troops to fight in Asia.

Thus, the contributions toward war in Korea cannot be blamed on any single person. Rather, many individuals were involved. The establishment of a republic in the South seemed to be motivated by a desire in the United States to have a buffer zone against communism, but the U.S. government policy was indecisive, ambiguous and irresponsible to its commitment to bringing about a democratic government in Korea.

The Korean War was far more tragic than any war between two unrelated sections because it was fought by two politically split camps of one and the same people. A tragic war broke out at the 38th Parallel in the early hours of Sunday, June 25, 1950. When Northern and Southern Korean forces met, it became evident within a short time that the forces of North Korea were far superior to those of the South. Even though the South Korean army was only slightly smaller than the North Korean army, the fighting capacities of the two forces were not evenly matched. The South Koreans lacked tanks, medium-range artillery, heavy mortars, recoilless rifles, and fighter planes. The American support of ROK forces later revealed itself in the inability of South Korean forces to defend themselves against the North Korean army.

The information of the military clash was immediately reported to the United States and the United Nations by the South Korean government. A special meeting of the U.N. Security Council was called and it quickly approved by a vote of 9 to 0 a resolution that North Koreans had

committed a breach of the peace, and ordered them to withdraw from
South Korea and to cease military actions. President Truman then issued
three orders. He directed General Douglas MacArthur to evacuate
Americans from Korea, to repel attacks on airports, but to remain south of
38th parallel. General MacArthur also was ordered to get supplies and
ammunition to the South Koreans and the Seventh Fleet was to be moved
into a position to protect Formosa from attack.[10] Mr. Truman, hastily,
without consulting other U.N. members, ordered the preparation of
American troops for use if the U.N. should call for action against North
Korea.

It was quickly evident that the South Koreans could not cope with
the North Koreans. The capital city of Seoul fell on June 28, and the
northern forces marched swiftly to occupy most of the area south of the
38th Parallel line. President Syngman Rhee's government was forced to
flee Seoul and moved to Taigu, about 150 miles to the south. President
Truman feared that a victory in Korea by the communists would put their
planes very close to Japan, Taiwan and Okinawa. General MacArthur was
directed to aid South Korea with air and naval support south of the 38th
Parallel. This support was to come from elements already in his command.

The U.S. 24th Infantry Division was sent to Korea. According to
American intelligence, there were about 10,000 U.S. troops and about
25,000 South Korean soldiers holding off about 90,000 North Koreans.

On July 7, the Security Council voted that U.N. forces be united
under one command and requested the President of the United States to
appoint the U.N. commander. President Truman named General MacArthur to this position on July 8.

This decisive year in the U.N. had started with a proposal to remove
the Nationalist Chinese representative from his position in the Security
Council. The Soviet Union contended that the communists, not the
Nationalist government of Chiang Kai-shek, represented the people of
China. When this proposal was defeated, the Soviet Union boycotted
functions of the United Nations including meetings of the Security Council. Had the Soviet delegate been present to cast the U.S.S.R. veto, the
U.N. would have been powerless to act in Korea. The Soviet delegate
returned to assume the powers available to him in August.

On July 31, the U.S. Department of State received a report from
MacArthur that North Koreans had no chance of victory. New forces
arrived from the United States, the United Kingdom, Australia, New
Zealand, Canada, France, the Netherlands, and Turkey, with the U.S.,
of course, providing the largest number.

Nearly two-thirds of the U.N. members contributed aid of some type, from medical aid and foodstuffs to actual troop commitments. Although the help furnished by the United Nations was considerable, the military action was carried on primarily by the United States. Under the command of General Douglas MacArthur the South Korean Army was regrouped and strengthened and outfitted once more for the field.

Participating U.N. members in the Korean war (or "police action") felt that Northern Korean forces were challenging the charter of the United Nations. They further believed that it was Stalin's strategy to test the willingness of non-communist nations to defend Korea.

President Truman said: "The attack upon Korea makes it plain beyond all doubt that Communism has passed beyond the use of subversion to conquer independent nations and will now use armed invasion and war. It has defied the orders of the Security Council of the United Nations issued to preserve international peace and security." The President concluded, "I know that all members of the United Nations will consider carefully the consequences of this latest aggression in Korea in defiance of the Charter of the United Nations. A return to the rule of force in international affairs would have far-reaching effects. The United States will continue to uphold the rule of law."[11]

The resources which the President had at his disposal at the outbreak of hostilities were not impressive. After World War II the United States and the other non-communist nations had demobilized rapidly, and the United States with the atomic bomb was thinking in terms of fighting a global war. In such a war, it was believed, the bomb and the ability to drop it anywhere in the world were more important than ground troops. In addition, the United States had not included Korea in its defense line against communism. Commenting on the condition of the United States armed forces, President Truman says in his *Memoirs* that the armed forces had been drastically reduced from their wartime peaks, and there was strong congressional pressure to reduce military spending even further. American commitments were many, but the forces were limited. The United States had some occupational troops in Japan, and the only other immediate military resources were air and naval forces. The South Korean Army was armed only for defense, not to fight tanks and heavy artillery.

Considering the reduced state of military forces at hand and the possibility that the United Nations might not support active military aid for South Korea, it would seem that President Truman did make an adventurous decision. In addition, when considering the possibility that United States action might bring the Soviets into the war and precipitate World War III, the Truman decision seems even more dangerous. The United

States "frankly did not know" if Russia would become involved, but Truman sent word to Stalin through channels that the United States would keep the peace in Korea even if it meant fighting Russia to do so.[12]

Another limit on President Truman's ability to make decisions was lack of information. At first, it was almost impossible to get any verifiable information, and there did not seem to be any existing plans to respond to an invasion by North Korea. Apparently the possibility of such an act had not occurred to anyone.

The Security Council had already condemned North Korea as an aggressor, and after all the talk of the previous five years about collective security, neither the United States nor the United Nations was willing to settle the situation peacefully, only to meet force with force. The doctrine of containment was a reality. The United States following its doctrine of containment was duty-bound to step into the action in Korea, and the United Nations with its concept of collective security was obliged to participate under American pressure at the Security Council.

"The decision of the free nations to withstand aggression in Korea, is of course, the first and essential step toward the fixing of a firm line containing Communist expansion. Notice has been served on the Russians . . . that any attempt to cross the present frontiers of the non-Communist world by force will be resisted, and will, if pressed home, lead to a general war."[13] This was a typical European reaction to the firm steps taken by President Truman and the Security Council. In light of previous commitments to the United Nations, the philosophy of collective security, the policy of containment, the decisions at Teheran and Yalta proposing an independent Korea, it seemed that President Truman had acted in a consistent manner. He acted, however, on an ideological basis—certainly not on the basis of military necessity.

In addition to the limitations we have been discussing, there were also certain influences which affected the decisions the President made during these first few days of the Korean conflict. It was quite clear that President Truman was going to get the backing of the Security Council, for it had already branded North Korea as the aggressor. He also received almost unanimous support from Congress, and he must have anticipated this before he made public his decisions.

One of the major influences on the President would have been the role played by his advisors. It is clear, for example, that Dean Acheson had great influence on Mr. Truman. Acheson, when he first called the President about the "invasion," suggested a Security Council meeting and Mr. Truman agreed. The following day, Acheson spoke to the President

again and made it clear that although the Security Council would probably call for a cease fire, the United States should expect that order to be
ignored by the communists. He said that some decision had to be made
at once as to the degree of aid or encouragement which the United States
government would be willing to extend to the Republic of South Korea.
Over and over in his *Memoirs*, Truman indicates how much Dean Acheson
had to do in influencing his thinking by his suggestions and command of
the situation.

At the first meeting with his advisors, Truman recalls, "The complete, almost unspoken acceptance on the part of everyone that whatever
had to be done to meet this aggression had to be done. There was no
suggestion from anyone that either the United Nations or the United
States could back away from it." He continued, "General Bradley said we
would have to draw the line somewhere. Russia, he thought, was not yet
ready for war, but in Korea they were obviously testing us, and the line
ought to be drawn now. I said that most emphatically I thought the line
would have to be drawn."[14] With the views of his advisors, the President
took the actions which followed.

The final factor in influencing the President's decision is simply his
own perspective. He is alone; he is unique, and only he can really know
what goes on in his mind. Truman told of his thoughts in the presidential
airplane as he returned from Independence to Washington before he met
with his advisors.

> I had time to think aboard the plane. In my generation, this was not the first
> occasion when the strong had attacked the weak. I recalled some earlier
> instances: Manchuria, Ethiopia, Austria. I remembered how each time that the
> democracies failed to act it had encouraged the aggressors to keep going ahead.
> Communism was acting in Korea just as Hitler, Mussolini, and the Japanese
> had acted, ten, fifteen, and twenty years earlier. I felt certain that if South
> Korea was allowed to fall Communist leaders would be emboldened to over-
> ride nations closer to our own shores. If the Communists were permitted to
> force their way into the Republic of Korea without opposition from the free
> world, no small nation would have the courage to resist threats and aggression
> by stronger Communist neighbors. If this was allowed to go unchallenged it
> would mean a third world war, just as similar incidents had brought on the
> second World War. It was also clear to me that the foundations and the
> principles of the United Nations were at stake unless this unprovoked attack
> on Korea could be stopped.[15]

As much as Mr. Truman was willing to support the Republic of
Korea, he did not mean to send American troops to defend her. He
probably trusted that the Republic of Korea could defend itself with

American material aid. After all, the Seoul Defense Minister, Shin Sung Mo, said publicly that ROK troops could defeat the communists within a few days.

The event which involved American troops in the conflict came about through the military and political manipulations of General MacArthur. The opportunity to confront the communists in Asia had arrived, and MacArthur was trying to make the most of it.

In the United States, it was not only President Truman, but conservative policy makers in the Congress, too, who were not thinking in terms of sending American troops to Asia. Senator Robert A. Taft, leader of the Republican party, made clear that American troops should not get involved in an Asian war by saying that the United States was not prepared to use its troops to aid Chiang Kai-shek's nationalist government against communists in China, and he did not agree to using American troops in the Korea War.[16]

Even after clear signs of the Southern Korean armies' defeat, the American government hesitated to commit American troops in Korea. Secretary of Defense Louis A. Johnson made clear that he did not wish to see ground troops sent to Korea.[17] Air power was to be used, although limited to south of the 38th parallel.

As much as the Truman administration was trying to control the Korean situation by not involving American ground troops, President Truman was unable to control the events which followed, and General MacArthur, not President Truman, made major decisions on them. For instance, MacArthur made up his mind to bomb North Korea without Washington's approval.

> MacArthur emerged from his private cabin and remarked almost casually: 'I've decided to bomb north of the 38th parallel. The B-29's will be out tomorrow. The order has gone to Okinawa.[18]

A similar historical event can be recalled. The Kwangtung Army attacked Chinese forces in Mukden in September, 1931, initiated the "Manchurian Incident" without the Tokyo government's knowledge. The Tokyo government had to accept the Japanese military action and this gradually led to the Sino-Japanese War. Truman and Acheson accepted what MacArthur had committed. General MacArthur intended to escalate the Korean war to an Asian war. He had committed American ground troops to a combat front against the will of the Joint Chiefs of Staff in Washington. The primary reason for sending American troops to Korea by the Joint Chiefs of Staff was to protect the evacuation of American citizens.[19] MacArthur, however, had a different idea. He even made a trip to Taiwan to discuss with Chiang Kai-shek the military problems in Asia without the approval of the White House. Even Winston Churchill was opposed to MacArthur's adventurism in Asia, stating that he would have stopped at the neck of the peninsula north of Pyongyang, keeping clear of the sensitive Yalu River region.[20] MacArthur wasn't interested in peace either in Korea or with China at this point. Just as he decided to bomb North Korea and decided to commit American troops at the combat front, he decided to escalate war in Korea, in spite of serious opposition in Washington. Later MacArthur became so great an embarrassment that he was relieved of duty by President Truman.

In a military sense, it seems clear that Korea was not vital to United States security, but considering the ideological Cold War which President Truman initiated himself, he now became the prisoner of his own concept. President Truman had to practice what he had been preaching. He wasn't able to see, as President John F. Kennedy saw later during the Cuban crisis, reasonable alternative policies. One of the most important decisions since World War II was Harry S. Truman's decision to take military action against North Korea and this created the most tragic situation in the history of Korea. For whom was the war fought? For the benefits of the Korean people or for the defense of the Truman doctrine?

The war in Korea began with a retreat for United Nations forces. The first United Nations offensive started on September 15 when United Nations forces were coordinated with an amphibious landing at Inchon under the personal leadership of General MacArthur. The landing to cut North Korean communications was a great success and led to the eventual retreat of North Korean forces to the north. It turned the tide in favor of the United Nations forces, which recaptured Seoul on September 28. United Nations forces cleared South Korea and pushed to the 38th Parallel. The government of South Korea returned to Seoul on September 29.

With its forces in the process of securing the 38th Parallel and all territory south of it, the U.N. General Assembly was faced with the question of whether or not to cross the parallel into North Korea.

On September 30, 1950, in a resolution, the General Assembly reaffirmed the U.N. objective of unifying Korea and of holding elections for the establishment of a "unified, independent, and democratic government" for the whole of Korea.

In a meeting at Tokyo with Averell Harriman, MacArthur made known his views on the war. He thought that the North Koreans should be completely defeated as soon as possible, before they could be strengthened by the Chinese or the Soviet Communists. He did not, however, believe that the Chinese or the Soviet Communists had any intention of entering the war directly.[21]

The Truman administration thought it safe to take action in Korea despite threatened interference by Communist China. It was considered that the conflict between the Soviets and China would keep Communist China busy. Secretary Acheson had said, "Now I give the people in Peiping credit for being intelligent enough to see what is happening to them. Why should they want to further their own dismemberment and destruction by getting at cross purposes with all the free nations of the world who are inherently their friends and have always been friends of the Chinese against this imperialism coming down from the Soviet Union I cannot see."[22] There was nothing to fear.

On October 2, MacArthur announced that Republic of Korea troops were operating north of the 38th parallel, and that resistance was light. Thus, his action became official knowledge.

Meantime, Premier Chou En-lai was trying to tell Washington that China wished to avoid war with America, but would not be intimidated by MacArthur's aggression. Premier Chou had informed Indian Ambassador Kimi Panikkar at Peking to convey a message to Washington on China's position:

> No country's need for peace was greater than that of China, but there were times when peace could only be defended by determination to resist aggression. If the Americans crossed the 38th Parallel China would be forced to intervene. Otherwise he was most anxious for a peaceful settlement. . . .

Ambassador Panikkar then asked the premier, "Whether China intended to intervene if only the South Koreans crossed the parallel." Premier Chou " . . . was most emphatic: 'The South Koreans did not matter but American intrusion into North Korea would encounter Chinese resistance.' "[23]

India's warning of China's intentions drew little reaction. These warnings were credible since the content and channels gave them validity and the means of carrying out the intervention threats were obviously available. Intelligence had reported troops massing in Manchuria for months, and finally, the advantages of intervening outweighed the disadvantages.[24]

On October 3, word was received in Washington that the Chinese would intervene if U.N. troops crossed the 38th parallel.

On October 7, 1950, the U.N. General Assembly passed a resolution by a vote of 47-5 calling for a peaceful settlement of the Korean dispute.

MacArthur was given the word and once more a cease-fire proposal was offered to North Korean forces. No reply was received and U.N. forces crossed the parallel. With South Korean forces driving up the east coast, the X Corps set out for another amphibious landing. The United States I Corps moving along the west coast took the city of Pyongyang on October 19. The operation was complete when United States airborne elements were dropped just north of the North Korean capital to cut off a possible retreat. The forces continued northward on all fronts toward Manchuria. By the end of October, 135,000 North Koreans had surrendered and U.N. forces were approaching the Yalu River. In support of these forces were armed contingents from Britain, Thailand and South Africa. The conditions seemed perfect for a final push and victory. But victory was not coming to the U.N. forces.

On October 14, "volunteer" units of the Chinese Peoples' Liberation Fourth Field Army began secret movements into Korea. The final compromise proposal by the Russian delegation to the U.N. had been defeated as U.N. troops had marched into North Korea. The U.N. ignored Peking's warning and accepted its challenge. Great Britain and France, contributing to the U.N. offensive, grew wary of the total disregard of China's warnings. Both, of course, had their own interests to protect: Britain feared encroachment knowing the vulnerability of Hong Kong; France feared a cutback in her rearmament program, and both urged halting the advance at Pyongyang and creating a "buffer zone." To create a "buffer zone" in Korea was not going to solve the central fact of the international status of China at this stage.

Many American militarists and politicians still believed that China would not commit large forces to battle in Korea.[25] Even General MacArthur did not believe in the possibility of Chinese intervention. The general said: "Had they interfered in the first or second month it would have been decisive. We are no longer fearful of their intervention."[26] General MacArthur was basing his judgment on erroneous informations. The General's chief intelligence aide, Colonel Willoughby, was fooled by the Chinese Communist usage of the words "unit" and "battalion" to disguise full armies and divisions. Also the general's aerial reconnaisance failed to locate Chinese armies in the daytime because they moved by night and cleverly camouflaged themselves by day.[27]

On the eve of the great Chinese offensive American policy makers were faced with several disillusioning facts. First, China was apparently less the "agrarian reformer" and capable of competing militarily against major forces. In addition, the Chinese, rather than explaining their as-yet-unclear position on Korea, constantly and vehemently branded the United States as aggressor in Formosa. Equally unsettling was that the British and French were completely abandoning the U.S. offensive policy in North Korea.

At this point, there were policy-making disputes between President Truman and General MacArthur, especially in regard to the bombing of Chinese soil. Over the weekend of October 13–17, the President conferred with General MacArthur at Wake Island. When Truman returned, his public statements declared that he had complete confidence in MacArthur and his ability to handle the situation.

In their northward advance, U.N. troops met with increasing numbers of Chinese forces. On November 7, MacArthur reported to the Security Council that U.N. forces had engaged in hostile action with "Chinese Communist military units." With this development, U.N. members sought to reduce the scope of the war effort. Six members of the Security Council sponsored a resolution suggesting that all nations refrain from supporting North Korean forces. It was emphasized in this proposal also that the U.N. forces would respect Chinese boundaries.

On November 24, General MacArthur issued a statement that the war might well be near its end, that his army had started on a major attack to "end the war," and he promised the troops would be home by Christmas. The general should have known that it was an over-optimistic promise. The next day, Chinese forces engaged several U.N. units in action. Surprised, the U.N. forces withdrew southward. On November 28, President Truman blamed the Soviets for the original attack by the North Koreans, and asserted that the Chinese, who were traditionally friendly toward the United States, were being forced to fight U.N. troops. As later events indicate, Chinese Communists were no more friendly than Soviet Communists. Just as the interpretation of the Chinese Communists as agrarian reformers had been erroneous, classifying Chinese Communists as "friendly" toward the U.S. but forced by the Soviets to fight against U.N. forces, was also false. The Chinese acted very much independently.

General MacArthur wanted authorization to stop "the invaders" in Manchuria, their origin, but it was feared that this might start World War III. Truman, weary of MacArthur's policy statements, ordered all government agencies that " . . . no speech, press release, or other public statement concerning foreign policy should be released until it has received clearance from the Department of State." "And also that "everything relating to military policy must first receive clearance from the

Department of Defense." MacArthur's violation of this directive was the basis for one of President Truman's most debated actions.

The U.N. now faced a ticklish situation. The U.N. had passed a resolution labeling the Communist Chinese as aggressors, yet what could it do? The Communist Chinese had their bases in Manchuria, and if the U.N. forces attacked their bases in Manchuria, this would be construed as an act of aggression, and would probably plunge the world into World War III, with the U.S. and others pitted against China, and possibly the Soviet Union. At least, this was the main concern of the Truman administration at this time. On the other hand, the Soviet Union probably enjoyed the situation where she could keep a neutral position while the United States and Communist China engaged in "undeclared war." It had to be an "undeclared war" since there was a military alliance between China and the Soviet Union. The more involved the United States was in the Far East, the less the U.S. could do in the rebuilding of Europe. Korea was not the only place in which communists were active. Communist forces had moved against Tibet, and communist forces were also making themselves felt in Indo-China.

Confronting the Chinese forces placed General MacArthur in a dilemma. He was not allowed to expand the war to Chinese territory and he was not used to fighting "limited war," nor was he in a mood to compromise with opposition. He made it plain that no blame for the defeat should be placed on him or his staff, but should be placed on those politicians who limited the war. He did not believe in "limited wars," and wanted to attack the Chinese full-scale.

MacArthur wanted to use the Korean war to make an Asian war. He proposed that the U.N. continue fighting to unify Korea and change the strategic picture in the Far East by crippling and neutralizing China. MacArthur proposed accomplishing this by a naval blockade of China, aerial bombardment of Chinese airfields in Manchuria and the coastal cities of China and by leading a counter-invasion of Mainland China by Chiang Kai-shek forces from Formosa. MacArthur was advocating a total war against China, not just defending South Korea. MacArthur's concept of the unification of Korea coincided with the destruction of Chinese power. He promised President Rhee, his loyal admirer, as early as 1948 to help the unification and now time had arrived for the unification of Korea. President Rhee said: "When General MacArthur was here on September 29th and had a talk with the president [Rhee] in regard to the 38th parallel, the general wanted to wait two to three weeks and get all the supplies ready and march on. It was the directive from the higher-up not to cross the parallel but to wait for the U.N. decision and act accordingly. The president [Rhee] told him that . . . the Koreans will move on and nobody can stop them. . . . MacArthur finally agreed. . . ."[28]

President Truman was unwilling to back MacArthur, as were the Joint Chiefs of Staff. General Omar Bradley gave strong support to President Truman's position. Even if President Truman had decided to support MacArthur's position, the United States would have had to go it alone. This was not an acceptable position because it would probably have destroyed the unity of the North Atlantic Treaty Organization.

The rejection of MacArthur's proposal was a rejection of the October 7 decision to achieve a military unification of Korea and affirmation of the original objective of the war, the restoration of the status quo before the war.

When United States forces acted in Korea, the administration wanted to move under the aegis of the U.N. There were two reasons for this. First, by virtue of the "free election" it had sponsored in South Korea, the U.N. had been intimately concerned with the birth of the young state. Secondly, one of the aims of American foreign policy was to associate its cold-war policies with the symbolic, humanitarian values of the United Nations.[29] The United States had to maintain its public image of altruism and acting on moral principles. It had to maintain the image of acting for the public welfare and for the advancement of peace, not for political power and national interests.

On the other hand, United States policy in the United Nations was to get the U.N. to play "follow the leader." On June 25, 1950, the U.S. representative to the U.N., Warren Austin, gave the first statement on the actions of North Korea. The protest by Austin reviewed the efforts of the U.N. to provide ways and means of granting the Korean people the independence which it was agreed was their right.

Strangely enough, many American militarists and politicians believed that China would not commit large forces to battle in Korea. Mirroring the American public's concept of the war's progress was the *Life* magazine article of October 30, 1950, entitled "Hard Hitting U.N. Forces Wind Up War." It said:

> The next day General MacArthur dropped 4,100 paratroops north of Pyongyang to trap what was left of Kim's army—some 27,000 men. Now MacArthur could say confidently, "The war definitely is coming to an end shortly."

On December 16, President Truman issued a Declaration of National Emergency, the idea being to step up production so as to produce by 1952 what had been planned to be produced by 1954. On December 29, MacArthur announced that he felt if he were not going to expand the battle, then America's only recourse was to gradually back off to the Pusan beachhead and then quietly leave, though realizing that this move would leave a most unfavorable impression for Asians in general. He felt that the U.S. could in no way provoke China more, but agreed that it was difficult to tell what the Russians might do if U.N. forces attacked the Manchurian bases. He was frustrated. In March, 1951, however, the Chinese had been pushed back, roughly past the 38th Parallel.

But erroneous estimates by American military leaders of Chinese Army numbers, morale, and capabilities were the critical components of the disaster that befell the U.N. army in the winter of 1950–1951. For example, here was the assessment by an air force general.

> It is difficult to believe that the Chinese will commit their forces in major strength unless guaranteed at least the support of the Soviet Russian Air Force. And if it is true that Soviet Russia does not want to enter the conflict at this time, the Korean War should be liquidated within a few months.[30]

It was not thought that China would employ all 500,000 troops known to be in Manchuria because the munitions necessary to support a Western-style war were beyond Chinese industrial capability and, the Korean "waistline" could be defended by ten U.N. divisions, against which the Chinese masses would be ineffective, even with supply lines intact. General MacArthur became the target for opposition in the U.N. It was MacArthur's interpreters who failed to understand the Chinese prisoners' demoralization and unwillingness to fight U.N. troops. It was also misunderstanding by MacArthur's intelligence aide, Colonel Willoughby, upon which the general based his judgments during the months of October and November, 1950. General MacArthur commented on possible Chinese intervention:

> Very little. Had they interfered in the first or second month it would have been decisive. We are no longer fearful of their intervention. We no longer stand hat in hand. The Chinese have 300,000 men in Manchuria. Of these probably not more than 100–125,000 are distributed along the Yalu. They have no Air Force. If the Chinese tried to get down to Pyongyang there would be the greatest slaughter.[31]

After an initial token attack on November 2, China pulled back to Manchuria. U.N. forces numbering 180,000 troops began their "end-the-war" offensive on November 24 and on November 26 were smashed by a counterattacking Chinese Army of 200,000 who split the U.N. forces into east and west fragments and ended hopes, for the forseeable future, of either the unification of Korea or MacArthur's dream to destroy communism in Asia.

In the light of the new situation, cease-fire talks renewed. On March 24, MacArthur released a statement on the war. This was directly in violation of the decree by President Truman and the U.S. Joint Chiefs of Staff. MacArthur's statement was contrary to views in a statement prepared by President Truman, his staff, and the heads of several other governments, which had not been released yet.[32]

General MacArthur was replaced by General Matthew Ridgeway as Supreme Commander of Allied Powers and as Commander-in-Chief of the U.N. Command on April 10, 1951. President Truman regarded the recall of General MacArthur as necessary to maintain civilian authority over the military, which is required by the American Constitution. On the other hand, many Americans opposed Truman's action. "The nation and the entire world were shocked by the precipitate action. The free world was stunned," commented one source. It further stated: "The Communist dictators in Russia and China were exultant. The one strong man that they feared, the world's greatest enemy of Communism, had been eliminated from the world combat. It was to them the greatest decisive battle they had ever won."[33] On the eve of this hisotry-making decision, President Truman spoke on a national radio broadcast to restate the government's policy to the people. The President said: "The free nations have united their strength in an effort to prevent a third world war. That war can come if the Communist leaders want it to come. But this nation and its allies will not be responsible for its coming."[34]

With General MacArthur's return to the United States, congressional hearings were held during the months of May and June. Meanwhile, in Korea, U.N. forces moved beyond the 38th parallel, and captured the capital city, Pyongyang, of North Korea. On June 1, the Secretary-General of the U.N., Trygve Lie, suggested a cease-fire approximately along the 38th Parallel. On June 7, Secretary of State Dean Acheson made a similar proposal. On June 23, Jacob Malik, Soviet representative to the U.N. Security Council, suggested that the time was right for discussions to begin between the belligerents.

At the end of a United Nations radio address in New York City Malik said: "The Soviet people believe that as a first step, discussion should be started between belligerents for a cease-fire and an armistice providing for the mutual withdrawal of forces from the 38th Parallel."[35] Obviously China's reaction was important and it reacted favorably but

with an exception. The Peking government approved the cease-fire proposal a few days later but said it had not given up hope of pressing its own
terms. At first it wasn't known if the statement was to be taken seriously,
for many tentative statements of similar nature had been discredited
before. But the position was reaffirmed by Admiral Alan G. Kirk, United
States Ambassador to the U.S.S.R., after a conference with Soviet deputy
foreign minister, Andrei Gromyko, in Moscow on the 27th of June. He
had informed Kirk that the negotiations should be by the field commanders and strictly concern military matters, leaving to others political or
territorial matters.

The fact that the cease-fire proposal was delivered by the Soviet
Union is extremely important. This meant that neither Washington nor
Moscow, the two super powers of the world, wanted this engagement
fought to a conclusion. Russia, although somewhat materially committed
to the Chinese, had no intention of involving its own troops in the war.
The U.N. (mainly the United States) had no desire or inclination to
extend its losses by advancing past the 38th Parallel in the interest of
Korean unity. Western powers were beginning to feel the strain of trying
to support a conventional force against the military resources of China and
the U.S.S.R. The West welcomed the Soviet proposal.

Secretary of State Acheson now saw it clear to use the reported
statements of China as a chance to restate the United States position.
While he was appearing before the House Foreign Affairs Committee,
Acheson dropped the line that the United States military aims would be
satisfied if the communist forces withdrew behind the 38th Parallel and if
these forces gave assurances of no further attacks. The United States was
then given clear sailing in the negotiations with the communists. This was
done when Abraham Feller, the United Nations legal adviser, informed
Secretary General Lie that the United States had the right to arrange an
armistice or a cease-fire so long as terms of the agreement dealt only with
military matters and the results were reported to the Security Council.
As a result, General Ridgeway, the Commander-in-Chief of the United
Nations Forces in Korea, replied to the Chinese statement on June 29. He
said, "I have been instructed to communicate the following: I am informed
that you may wish a meeting to discuss an armistice providing for the
cessation of hostilities and all acts of armed force in Korea, with adequate
guarantee for the maintenance of such an armistice."[36] On this same day
Ridgeway was told the principle military interests and the specific details
that the United States wanted established in the negotiations. The principle military interests were the stopping of hostilities, an assurance that

fighting would not start again and the protection of the United Nations forces. Also sought was a military agreement that would be acceptable over a long period of time. Ridgeway was instructed not to speak on any political questions. Specifically, United States policy-makers wanted a commission to insure the terms of the armistice were met, a twenty-mile demilitarized zone established between the lines at the date of the armistice, no troop buildup except on a one-for-one basis and the quick exchange of prisoners. After receiving this information, Ridgeway appointed his delegation. Admiral C. T. Joy, Commander Naval Forces Far East, headed the delegation. The Communist delegation was headed by General Nam-Il.

On July 10, the first meeting of the delegations began. The meeting place changed from Kaesong to Panmunjom. On July 22, the Chinese halted the talks, demanding that "all foreign troops must be withdrawn from Korea." Unable to achieve the withdrawal of all U.N. troops, the Communists resumed negotiations on August 11. The fighting continued while the talks were going on. On November 27, a cease-fire line was agreed upon.

By the end of 1951 the agenda was complete and the first matter—the adoption of the agenda—concluded. Item 2 fixed a demilitarized zone between the two lines so as to provide a basis for the ceasing of hostilities. Item 3 provided concrete arrangements for the realization of a cease-fire and armistice in Korea, including the composition, authority and functions of a supervising organization for carrying out the terms of a cease-fire and armistice. Item 4 concerned arrangements relating to prisoners of war. Item 5 provided for the withdrawal of troops by stages after a military agreement.[37] As soon as the agenda was agreed to, General Nam proposed that the 38th Parallel be used as the dividing line since it had been so before the war. But Admiral Joy wanted a truce line established by the actual battle lines, not on an imaginary geographic line or on political objectives. The Communists eventually gave way on this point.

There were still four problems to be resolved before an armistice could be signed: the rehabilitation of certain North Korean airfields; control of airfields in North Korea; the exchange of prisoners on a one-for-one basis, and the right of individual choice in repatriation; and exchange on an all-for-all basis.

Before negotiations were suspended in 1952, on the insistence of the United States, the delegations had reached an understanding on three of the four main aspects of the proposed armistice. First, the military line of demarcation was to be established along the line of contact and each opposing force was supposed to withdraw two kilometers from the demarcation line to form a four-kilometer wide demilitarized zone. Supervision of the armistice was to be by a commission made up of officers from the Communist forces and the United Nations forces plus a commission made up of four officers from neutral countries. The United Nations chose Sweden and Switzerland, with the Communists choosing Czechoslovakia and Poland for the neutral commission. The commissions were the Military Armistice Commission and the Neutral Nations Supervisory Commission. The two sides agreed also to recommend a political conference to be held after three months to settle unresolved questions. The fourth point that remained unsettled concerned exchange of prisoners of war.

At this point it is important to point out that the United Nations delegation were all United States officers. Therefore, the decisions they made reflected the wishes of the United States government.

Even though it had been arranged that a prisoner exchange would take place two months after the armistice, it was discovered by the United Nations that 72 percent of the Chinese Communist prisoners captured by the U.N. did not want to be repatriated or exchanged. This was a real blow to the Communists and they demanded repatriation without exception. The United Nations command, backed strongly by Washington, refused to force anyone to be exchanged. From December 14, 1952, until March 30, 1953, when Premier Chou En-lai broke the ice, the truce talks were at a standstill. Chou En-lai proposed that prisoners who were afraid to return home should be handed over to a neutral state.[38] The proposal did not mean that China or North Korea were bending to the United Nations. Behind Chou's proposal was the Communists' acceptance of a proposal that had been suggested in 1951 for the exchange of sick and wounded prisoners. It had little bearing on the issue of the exchange of healthy prisoners after the armistice but it could be used to gauge the Communists' intentions. This exchange was called "Little Switch" to distinguish it from the general prisoner exchange called "Big Switch."

In 1953 there was a new commander, General Mark W. Clark, a hard-line advocate, and a new party in power in the United States, the Republican party. When the issue of repatriation was taken up again at Panmunjom on April 26, the Communists wanted a chance to question prisoners and hear explanations by them as to why they did not return. The extent of the free hand given to the Communists, which was approved in Washington, prompted the field commander to say, "The Republicans were ready to go further than the Democrats to achieve a truce." But the Communists seemed less willing, for their first proposal on prisoners was totally unacceptable. The one presented on May 7, however, provided the basis of the armistice agreement. They wanted a commission made up of five neutral nations to hold and take charge of prisoners during a four-month "explanation" period. After studying the proposal, the United Nations suggested a number of amendments. At this General Nam exploded and abandoned negotiations.

General Clark then suggested to Washington that the time had come for action. In reply he was instructed to give way on the matter of the Koreans and other points but to stand firm on the policy of no forced repatriation. He was also authorized to carry the war in Korea on in new ways if the final offer was rejected. The final offer was put forward by the United Nations and accepted by the Communists. This led to the signature of agreed "Terms of Reference" for the Neutral Nations Repatriation Commission established 60 days after the armistice became effective. The terms provided for the five-nation neutral commission headed by India and 90 days were allowed for groups to pursuade prisoners to come home. Any prisoner who did not exercise his right of repatriation became part of the post-armistice political conference which was to have 30 days to decide the issues. If there was no decision within these 180 days, the prisoners would have civilian status and their freedom. The neutral commission would dissolve in one month.

President Rhee of South Korea was totally unsatisfied with the truce negotiations, and threatened to release anti-communist prisoners in camps in South Korea as a protest against a "compromise truce." Feeling that he had been "double-crossed," Dr. Rhee released 25,000 prisoners of war. This action greatly embarrassed the United Nations, for the U.N. had promised that these prisoners would be brought before the repatriation committee.

General Clark had earlier favored Rhee's plan and now recommended it to Washington. The United States government rejected the proposal for it did not want to upset the negotiations. The United States government went to great lengths trying to please Rhee but to no avail. Seeing that the delegations at Panmunjom had almost completed their task Rhee released the prisoners. At this crucial moment, the Communists posed some questions: "Is the U.N.C. able to control the South Korean government and army? If not, does the armistice in Korea include Syngman Rhee's clique? And if it is not included, what assurance is there for the implementation of the armistice agreement on the part of South Korea?" Then the Communists recessed the Punmunjom negotiations. Rhee had succeeded in upsetting the apple cart.

The American government induced Dr. Rhee to calm down and cooperate with the U.N. truce team. The inducements were a mutual security pact, military and economic aid and a concession dealing with the political conference to be held three months after the armistice. It was agreed that if nothing was accomplished at the conference table within ninety days, both the United States and ROK governments would withdraw, calling it a hostile trick and a sham. While this was going on, the fighting front was being made ready to be turned over to ROK forces if Rhee decided to fight on alone. The negotiations were resumed in the second week of July. The signing took place on July 27 at three separate sites.

Thus ended, after three years and thirty-two days of fighting and more than two years of negotiations, the military phase of a conflict whose impact on modern civilization had been too strong and too varied to be adequately assessed by any contemporary. Some of the direct costs of the war could be approximated, among them the 300,000 South Korean and 155,000 United Nations casualties, one and one-half to two million Communist casualties, perhaps a million other lives lost in South Korea and three million in North Korea. Under the armistice agreement, the Korean Republic would gain some 1,500 square miles of territory, five million of the destitute, 600,000 destroyed houses, and devastation estimated at anywhere from one to four billion dollars. The monetary cost of the war to the United States was later estimated at $18 billion, exclusive of servicemen's pay.

The armistice had four main provisions. A military demarcation line and a demilitarized zone were established roughly following the line of battle at the conclusion of the hostilities, and lying mainly just to the north of the 38th parallel. The agreement stablized the military strength of both sides with guarantees and supervision to prevent new forces being added. Repatriation of prisoners of war on the basis of the free choice of the prisoners had been accomplished and there was a call for a "political conference of a higher level" to settle "through negotiation the question of the withdrawal of all foreign forces from Korea." The armistice agreement merely brought to an end the fighting; it did not solve the basic issues involved in the unification of the country. To supervise the truce, a commission composed of representatives of the neutral nations of Sweden, Switzerland, Poland and Czechoslovakia was appointed. Further negotiations planned by the neutral commission failed to materialize as North Koreans insisted on complete United Nations withdrawal and refused to allow U.N.-supervised elections to be held in the north. With a military as well as political stalemate in evidence, the U.N. set up a commission to represent it in Korean affairs. The U.N. Commission for the Unification and Rehabilitation of Korea (UNCURK) was established to carry out the goals and interests of the United Nations in unifying Korea.

Why did Peking choose to intervene in Korea? What were the motivations behind the decision to send "volunteers" to Korea? Was this token payment for their "Korean comrades" who had helped the Chinese revolution during the Chinese civil war? There was no immediate threat to their territories. The threat of a U.N. attack on the mainland would have become more acute with actual engagement, but there was no clear and present danger, at least, in the minds of decision-makers in Washington. The Chinese, however, had a different impression. They felt threatened by MacArthur's manipulations.

Mao Tse-Tung told the West that China was obliged to intervene because first of all, the United States was bent on world domination, as evidenced by the invasion of Korea and Formosa, and the bombing of Chinese towns indicated that China was the next American target. He also charged that "American employment of Japanese troops" in Korea made intervention imperative, in accordance with the Sino-Soviet Mutual Assistance Treaty, and finally, China could not stand by while North Korea was wiped out.[39]

There might be other explanations why China entered the Korean War. For instance, Dr. Hu Shih, a well-known author and a former Nationalist Chinese ambassador to Washington, said: "Months ago I predicted that the Communists would come into the war . . . for two main reasons. In the first place the Korean Communists and Chinese Communists, the Korean Red Army and the Red Chinese Army are more than blood relations. They have for years fought together as brothers in distress." Many hundreds of Koreans fought alongside Red Chinese forces and some of them held important positions. For instance, Mu Chung, a Korean, was in charge of the Artillery forces of the Red Chinese Army ever since the days of the Long March, and joined the North Korean Army in 1945. The Russian-trained North Korean Army helped China conquer Manchuria. The situation now being reversed, the North Koreans needed help from the Chinese.

According to Dr. Hu Shih, there was a second and more important reason for Red Chinese forces to intervene in Korea. He said: "If the Communist State in North Korea should be permitted to be conquered by the U.N. army, while Soviet Russia on the northeastern border stands by without helping, and the Chinese Communists on the northwestern border stand by without helping, if that were to happen, the prestige of world Communism would fall to pieces. Soviet Russia cannot permit it. Hence Communist China must come in."[40] Dr. Hu Shih's analysis of ideological aspects of intervention was reasonably accurate observation. But if it were for purely ideological reasons, why didn't Soviet forces intervene with the Chinese? The Soviets certainly would have been concerned as much as the Chinese, if not more. Who was to play a big brother's role in saving North Korea? Was Soviet policy the determining factor in Chinese Communist participation in the war? Did China, on the other hand, fear aggression in Korea by the Soviet Union and a continuous dominating influence there? It seems that there had been jealousy and uneasiness between the Soviets and the Chinese as to the war in Korea. Since the North Korean forces were not able to defend themselves with the military aid from the Soviets alone, it was inevitable that help was needed from the Chinese "volunteers." This help saved the communist state, and avoided the danger of a major war in the Far East.

It seems that Chinese authorities were undecided whether to believe U.N. officials, who repeatedly emphasized their desire to recognize Chinese territorial integrity, or to believe the "MacArthur-Chiang clique," who were outspokenly desirous of extending the war into China proper. Chairman Mao believed that Manchuria was the teeth and Korea the lips—if the lips were lost, the teeth became cold.[41] It was also entirely possible that Mao was displaying "a screen of foreign intervention and foreign adventure for internal troubles,"[42] hoping to divert neutralists' eyes from China's domestic problems to a front of military might.

Another possible factor in China's decision to enter against the U.N. forces probably was America's reluctance to employ nuclear weapons in the Korean War. Assured by the British diplomatic defectors, Guy Burgess and Donal Maclean, of American intention of respecting China's "privileged sanctuary" of Manchuria, China was relieved of a primary obstacle to a successful intervention.[43] China could employ her fluid offense against the stabilizing defense of U.N. troops, confident of unharassed supplies and reserves. In any event, Chairman Mao knew the moral criticism that the United States would be forced to bear should she attack with A-bombs, and Mao also was informed that the United States was incapable of effectively delivering its small stockpile and he probably assumed that the Soviets would retaliate in event of a nuclear attack. China's massive population and vast land mass and scattered industry could swallow dozens of nuclear weapons without being decisively affected. Therefore, we can conclude that the final decision to fight against the U.N. forces appears to have been basically a Chinese one.

China did have more than casual interest in North Korea's success. A communist victory would severely damage the American image in Asia. In view of the rapid rebuilding of Japan under the American influence, to destroy the American image was an important political factor. There is no evidence that China participated in planning the war. China observed patiently the development of the war, although her Fourth Field Army was ready to cross the Yalu River at a moment's notice.

Chinese war preparation, originally for the Taiwan invasion, had slowed with the Russian negotiation proposal, but it again became apparent with the U.N.'s crossing of the 38th Parallel. This time Chinese forces were destined for a different location and aimed at a different enemy. When high American officials, particularly MacArthur, began advocating more aggressive action in the Far East, when U.N. aircraft allegedly attacked Chinese territory, and when U.S. President Truman and Representative to the United Nations Austin publicly warned Peking to stay out, China retaliated with bitter diplomatic protests and vicious Hate-America propaganda attacks, exemplified by:

> This mad dog [the U.S.] seizes Formosa between its hind legs while with
> its teeth it violently bites the Korean people. Now one of its forelegs has been
> poked into our Northeast front. Its bloodswollen eyes cast around for some-
> thing further to attack. All the world is under its threat. The American
> imperialist mad dog is half beaten up. Before it dies, it will go on biting and
> tearing.[44]

China, sponsored by Russia in the U.N., also protested against American air attacks on Chinese civilians in Manchuria and the American "invasion" of Formosa.

The war ravaged most of Korea and a great task of rehabilitation lay ahead for the United Nations Command. It was evident that the same type of united effort that was put together by the member nations during the war was needed desperately for rehabilitation. The war had spread destruction throughout the peninsula. Korean citizens were killed, captured or forced to fight in their own forces. The people were tired and distressed and in need of economic help. The forces which strove to restore peace and order now turned their attention to bringing back this proud people to its rightful state.

During the early stages of the conflict, U.N. aid and service were seen in such organizations as KMAG and the Civilian Relief in Korea program, which financed the bulk of the assistance program. The post-

war need for financial aid outside of these American programs came
without request for the most part and without delay. By June, 1953,
the civilian relief investment and economic aid contributed totaled almost
$750 million. The United States bore the major burden of military re-
sponsibility in the war, and of this total, it contributed $650 million. The
United Nations Korean Reconstruction Agency (UNKRA) added $64
million and other U.N. donations added to the total pledged.

The war had intensified health threats which already were serious in
some parts of South Korea before the war. Overcrowding, filth and
conditions conducive to the spread of disease were the result of destruction
and decay. The first step taken by the United Nations Command (UNC)
was to innoculate and vaccinate as many as possible. Those who were sick
or injured were given primary emergency care and then treated at temporary hospital locations. As a result of these efforts the effects of plague and
disease were kept low.

Established sanitation systems had been wiped out for the most part
and new ones had to be designed and built. Dusting, construction of
wells, and purification of water supplies were only a few of the jobs which
had to be undertaken. Medical and sanitation supplies contributed by the
U.S. alone by June, 1953, totaled $8.6 million. United Nations agencies
and voluntary contributions added up to $1.3 million worth of medical
and health supplies.

The Korean War was an unfortunate war, begun as a result of a
dividing line intended to facilitate return of Japanese prisoners-of-war in
1945. Why, then, was it not avoided?

> Inadequate communications, or the failure to convey accurately to an oppo-
> nent one's intention and one's probable responses, played a pivotal role be-
> tween August and October of 1950 in precipitating war between the Chinese
> People's Volunteers and the United Nations forces.[45]

Was it true that Peking listened to Tokyo and MacArthur too much,
to Washington and Truman not enough? Did Chinese appraisals, dependent upon Russian interpretations, exaggerate the threat posed by American policy? America, listening through Indian channels and convinced that
China was only trying to increase neutralist pressure on the U.S. through
India, diminished the seriousness of the Chinese concern.

> In the conduct of military operations (as in any aspect of human behavior),
> great illusions are born out of a poverty of information coupled with a wealth
> of confidence that the enemy in any case is unequal to the task of promoting a
> decisive change in events. This illusion (concerning China's intervention) was
> nearly complete.[46]

Even had China been assured that her territory would not be physically attacked, she would probably have intervened in Korea at the time she did. There was very little possibility of compromise between Peking and Washington. To China, the ever-increasing aggressive actions of Washington in Asia were signs of troubles. Time had come for Peking to demonstrate to the world that she would not be intimidated by the arrogance of American power.

Mao was dedicated to halting American imperialism in Asia and the time had come. It was Mao's strategy to force the American force to withdraw from North Korea in defense of Chinese sovereignty and her prestige as well as for the interest of Korea's territorial integrity. Ideologically, confronting the super American power in Korea was a significant movement in the development of Maoism. As it expanded later, the Maoistic strategy of world revolution was to increase national liberation wars all over the world wherever American imperialism was involved. To attack the American world position from all directions became an important key in the Maoistic world strategy. Peking was looking for a breakthrough. The concept of driving out American imperialism from Asia, Africa, and Latin America motivated China to intervene in Korea.

As we indicated earlier, the main reason for the United States to intervene in Korea was to contain Chinese communism, or if possible, to destroy it while it was still in its infancy. Saving the Republic of Korea from North Korean domination was an after-thought. Examination of Acheson's public statements which were endorsed by President Truman, probing attitudes among American law-makers, and above all, "the MacArthur school" reveals more than enough to convince us of the U.S. intention in Korea. Consequently, the prime motivation of both China and America in the Korea War was to protect their own national interests. The Korean War was a political war of two big powers, China and America, rather than one based on morals. A Korean proverb says: "A shrimp becomes victimized when two whales fight." The wound of the war has not healed between the two Koreas yet. Two powers should perhaps contribute toward the unification of the two Koreas as a token of friendship.

7 Syngman Rhee

Winston Churchill, the wartime Prime Minister of England, interestingly described Dr. Rhee as "a self-constituted dictator." Yet, the United Nations, led by the United States, fought a war in Korea to keep Dr. Rhee in power. Why did the United States deliberately ignore the fact that Dr. Rhee was a dictator, and pretend to preserve a non-existent democracy in Korea? Did Dr. Rhee set a trap for America to commit it to a war in Asia? Why did America conveniently overlook Rhee's regime advocating unification by force? Professor Robert T. Oliver, a long-time friend and advisor to President Syngman Rhee, wrote to Dr. Rhee on October 10, 1949 that: "We who are here [Washington] can and will try, of course, to change the opinion that the Republic [of Korea] must not attack the north, but until and unless that opinion does change, . . . either to attack or to indicate that you may plan to do so, would be to take a great risk of losing all support by either the U.S. or the U.N. Meanwhile, if we do lose the 'cold war,' that would only result in its becoming 'hot' . . . and that may well be the only way in which the issues finally can be settled."[1]

This letter clearly indicates that Dr. Rhee and his American advisor had had serious discussions about the possibility of a "hot" war which could be initiated by South Korea, which would get the United States involved in it. It was a common understanding among Koreans in the South that Dr. Rhee wanted to achieve the unification of Korea in his lifetime. Understanding this, many of his close associates, including Minister of National Defense Shin Sung Mo, openly advocated the unification of Korea by force. Many young Korean army officers believed that the time for the use of force was getting near. Professor G. Henderson, an American embassy staff member at that time, recorded an interesting conversation with a group of young Korean officers who shared this belief:

> Col. Kim (Paek-Il) laid some emphasis on the great sentiment existing in the army (ROK) for invasion of the north. Col. Kim stated that he felt that the troops needed about six months more training before being really prepared. The implication of what they would be prepared for seemed understood by everyone.[2]

Col. Kim, commandant of the School of Arms, and several other high ranking young officers were interviewed by Dr. Henderson. All of them agreed with Col. Kim's view on preparing for the invasion of the north. Another officer, Col. Kin, was a bright, aggressive young man, according to Dr. Henderson, and stated confidently, "One usually hears the army [ROK] never attacks North Korea and is always getting attacked. That is not true. Mostly our army is doing the attacking first and we attack harder. Our troops feel stronger." The conversation took place in Seoul on August 26, 1949, nine months before the war.

Tragically, Dr. Rhee was as convinced as these young officers and Minister Shin that they could win the war. On November 1, 1949, Minister Shin said at a press interview, "We are strong enough to march up and take Pyongyang within a few days."[3] The minister complained about the delay of the invasion saying: "If we had our way we would, I'm sure, have started up already." On March 2, 1950, President Rhee told the Korean people that despite advice given by "friends from across the seas" not to attack the "foreign puppets" in North Korea, the cries of "our brothers in distress" in the North could not be ignored. "To this call we shall respond,"[4] he said. The sentiment of this Korean independence speech was clearly to unify the country by force if necessary. To create a national emergency, President Rhee employed the unification theme as a patriotic movement. The national emergency was to keep him in power indefinitely.

Wasn't this speech a broad enough hint for American authorities to guard against the possibility of invasion if the Americans wanted peace in Korea?

The problem was that there were conflicting views among American leaders, as we discussed earlier. According to Kim Youngjung, "By violating the constitution, terrorizing the National Assembly and imprisoning its members to retain his position, South Korean President Syngman Rhee is strengthening Communist prestige in the eyes of the democratic people of the world faster than the Communists could hope to do themselves. By making a mockery of democracy, he is undermining the foundation of his country and the American position in all Asia."[5]

A year after the cease-fire between United Nations Forces and the Communists, Dr. Rhee was still trying to maintain his power against the will of Korea and also the very principles of democracy and freedom for which the United Nations Forces had supposedly participated in the war. When Dr. Rhee lacked spontaneous support, he resorted to force. Mounting tension between Dr. Rhee and the assembly finally exploded on May 24, 1952, when Rhee declared martial law "to maintain peace and order." On May 28, the National Assembly voted unanimously not to adjourn until government officials explained the imprisonment of assemblymen,[6] and rescinded the martial law edict. Dr. Rhee ignored the resolution. Vice-President Kim Seung-soo tendered his resignation on May 29 in protest against President Rhee's "assault on the constitution," but it too was ignored by Dr. Rhee.[7] Dr. Rhee said he imposed martial law because of an "international plot" against his government, saying the communists were smuggling money into South Korea. Eight of the arrested assemblymen were accused of being involved. One United Nations source called this charge "eyewash" and said, "The chances are perhaps one in 10,000 that any of these assemblymen are getting paid by the communists."[8]

If Dr. Rhee's accusation of an "international plot" were true, such developments could have well threatened the security of the Korean government and of the entire United Nations effort in Korea, yet Dr. Rhee never informed United Nations military authorities, who would have been vitally concerned. Dr. Rhee's Home Minister Lee Bum-suk, founder of the Nazi-type youth movement in South Korea, charged that the communists were plotting to elect Dr. John Myun Chang, former ambassador to Washington and premier of Rhee's government, who would collaborate with the North Korean regime.[9] Rhee's real reason for declaring martial law and cracking down on opposition members of the National Assembly was to maintain his absolute power. President Rhee was elected by the assembly for a four-year term which should have expired in July. The seventy-seven-year-old president was opposed by a majority of the assembly then, and there was no chance for him to be re-elected by the assembly. Thus, Dr. Rhee proposed to change the constitution so the president would be elected by the people instead of the assembly.

On the surface, Dr. Rhee appeared to be a champion of the people. He said that he defended the "will of the people" against the legislators who were "selfish minorities." Some Americans defended Dr. Rhee by

saying that United Nations efforts in South Korea would have collapsed
without Dr. Rhee as the head of the government. Dr. Rhee's advisor, Dr.
Paul F. Douglas, former president of American University in Washington, D.C., said that the United Nations could not afford to intervene
because Dr. Rhee had the support of his people. Dr. Douglas added in a
newspaper interview on July 14, 1952, that: "Dr. Rhee is staging 'a
one-man revolution' and is determined to change the constitution, illegally
if necessary."[10] Dr. Douglas had reason to fear intervention by the United
Nations in the Korean internal dispute as it could have caused open
warfare behind the lines and collapsed the war against communism. In
those extraordinary circumstances, an American editorial commented: "It
may be that the sounder—yes, the more democratic cause—is to stand
clear and let Rhee, with his solid backing by the people and the Army,
revise the constitution in his own way, even though his means appear to
outsiders the very antithesis of the democratic process." The editorial
continued: "Rhee is not wholly without legal sanction for his program, the
constitution providing that: The sovereignty of the Korean Republic shall
reside in the people."[11] No one was so naive as to believe in South Korea
that Dr. Rhee was the indispensable national leader. On May 29, an
American correspondent reported from Pusan: "There are growing signs
that Rhee stands almost alone within his government except for the
support of Home Minister Lee Bum-suk."[12]

In a parliamentary government system, if the legislators do not
represent the people, where do we find the will of the people? Dr. Rhee
contended that the time had come for action and he had advocated the
revision of the constitution to retain power. He said, "The real struggle for
power is between the entire nation and a group of Assemblymen. There is
no one more anxious than I am to see this country firmly established as a
truly independent and democratic state. This has been the sole objective
of my life-long struggle." He might have been sincere, as he had expressed
such sentiments, but the words were meaningless when he acted contrary
to them.

After he proposed popular election of the president and a two-
chamber legislative body proposition was defeated, Dr. Rhee and his
supporters went to work in a different manner. Posters appeared in Pusan,
wartime capital, and elsewhere demanding the recall of the assembly and
holding of new elections. Dr. Rhee said the assembly's action showed it no
longer reflected the "will of the people." The constitution made no provision for the recall of assemblymen. Thus Dr. Rhee now had cast aside the
Korean constitution. Whether motivated by desires for personal power or

not, he had by-passed the law and set himself up as the sole interpreter of what was best for Korea. It should, however, be noted that the constitution itself was only four years old, and was drafted on a somewhat experimental basis. The document was not flawless, and there was room for improvement. At any rate, this was hardly a time for Dr. Rhee to rip apart the document on the basis of personal gains, in the midst of struggle against "communist aggression."

In Washington, Presidential News Secretary Joseph Short said that President Truman "discussed fully with Ambassador Muccio his concern over the domestic situation in the Republic of Korea." At the same time, Secretary of State Dean Acheson sent Ambassador Muccio back to Seoul because he regarded the situation as "pressing and serious."[13] Meantime, President Truman had sent a strong personal note to President Rhee on June 3, and Prime Minister Churchill also communicated his concern to Dr. Rhee and made clear that British troops were "fighting in South Korea to protect that country from aggression and not to secure the establishment of a self-constituted dictatorship."[14]

In view of the serious political situation, Churchill sent his ministers to Korea to check the condition. The foreign office spokesman announced that Selwyn Lloyd, Minister of State for Foreign Affairs, and R. H. Scott, Assistant Foreign Undersecretary in charge of Far Eastern Affairs, would go to Korea with Lord Alexander, Minister of Defense. They left London on June 6.

Following the lead of London, other United Nations members also protested. A Netherlands foreign office spokesman said in the Hague that the United Nations Commission for the Unification and Rehabilitation of Korea sent a protest to President Rhee, and Richard G. Casey, Minister of External Affairs, said in Canberra that Australia had expressed concern in a note to Dr. Rhee. The French charge d'affaires in Pusan also delivered an official protest note to Dr. Rhee.[15]

U.N. Secretary-General Trygve Lie disclosed on June 6 that he had asked UNCURK (United Nations Commission for the Unification and Rehabilitation of Korea) to express to Dr. Rhee his "deep anxiety" over Dr. Rhee's "arbitrary" acts. Lie stated, "Strict adherence to constitutional and democratic processes are all the more necessary in a country which must nurse and develop all of its resources to join members of the U.N. in repelling aggression and in prompting economic recovery." The United Nations, he said, "and especially those members providing assistance in Korea, cannot remain unconcerned when arbitrary methods are used which threaten to destroy the roots of democratic government." Dr. Rhee responded by countercharging that the protests were made "on the basis of second-hand reports and premature conclusions."[16]

In response to the U.N. Secretary-General's message, Dr. Rhee's spokesman said: "Trygve Lie apparently has leaped to see the conclusion that the Korean government is using 'arbitrary methods.' It is very regrettable that Mr. Lie has chosen to arbitrarily evaluate local conditions on the basis of second-hand reports and premature conclusions."[17]

From this point on Dr. Rhee enforced strict censorship, instead of rectifying his authoritarian policy. He banned the June 9 issue of *Newsweek* which carried an article critical of Dr. Rhee's method of running Korea. The *Newsweek* article said: "President Rhee's autocratic action, in the frank opinion of United States and U.N. officials, appeared to threaten the Republic's democratic form of government." It was only the beginning. Even the "Voice of America," an American official broadcast, which had been the official news medium, was suspended as of June 12 because it had been broadcasting American public reaction and editorial comments on current issues in South Korea. "The Voice of America has been broadcasting adverse and distorted news about the feud," the Rhee government spokesman complained, adding the government could not permit its own monopoly radio to "rebuke the government." The ban continued for sixteen days.

Dr. Rhee, facing almost certain defeat for re-election to the presidency by the National Assembly, insisted that the Korean people be allowed to pick the president directly. A constitutional amendment to that effect was defeated by the assembly in April, 1952, 143 to 19. Dr. Rhee charged that the legislature's action violated the "will of the people." Imposing martial law and imprisoning the opposition members of the assembly did not solve the situation. Pressure from members of the United Nations did not allow him any freedom of action.

Dr. Rhee now mobilized the "representatives" of town and city councils and provincial assemblies. Supposedly they represented the "will of the people." There were six hundred of them, and more than eighty assembly members were imprisoned in the hall of the national assembly building by these "representatives." One member of the National Assemby, Pak Sung-ha, was seized and beaten by the mob, and others were pushed, slapped, and forced to return to the assembly hall after some tried to leave. Police stood by and watched the blockade of the assembly without intervening until the Home Minister Lee Bum-suk took charge personally. While this was going on, Dr. Rhee was away on a fishing trip with American Ambassador Muccio. The amicable relationship between

President Rhee and Ambassador Muccio left a strong impression on Koreans that the United States government approved Rhee's authoritarian policy, although President Truman registered his complaint openly. The dual policies in regard to the Rhee regime encouraged the dictator to pursue his authoritarian style with enthusiasm.

On June 30, Dr. Rhee issued an ultimatum to the National Assembly to transfer the power of presidential election to the people or face dissolution. In his message to the assembly, Dr. Rhee said that he could not wait any longer for the Assembly to pass the constitutional amendment bill. He could not wait any longer for the Assembly to take action. He was studying the ways and means of dissolving the National Assembly. He claimed that he must follow the will of the people.

Faced with their own discharge, the assemblymen re-elected Rhee. The *New York Herald Tribune* reported on June 24 that Dr. Rhee would never relinquish his office until he died of old age or an assassin's bullet.

In November, 1954, Dr. Rhee again forced the National Assembly to amend the constitution, enabling him to be president for life, while all successors were to be limited to two four-year terms. He was re-elected with a one-vote margin. In the third presidential election, held on May 15, 1956, Dr. Rhee became the presidential candidate of the Liberal party. A third term was prohibited by the constitution, but Dr. Rhee changed its contents once more to suit himself. The restriction on the number of terms was not to apply to the first president—Syngman Rhee. He was not to be restrained by the national law of which he was the chief administrator.

One of the most significant results of the 1956 election was not the re-election of Dr. Rhee, but the surprising election of Dr. John M. Chang as vice-president. Dr. Chang was one of several vice-presidential candidates, including Lee Ki-poong, Dr. Rhee's running mate. The number of votes Dr. Rhee received indicated that he might have lost had not his opponent, Shin Ikhi, been dead. A democratic candidate, Shin Ikhi died ten days before the election. He received almost two million votes, and the third candidate, Cho Bong-am of the Progressive party, polled more than two million votes, while Dr. Rhee received a little more than five million votes. Moreover, most of the Liberal party votes came from rural areas which were under absolute police control. The people had been warned not to vote for a dead man and they knew their ballots would be thrown out if they did. The vote for the dead man was a protest against the Rhee government, and it was made under an atmosphere of fear.

Democratic candidate Shin Ikhi charged "only a few hours before leaving for Iri (where he died) that national police were trying to intimidate voters into casting their ballots for Mr. Rhee."[18] On May 15, according to a United Press report, Progressive candidate Cho Bong-am was "in hiding, fearful of his life" for over a week before the election. Cho also charged that his supporters "were subjected to terrorism, their houses were destroyed and property robbed and they were placed virtually outside the realm of protection by the laws," according to a report on May 17 by the Associated Press.

The situation became worse. On December 24, 1958, opposition legislators were locked out of the National Assembly Hall and twenty-two bills were "passed" in their absence. Four months later the opposition Catholic daily newspaper, *Kyung-byang Shinmun*, was closed down for carrying editorials and news stories of a "false nature."

At the end of his third term, Dr. Rhee decided to run for a fourth term. He needed a new political strategy to fool the people once again.

On February 3, 1960, Dr. Rhee moved up the 1960 presidential election date to March 15 instead of the usual May date, claiming it would be a convenience to farmers. The election date announcement came soon after the chief opposition candidate, Dr. Chough Byong-ok, entered Walter Reed Hospital in Washington for a major operation. Dr. Chough died in the hospital on February 15. Since the constitution provided, in Article 56, that the election should be held "at the latest" thirty days before the outgoing president's term expired, and Dr. Rhee's third term was to end August 15, there was no reason for haste, except to take advantage of his opponent's illness. Dr. Rhee forced through his fourth term on March 15, 1960, which brought an end to the people's patience.

A revolution took place. More than 100,000 students participated in bloody riots all over South Korea against Dr. Rhee's regime. The student revolution was a spontaneous movement without political party involvement. On April 27, student demonstrations were renewed, and threatened the presidential mansion and other government office buildings in Seoul. The situation was uncontrollable. Seeing that Rhee's days were over, Rhee's running mate Lee Ki-poong and his family committed suicide and Dr. Rhee reluctantly resigned his presidency. He was eighty-five years old when he left Korea for exile in Honolulu where he remained for the rest of his life. He wanted so much to be known as the "George Washington" of Korea, but he abused his country's infant democracy more than he could have imagined in his aged years.

The presidency of the Republic of Korea is a constitutional organ heading the executive branch, and as such represents the republic in relations with foreign nations. The governmental organization law, promulgated on July 17, 1948, as the first law of the republic, provided that "the president, as the head of the executive branch, in accordance with laws and regulations, may suspend or repeal administrative orders or dispositions of the cabinet ministers in case such orders or dispositions are deemed improper or illegal." The constitution of the Republic of Korea adopted a presidential system patterned after that of the United States, with some features of the British parliamentary cabinet system added to it. The latter was more characteristic when the Democratic party controlled the government after the April Student Revolution. The Inspection Committee and the Civil Service Committee were established as independent government agencies directly responsible to the president.

A Western-patterned parliamentary system was instituted in South Korea following the first election in Korea in May 1948, and remained through three elections until the military coup on May 16, 1961. Dr. Rhee was elected as first chairman of the National Assembly by an overwhelming majority, then lost his influence steadily as time passed, finally to be overthrown by the spontaneous popular movement.

Dr. Rhee's Liberal party introduced and passed by force a constitutional amendment enabling the first president to run for more than two terms, despite constitutional restrictions, and this act disillusioned the people of Korea who lost faith in the government.

Dr. Rhee was probably the most fanatic foreign supporter of the American struggle against communism. He had received an American education, holding a master's degree from Harvard and a Ph.D. from Princeton, majoring in political science. On the other hand, he was also a revolutionary preaching liberty and democracy. The last Korean Royal House sent him to prison for his anti-government activities. He suffered in jail from both the Royal Koreans and the Japanese militarists. They gave him the "water torture"—drops of water at measured intervals dripped on the victim until he was driven to frenzy and madness. The jailers put his fingers between steel rollers and smashed them. He was released from prison in a general amnesty in 1904 as the Russo-Japanese war was beginning—the main issue of which was the domination of Korea. Dr. Rhee fled to the United States where he spent his long exile until 1945 when a United States Army plane brought him to Seoul in mid-October.

Dr. Rhee had been unveiled before the Korean people by Lieutenant General John R. Hodge, then the commander of the United States 8th Army which occupied Korea. Dr. Rhee was merely one of several Korean politicians being tested hopefully by American policy-makers. Dr. Rhee's

public statements sounded like Fourth of July oratory. His 1948 presidential inaugural speech was packed with fine Jeffersonian phrases. His
American friends were pleased. His actions, however, proved an embarrassment to democratic people. Dr. Rhee adopted a pattern of government
that had been consistently dictatorial. Few men in Korea have ever been
safe from the coercion of Rhee's large police force. Two of Dr. Rhee's
major political rivals were mysteriously assassinated. A third, the American State Department's main choice for the presidency of Korea, fled to
the security of a United States Army hospital in fear of his life, and
eventually moved to North Korea. Dr. Rhee alone survived.

Men who had been mentioned as opposition leaders usually found
one of the following courses advisable: first, prompt disavowal of their supporters; second, a hasty trip to United States territories; third, convenient
illness demanding care in a safe hospital. Dr. Rhee believed that he alone
could bring the "will of the people" to fruition, since in his opinion other
Korean leaders were hopelessly incompetent for the job. Some Americans, particularly generals, including General Douglas MacArthur, liked
him and respected his leadership abilities. He was intransigent and in-
tractable. From the outset, he had set himself up on a narrow but very
solid platform. He was against the political monstrosity which split his
country along the 38th Parallel; he was against communism; and he was
for the revival of one Korea. He wanted both American and Russian
troops removed from Korea and the nation united, by force and violence if
necessary. In commenting on a truce at the end of the Korean War, Dr.
Rhee said: "My country today, like Great Britain in 1940, believes that
rather than accept a truce of appeasement—the kind of truce we truly
believe to be suicidal—it is best to fight on. The alternative is that this
monster [Red China], by feeding on its new conquests, will develop power
and appetite for all Asia."[19]

Rhee's Korea suffered from economic instability. A characteristic of
Rhee's regime was a monopoly control of the economic life of the new-
born nation.

In 1941, 94 percent of southern Korea's capital investment was in the
hands of Japanese monopolists. When the American Military Government
confiscated enemy properties and redistributed them to Koreans, the
redistribution method favored the "haves" rather than the "have-nots."
This policy escalated when Dr. Rhee was elected as president of the
republic. In other words, Rhee's regime enhanced the position of the
monopolists, beginning the Korean monopoly system. As a result, small
business enterprises did not grow and the gap between the rich and the

poor increased. With the increase of monopoly, free competition was eliminated, and prices were dictated by suppliers rather than regulated by the law of supply and demand, and the nation was confronted with uncontrolled inflation. On top of that, the price of manufactured goods in the city markets went sky high, but the price of farm products went down. During the last days of Dr. Rhee, during 1950s–1960s, the price of fertilizer had gone up 500 percent in five years while farm products went up only 20 percent in the same period. When I visited farmers in the Taejon area in the spring of 1961, a year after the April Student Revolution, farmers were searching for grass roots to substitute for more substantial food in their diets. The starving farmers were ready to revolt against the Rhee regime, and they were more than happy to participate in the April Student Revolution. The students, of course, were well aware of conditions in the country-side. There were, however, no rewards for the farmers after the revolution.

Failure to deal with social problems was the third characteristic of the Rhee regime. Not able to support themselves on farms, tens of thousands migrated to the cities looking for jobs. There were no jobs for them. As a result, millions of unemployed gathered in the metropolis. Dr. Rhee's government had no policy to cope with this serious national problem. If there was a government policy, it was to ignore the starving and jobless population. The apathetic policy increased tensions between newly-created entrepreneurs and the newly created unemployed class. The job-less saw the Rhee regime as the protector of the rich.

Paradoxically enough, these unbalanced conditions simultaneously produced both modern air-conditioned skyscrapers and slums in the capital of Seoul and other major cities. Seoul, for instance, has had everything a modern city should have as the capital of a newly emerging nation: many tall modern buildings, well-trained bureaucrats, disciplined police forces, paved boulevards, a booming tourist business, a center of modern cultural activities, and, of course, many green golf courses in neighboring areas. No foreigner would ever suspect that there could be a revolution in such a prosperous city. Nevertheless, it happened. It happened, because of the more than one hundred thousand jobless men and women from the country-side, added to the tens of thousands of war orphans and widows living in urban slums, and the estimated several million beggars. The Rhee government did not keep statistics on these unfortunates. With high unemployment, war orphans, beggars, and resulting high crime rates, one could not walk safely in the streets of Seoul after dark.

The Korean War, of course, had worsened the situation, but Dr.

Rhee's government didn't understand the seriousness of the problem. More and more people were alienated from their government, and the government became more regulative and authoritative, and evolved into a totalitarian regime. Dr. Rhee became a dictator when he declared martial law in the war-time capital of Pusan in July, 1952. The possibility of autonomy for political sections diminished, and the entire governmental system was controlled absolutely by one man. The end of the dictator's regime was inevitable.

The fourth characteristic of the Rhee regime was the style of bureaucratic politics. In spite of laws prohibiting political participation by bureaucrats, the civil servants openly took active roles in politics. They overwhelmingly supported the government they worked for rather than maintaining neutral positions as the law required. As a result, Korean civil servants became inheritors of the traditionally notorious bureaucrat systems of the past—the days of the Japanese occupation, and the later days of the Yi Dynasty.

Under Rhee public administration was primarily a police function, and more and more it was concentrated in the central government. Therefore, public servants' careers depended on the success or failure of governmental control over the public. To preserve their position in the public office, they had to exercise influence over citizens. The situation created an inevitable result. Public servants became the servants of the political party in spite of legal strictures against the practice.

The Korean people had experienced how government operated during the days of the Japanese occupation and the Yi Dynasty, but the public was not experienced in dealing with a democratic system of public administration. When Korea adopted a democratic system, the public was not ready to appreciate the change. Lack of democratic experience by the people made it possible for bureaucrats to follow the autocratic and political traditions of the past rather than to identify with democratic concepts. Consequently, bureaucrats maintained strategic political positions during the Rhee regime and set a pattern for the new system following the old line.

Complaints, mostly unheard by the government, were caused by increasing economic and social problems among the people, especially, intellectuals who had been alienated from the government. The Rhee regime paid little or no attention to the complaints and suppressed them.

The public servants who were nourished by taxpayers worked for Rhee's ruling political party, the Liberal party. An outstanding example is the case of Choi In-ku, the Minister of Interior during the presidential election in 1960. Choi ordered his subordinates, including the national police force, to campaign to re-elect Dr. Rhee. Instead of a fair and just election, the man who was charged legally with enforcing election law actively campaigned in favor of the current president and against his opponents. As a matter of fact, bureaucrats were instructed to ignore violations of election laws, and they justified their illegal actions as it served the incumbent. It was a characteristic exhibition of government by force rather than by law.

Korea's problem, now, was not of communism, as Dr. Rhee frequently claimed, but the treatment accorded the citizens of his republic. He exercised more and more dictatorial power, and became an absolute power with a 50,000-member police force to back him up. Dr. Rhee's regime became a police state. With or without his knowledge, his subordinates became little dictators in their own territories. The nation was ruled by fear and terror. The result of such government is inevitably corruption. Entire government machineries were under the influence of bribery and corruption. The government lost its dignity, influence and ability to function. Since it did not fulfill its duty as a government, it produced anarchy.

Under the Rhee regime, a potential modern and liberal democracy was hopelessly suppressed under the pretense that internal stability and unity of the nation required such suppression. Finally, the government was unable to maintain itself. Remaining were the same autocratic rule, the same corruption, the same indifference to misery and the same misuse of the American aid, which characterized China in the last year of the Kuomintang rule. Dr. Rhee trusted no one, and no business was too petty to escape his attention. For instance, the Korean treasury was under orders to make no foreign exchange allocations in excess of $500 without Dr. Rhee's personal approval. He also had no friends.

Dr. Rhee's speeches were packed with Jeffersonian phrases and his American associates were pleased. His actions, however, betrayed his people too many times. The regime could not free itself from the common practices of graft and bribery. No one expected miracles. No one even anticipated the government would be completely free over night from the age-old practices of graft and bribery. But the people did expect there would be sufficient control so that the nation could survive. Dr. Rhee, like King George III who refused to believe the reports from Boston, had not believed the news of the student revolution. It was, however, too late to take the necessary action when he finally realized that the student revolution was real and discontented citizens were at his doorstep. He was no longer able to control the situation and his political adventure ended.

8 Modernization and Traditional Value Systems

President Park is known for his modernization program and receives strong support from the United States because of it. To modernize a country like Korea, it is necessary to find a socio-political system which is adaptable to local customs and traditions. There are, obviously, many conflicting views on this subject, based on individual background, training, and experience. Some are working to build a new nation based on a democratic socio-political system with a modern economic system while others are interested in preserving the traditional socio-political structure of Korea.

The differences between these two basic attitudes are acute and tense. It is a conflict between the old tradition and new concepts of socio-political systems and human life, and it is being waged not only between the North and South, but also within the regions themselves. President Park demonstrates he favors traditional ways, preserving the traditional elite system of Korea, in spite of his "revolutionary" rhetoric and desire for modernization.

The socio-political system of traditional Korea goes back to the Confucian feudal philosophy which dominated Korean society during the Yi Dynasty (1392–1910). The Yi Dynasty had inherited the Confucian ideological system from the Koryu Kingdom (936–1392) when the growing ascendency of Confucianism had been deeply rooted in the Korean mind. Koreans believed that Confucian ideology is far superior to other ideologies and that it should remain as the basis for Korean society. It was convenient for the Yi Dynasty to adopt the theory of harmony and obedience which is the moral precept of Confucianism. The dynasty's

115

rulers understood fully that the ruler enforces absolute obedience of his subjects through the offices of the bureaucracy or scholar-gentry class. The Confucian philosophy served the rulers as it justified the monopoly of power by a privileged elite.

Traditional patterns of life based on Confucian teachings left no room for independent thought and teaching, and the subjects were required to obey absolutely the rules and laws that the elite considered appropriate for society. Thus, the members of the bureaucracy using their official positions gained fame, position, and above all, property. They became landlords, money-lenders, wealthy merchants, and held political power as well. They wanted to preserve what they had. They were not interested in progress and changes which would threaten their security. If changes were accepted, they were for their benefit, not for the ruled. Confucianism allowed self-seeking and profit-seeking by the bureaucracy. But these practices would not be recognized as acts of the "superior man." The superior man must protect the welfare of the ruled. The superior man, however, seldom appeared in reality, remaining only a concept, just as Plato's "philosopher-king" had not emerged on life's stage. The "superior man" recited the classics and lived a different kind of life than that of the people, and he provided audible and visible proof that the rulers had no common connection with the ruled.

How much has Confucianism influenced Korean political, social, and economic orders? How much has it influenced her educational system, family system, and other aspects of life? Can the Korean people learn to live in modern society, coming out of their traditional shelter? What should be discarded and what should be treasured of their tradition? What efforts should be exerted to uproot Confucian ideology from Korean culture?

We must examine the meaning of modern man in order to distinguish him from traditional Confucianism at this point. In modern times we experience a process of change which affects everything, yet is controlled by no one. We must all be concerned with these changes because, try as we may, we cannot escape them. Man is being transformed—sometimes spontaneously, sometimes over a period of time.

Modern man must be ready for new experiences and open for change. This is a psychological state of mind. Traditional man lacks this readiness to change. We all see this evidenced by the actions of older people in society. They are "set in their ways" and refuse to send out the old and bring in the new. Change, any kind of change, whether an improvement or not, is undesirable in their life space. Modern man is concerned and holds opinions on a large number of problems and issues, while the traditional man tends to be concerned only with his immediate environment and those problems and issues which affect him directly.

Modern man is flexible and does not think in a strictly autocratic and hierarchical manner. Concern with the present and future rather than with the past is an important characteristic of modern man. In the hectic world today, man cannot live in the past; he cannot cry over spilled milk—he must move with the times; he must progress. Modern man must plan and organize. He cannot sit back and wait for things to happen. Life is what we make of it, and it must be handled on those terms. Seeking to dominate his environment, modern man looks to achieving his goals of life. Environment, per se, will never overpower a modern man. Modern man has dignity and respects the opinions of others. He believes in fulfilling his obligations and responsibilities. Consider now how different is the philosophy of the traditional man whose intellectual basis is in the teachings of Confucius.

There are several dominant characteristics of Confucianism which contribute heavily to the failure of modernization in Korea. First of all, Confucianism is closely associated with the ruling class of the establishment; secondly, it presupposes a strong family system; and thirdly, it creates a vacuum between the rulers and the ruled.

Confucian teachings are feudalistic and autocratic. They are aimed at training elite members of the ruling class to rule the rest of the population. The Confucian system did not favor the lower class; it was primarily for the benefit of the "superior man." It assumed that there were different classes of people: those who could be educated and those who could not be. It also assumed that something crafty and insidiously undemocratic was afoot. In other words, the Confucian system advocated an anti-democratic system. Yet, the Confucian "mentality" has dominated Korean rulers for the past thirty years, since Korea's "independence" in 1948. The United States has, of course, endorsed from the beginning these leaders.

The Confucian scholar-gentry was almost identical with that of the modern state bureaucracy. Furthermore, political activity within the bureaucratic framework was in keeping with the Confucian ethical orientation. As a matter of fact, the societal structures were focused on the political center, or the monarchical center, which was strongly oriented to Confucian ideology.

The political center, therefore, became the sole distributor of honor and prestige. Nonpolitical groups did not develop independent status orientations as they did in the West.

The role of the scholar-gentry, or the intelligentsia, becomes most crucial at this point. Their special position enabled them to influence the decision-makers. The most important single political concept of the intelligentsia throughout the ages was contingent on the persistence of the political order and the unity of the kingdom. The scholar-gentry group, therefore, became the major bulwark of the ruling class against any changes or reforms of the existing system.

The second factor which is characteristic of the traditional society of Korea, and the factor which helps to explain the failure of modernization, has been a strong family system. The core of the Korean social structure has been the feudal family system. Like the old Chinese system, it is based on Confucian ideology. One of the basic elements of the system is the family's internal cohesion, similar to the political framework of the society. The morality of the old family system has been challenged today, especially by the demands of the poor.

The negative elements of the family system could, however, orient themselves to new symbolic centers. The contours of emerging modern systems depend on clear structural locations of autonomous institutional spheres. Without these, one cannot anticipate the development of flexible, viable, modern structures. And where family systems are closed, they are likely to undermine the development of new institutional centers which are sufficiently flexible and viable to survive in today's society. For instance, in Turkey, new institution building was achieved only at the negation of Islamic traditions.[1]

The third factor which is characteristic of the traditional society of Korea and a contributing factor to the failure of modernization is the vacuum that exists between the rulers and the ruled. The scholar-gentry was supposed to be a bridge between the two classes, but has become the servant of the rulers, rather than the guardian of the people. The alienated citizens lived in total bewilderment about affairs of their government and their country; the change from one dynasty to another had no effect on their lives. On the other hand, the scholar-officials worked in complete ignorance of what their bureaucracies were doing to the people. When some Koreans commented that they were "better off under Japanese imperialism than under Dr. Syngman Rhee's regime," certainly, they didn't mean it, or at least, they didn't understand the meaning of national freedom. Apparently the legal-political liberation of their nation had no meaning at the level of their individual socio-economic beings.

Traditional society cannot be identified with a single individual or group of individuals. There are certain impersonal forces over which all individuals are gradually losing control. It has happened in the Asian traditional society, and it is happening in the industrialized not-so-traditional society of the West today. That is, man has lost control over the man-made system, and the system dominates him.

With this background, let us now move into the area of the process of modernization. Modernization is associated with some definite structural characteristics. The most important factor is a high level of structural differentiation. However, these structural characteristics are not to be regarded as simple indices of successful modernization. There are many different interpretations about the meaning of modernization. Professor David E. Apter thinks that modernization is not different from industrialization. He says, "Industrialization is that aspect of modernization so powerful in its consequences that it alters dysfunctional social institutions and customs by creating new roles and social instruments, based on the use of the machine."[2]

Contrary to this view, there is an opinion that it is a fallacy to overemphasize industrialization in the continuous economic development of underdeveloped countries.[3] It is too simple and misleading to define modernization as an industrialization or a Westernization, but on the other hand, we should not minimize the significance of economic development as an important part of modernization. Modernization is, however, more than an economic phenomenon. We should deal with conceptual and social changes as much as economic changes. They are interrelated phenomena. A scholar has stated in the following manner, "It seems to me that the key problem in successful development is not to focus on a single criterion of growth, but rather to balance and measure development according to several different economic and social criteria."[4]

The antithesis of modernization is traditionalism, which is an attachment to the glories of the past, its beliefs and practices. Those traditional beliefs and practices are thought of by the traditionalist as immutable. However, tradition should not be confused with traditionalism as being antithetical to modernization. Tradition itself is not. Beliefs and practices handed down from the past and the manipulation of such traditional ways are a part of the modernization process. It is only when proponents of tradition disallow its reinterpretation and modification that a barricade to modernization is erected.

Modernization during the late nineteenth and early twentieth centuries referred to the growing tendencies toward rational leanings and secularism. It included a break from superstitious constraints and tyrannical regimes.

Although industrialization is not modernization *per se*, it is necessary to its achievement. In discussing the importance of industrialization of a society reaching for modernity, one authority on the subject proposes a definition of modernization that is more functional than encompassing. His definition focuses on the sources of power and the nature of the tools used by a given society, usually referred to as technological and economical. A society, he says, is considered more or less modernized to the extent that its members employ inanimate sources of power and/or the use of tools to multiply the effects of their efforts. Inanimate sources of power are those not produced from human or other animal's energy. Tools are considered physical devices that are separable from the body of an individual who applies them and are used to accomplish what could not be accomplished as well without them.[5] Thus, the greater the ratio of inanimate to animate sources of power and the greater the multiplication of effort as the effect of the application of tools, the greater is the degree of modernization.

But industrialization is not sufficient in itself to develop a modern state. While the chief characteristic of modernization is a central belief in rational and scientific control, the revolution of modernization is more far-reaching, involving the transformation of all systems of society. It is because of this that modernization must be studied from the complete spectrum of the social science disciplines rather than from any one major focal point. Some of the common functions of modernization include the promotion of knowledge, political integration, economic development and social mobilization. The way in which these functions are performed and their sources depend to a large extent upon the traditional institutions of each country.

Whether modernization means industrialization, Westernization, enlightenment or science, or all of these, there is no doubt that a basic criterion for the achievement of the ingredients of modernization is education.

Obviously there are good reasons why education is emphasized in any modernization program. For one, to promote economic and technological progress in a state creates a natural demand for well trained people. There is no such demand in a Confucian-oriented traditional society. National unification is also important. Men of an isolated village or tribe cannot communicate and understand others, much less understand what it means to be a nation, unless a statewide network of uniform educational programs is launched. Education also is important if administrative coordination is to be carried out over large areas. The success of such coordination is dependent upon literate public officials. Education for survival in the modern world is an absolute necessity.

The specific contributions that education has made and can make to modernization are many. Education is a tremendous force in promoting the development of new conceptions of the self, developing within the individual loyalties to new rules, new ideas and new groups. This is a threat to a traditional society. Education prepares men to transform the occupational structures of their society while working in it and teaches men to remold their traditional intellectual systems into new forms. Preservation of important intellectual systems, such as literature, law and science, is also a function of the educational process.

Education aids in the selection of those who will bear the burden of leadership, creativity and culture while reinforcing the political system through indoctrination, directing minds toward the present and the future. Lastly, it must not be forgotten that education in itself perpetuates, elaborates, and reinforces the educational system.

Although education can perform all the aforementioned tasks, it can also act as a stultifying force perpetuating traditionalism. Whether education acts as an agent promoting progress and new ways depends upon how much it is being influenced by the modernization process.

Edward Shils puts his stress on the university level of education. He feels that the success of a country trying to modernize is dependent to a large extent upon the quality of its university system. He gives top priority to the development of universities in underdeveloped countries, criticising present systems for having too many "ill-qualified" professors teaching too many "ill-qualified" students. He calls this a "problem of numbers," or quantity over quality.

Education in any society is viewed from an input-output standpoint. Developing countries investing in education strive for maximun beneficial outputs. An obstacle arises as to how much freedom of choice in education and job selection should be permitted. Officials must provide the widest array of choices while faced with a consistent need for procuring the right supply of trained personnel. Thus, education at times is limited to those influences that need and support it.

Levels of education and economic progress are closely related. Countries cannot escape from poverty until their citizens become literate, learn to carry on complex technical and business operations, and can administer complicated organizations. The benefits of schooling depend on how people use what they have learned. Poor countries find it difficult to spare resources for development, as there are many demands on existing resources. Investments of these resources are limited by the supply of people knowledgeable enough to make productive use of assets. The schools themselves absorb a large share of the trained people needed to teach new workers.

Whatever the size of the educational system, the problem of division also arises. Elementary, secondary, and university levels are all needed, but where is the line of priorities to be drawn? Most countries should resist political pressures to overexpand the institutions of higher learning. A basic test of how much education a country can afford is to ask what it would have to give up to achieve it.

Controversy over the kind of education to offer arises in every country. Should the emphasis be on general education or technical training? Developing countries usually adopt a policy of getting the most for the least cost. They train a large number to an intermediate level and only a few to the highest level. Emphasis on vocational training raises objections because it is argued that children taught a particular skill too early in life will dislike it later. Also, vocational training takes time away from studies of science which are basic to technical education. A good educational system, then, should be flexible. The educational system of South Korea is anything but flexible. It has been identified more with the old Japanese colonial system than with a democratic system. President Park Chung Hee has become an absolute ruler like the Japanese emperor during colonial days, and the influence of the Korean CIA dominates the educational system. The reason for tight government control is obvious. Education upsets traditional life. It helps to lay the foundation for a new way of life. The more effective education is, the more changes result. President Park and his supporters are evidently afraid of the results education could produce in Korea.

Mass communication is another important aspect of modernization. It enlarges the range of human experience. The more a person is exposed to mass communications media, the more modern his or her attitudes tend to be. There is much evidence available that those individuals who have access to newspapers, radios, and televisions have more modern attitudes, are more liberal, and more adaptable to new ideas than those who do not have such access. The mass media provide basic information, maintain accurate records, and communicate rapidly. The media coordinate various groups in a society, and open the gates for interpersonal actions. By doing these things, modern communication has changed the thinking and the attitude of people in developing countries by exposing them to a new way of life.

The development of communications media is dependent upon a number of variables, such as transportation and political organization. Other factors in their development include the conflicting goals of individuals and the controlling elements of the society. For example, communication may be important to unify a country but less important for exploitation of natural resources. Of course, investments in communications do not come with all the answers in one neat package. Preciseness in being able to calculate what type of a communication investment is necessary to meet desired ends is the goal but not always achievable. Radio may be needed for entertainment, propaganda, and education, or all of these. In some cases, telephones and roads might be more necessary for business-oriented plans. Policy decisions as to what extent the media can be used must be determined. Should they be free, for propaganda only, as is the case now in South Korea, or for open and sophisticated debate, or for what? The objectives for the use of the mass media must be closely linked with the aims and process of modernization.

Korean society has become a static society as a result of the lack of vigorous debate and intellectual activity. The government has discouraged intellectual originality. Change and progress were sacrificed for unity and stability. The assumed stability and unity, as a matter of record, were the major sources for the instability and disunity of the Yi Dynasty.

For instance, following the downfall of the Chinese Han Dynasty, a prolonged period of political division and weakness ensued. For more than three and a half centuries China knew no great unifying imperial line, such as she had under the Han Dynasty. The Han Dynasty had adopted Confucianism as its only political ideology, enforced Confucian rites at all schools, and used Confucian classics as the only standard text books. The seemingly unified society was actually preparing its way to collapse, as evidenced by its eventual weakening and loss of power.

To a large extent, Confucianism was the stabilizing element in the Korean political system; it motivated political actors in the system to resist change in the name of traditional values and beliefs.

In the process of modernization, those political actors became major obstacles to change and progress as we are witnessing now with the Park regime. The regime labors to maintain the status quo. One of the characteristics of modernization is change. But change for the sake of change is not progress. Change must take place in a free and creative atmosphere to have meaning. Neglecting to create such an atmosphere is damaging to the modernization process. Again witness the lack of this free atmosphere for change under Park Chung Hee.

Let us now turn our attention to the issue of political modernization. In spite of the long history of Korean civilization, Korea has been unable to bring about modernization from within, either through reformation of the system or through revolution. There were many sporadic reform movements within the system, ranging from conservative attempts to reform bureaucratic corruption, to the more radical movements attempting to transform primary value orientations. But none was very successful. The Confucian cultural primacy remained because foreign imperialistic powers always supported corrupted regimes, which in turn protected the foreigners' investments.

As far as the political corruption goes, there is no great deal of difference between old concepts and new concepts. Corruption is a corruption, although corruption may be more prevalent in some cultures than others. Yet, many American scholars, including Professor Samuel Huntington, stress that corruption may be helpful to the development of modernization in developing countries. Huntington states that "Corruption itself may be a substitute for reform, and both corruption and reform may be substitutes for revolution."[6]

This is representative of statements made by American scholars concerning political modernization in developing countries. These scholars have taken the position that there is some positive value in political corruption, and one should not totally dismiss the possible benefit of corruption. We know now how much these American scholars have influenced the process of modernization in South Korea.

The bribery scandal involving Tongsun Park is a good example. Park was just one of many thousands who had been educated at American universities, learning about Professor Huntington's concept of modernization, and now serves the Park regime of South Korea. There are many hundreds of young Koreans with Ph.D.s from American universities who are now serving the Park regime, as does Tongsun Park. He was rather successful in his assignment in Washington. He made many contributions to American congressmen to influence them to support President Park Chung Hee's dictatorial regime in the U.S. Congress. Of course, congressmen consider any contribution from a foreign source like Tongsun Park close to bribery, if not bribery in fact. They know they should avoid that kind of generosity, but they didn't. They, too, probably believed like the scholars that corruption is a good way to modernize South Korea. The concept that corruption is a substitute for reform, and may be a substitute for revolution, is not only reactionary in nature but also deceitful. Tongsun Park and many other American-educated Korean scholars are now helping President Park's dictatorial policy and are supported by Huntington's view.

From the political point of view, the primary concern with the modernization process is identifying an institutional framework that will be flexible and powerful enough to meet the demands it must face. In this connection, there are two basic characteristics of political modernization. The increased central power of the state with a simultaneous weakening of traditional power sources is one, and the other is popular participation in politics.

Under the first characteristic, the state has the prime responsibility for bringing together as a cohesive unit the diverse elements of a society, such as regional, ethnic, language or religious groups. Much depends upon the ability of the government to exert its authority throughout the state. The government must avoid problems of mutual suspicion, fragmentation, and alienation. Under the second characteristic, the new nations, freed from the shackles of colonial rule, are following a different pattern than that followed by Western nations where control and differentiation of political institutions preceded popular participation. Today, popular participation in governments of developing countries may be very high and often contributes to instability. Popular participation is, as Marion J. Levy, Jr. has pointed out, a contributor to psychological aspects of modernization by promoting "psychic mobility" or "empathy."

Through participation and awareness, persons become better able to see themselves in another's place. This increases the tendency to use rational, pragmatic norms in deciding issues, rather than relying on occult, religious and traditional forms. Also, participation aids in promoting a more optimistic outlook on the need and utility of change.

This participation should not be confused with mobilization, but rather it is concerned with the election of leaders and influencing the formation and conduct of public policy. In certain developing nations, the government has made a decided effort to limit participation because of the central values of the new elite, which may include only a desire for national unity, political stability, and economic modernization. In other words, the main populace is given few opportunities for participation because of the difference in goals. These governments are perhaps afraid of real political modernization because it often brings social conflict and revolt.

In the case of South Korea, there were at least three major conditions which promoted the development of a political participation movement. These were the growth of an urban population which created a mass labor force, the expansion of governmental activities affecting the lives of many citizens, and the growth of mass communication systems.

Any government can have a good economic growth if a sufficient amount of economic planning is included in modernization. During modernization a government, however, will run into certain crises which affect both its economic and its political development if there isn't sufficient participation of the masses. First of all, if there is no fair distribution of goods and services in response to generalized and fortified demands, there will be constant unrest among the people. Historically, this is true of Korean mass movements.

A nation must be able to maximize what it has and its benefits must be equally shared. A modernizing country must have successful economic planning. The government's capacity to meet the demands of distribution is related to the degree of its flexibility and creativity in anticipating those demands.

Because of this distribution crisis, it is sometimes advantageous for a developing country to have a one-party, tightly controlled government. There are other reasons also for advocating a one-party system. First, a new nation would not be able to stand excessive demands that are destructive to the national integrity of a two-party system, and in a country with no classes, what could be more logical than a one-party government? A single-party government can and does provide a context for genuine policy debate and constructive opposition.

In the development of a modern nation-state, crises are bound to occur. There are numerous types of crisis—identity, legitimacy, penetration, integration, participation, distribution, etc., just to name a few. "A firm sense of identity is necessary for building a stable and modern nation-state,"[7] said one authority, referring to the identity crisis.

A modern community is many things, but one thing it should not be is reliant on another country for its survival. Korean history reveals many shameful episodes where the country relied on external powers for solutions to domestic conflicts. On the other hand, there were as many incidents which called for foreign powers to stay out of Korean affairs.

We recall such movements as the Tong-hak Rebellion of 1894, the Independent Club movement of 1896, the "Righteous Soldiers' Movement" of 1905, and especially the 1919 national movement against Japanese imperialism.

The Tong-hak Rebellion was the earliest manifestation of the Korean people against both foreign subjugation and the rule of the landed gentry. This great peasant uprising established its headquarters in Jolla Province and overwhelmed Korean government forces. The revolt, however, failed, chiefly because of the armed support given to the Korean government by the Chinese and the Japanese. They intervened actively to prevent the overthrow of the Yi regime which had proved amenable to their demands. It was a devastating defeat for the people and a victory for foreign imperialism.[8] Interestingly, we find the leading bureaucrats who invited foreign powers to intervene and to suppress the revolt were Confucian scholars.

Even today, there is widespread acceptance of the thesis that Confucianistic Korea was good and that Confucian doctrines provided the right answers to all problems of socio-economic and political relationships. It is a temptingly simple solution for rulers to secure popular acceptance of such authoritarian doctrines, for "paternalistic" control over the lives of the Korean people is based on hallowed historical precedent. A repeated emphasis on the vast superiority of the ancient Korean civilization and the Chinese civilization over modern or "Western" civilization is one of the major obstacles impeding modernization of Korea today. Frequent visits of Lin Yutang to South Korea and the publication of his collected works demonstrates his popularity among Korean intellectuals and the elites. *Between Tears and Laughter* and *The Vigil of a Nation* by Lin Yutang are well known anti-modern books. Unlike his *My Country and My People*, Lin's later books emphasizes ancient Confucian morality as the ideal basis for China's future social structures. Chiang Kai-shek in his *China's Destiny* follows in the same vein.

Can Korean society be modernized and still retain autocratic Confucian ethics as its basic code of life? If it is not possible in China, as demonstrated by the modern Chinese, then how can an alien doctrine like Confucianism be accepted in Korea as its foundation of society? Confucianism has played its progressive and useful role in various stages of history. It has unquestionably contributed to Korean culture, but how relevant is it to the present age of science and technology? Even more doubtful is its value to any future age. The kind of teaching and training that is central to the Confucian educational system is obsolescent, if not obsolete. The people who call themselves "righteous" or "superior," moreover, will have to live up to their self-created image; they will refuse to come to self-knowledge and, by not knowing who they really are, they will fall deeply into the plight from which they wish to be freed. Confucianism teaches universal humanism. This humanism, however, was a class humanism comparable to that of the ancient Greek democracy. It was for the elite class, not for the lower classes. It was for the superior man, not for farmers, merchants, and artisans. A philosophy that helps all men to become human by helping them gain complete possession of all their natural powers would seem to be the only positive concept in a world of rapid technological change; only a positive philosophy, and creative concepts could help to build a healthy national community as well as the world community.

Modernization in the area of politics and government must include not only dominant themes of administrative structure, popular participation and development, but also such important themes as distribution, national integration, and political ideology, including the self-reliance concept. None of these concepts could be found in South Korea after thirty years of American tutelage.

The demonstrated superiority of democracy over dictatorship derives precisely from democracy's refusal to let the ruling elite make basic moral decisions and value judgments for society. The view that expertise is a prerequisite for holding competent opinions on public affairs is one that does not disqualify only *some* of us, it disqualifies *most* of us. No one today can be expert in all the fields that ideally he should be in order to make public moral decisions. What is called for in making public decisions, accordingly, is not omniscience or omnicompetent knowledge but something closer to wisdom and common sense, and an understanding of when and where and for what reasons to rely on the advice of experts. Modernization without such basic understanding of man and his life is anti-modern, anti-democratic, and furthermore, incapable of achieving a real sense of modernization. One only need look to the seemingly most modern society to find written large some of the basic problems of man today. Modern society is suffering from its mistakes in the process of modernization of the past.

Modern man is faced with a flood of external and internal stimuli. With the external, he faces his environment, and with the internal, it is attitudes, values and feelings he must wrestle with. For the external man faces urbanization, mass communications, education, industrialization, politicization, impersonalization, and bureaucratization. With this onslaught of cold facts he must be ready internally to breathe life and freedom into his soul. Attitudes expressing a disposition to accept new ideas and try new methods, a readiness to express opinions, a time sense that makes men more interested in the future and present rather than in the past, are all important to the modern process. Attitudes showing a propensity toward punctuality, planning, organization, and efficiency are necessary to the success of a nation changing from the traditional to the modern. Also needed is faith in science and technology.

There is reason to believe, however, that only as modernization occurs at grass-root levels in an open democratic manner will there be lasting success. The old traditional mentality has to be broken at grass-root levels. It is in this setting that modernization will grow to be lasting and effective. Such modernization processes will strengthen the political hold over all citizens by promoting the formation of consensus at the national level by stressing nationalism and economic and social integration. Modernization is a world-wide phenomenon that no people can ignore. The future of all mankind depends on the success of world modernization. Modernization is needed in Korea. But man cannot become modernized without undergoing a change in spirit. He must acquire new ways of thinking, feeling, and acting.

How should Koreans then rectify their traditional system and enhance the process of modernization? To overcome its weakness and bring about successful modernization, there is a need for a national symbolic center. As long as people feel pulled between two different poles and are without any roots in society, they cannot have a firm sense of identity—an identity which is essential for building a stable and modern nation-state. Unfortunately, Korean people are still under the strong influences of foreign powers and the modern center has been established in terms of Western or Japanese symbols. Thus, it is to some extent detached from the Korean people. For instance, President Park Chung Hee's "Yushin" system initiated in October, 1972, is modeled after the Meiji Restoration concept of Japan. Created as an imperialistic institution to monopolize economic and commercial activities and aid in developing the colonial economy, the Japanese *zaibatsu* system served the empire and its elite class. After achieving independence from Allied forces, Japan restored the life of this imperial institution. This seemingly paradoxical existence of an imperialistic institution under a democratic constitutional government is explained in the nature of the government which rules present-day Japan. The Park regime has chosen a model which is alien to Koreans.

The values of a new center in Korea today are expressed in terms mostly of Western or Japanese values on political and social justice. It appears on the surface as a strong institution, but it contains a serious weakness, that is, it fails to develop common symbols in which elements of the new culture could be combined with the traditional culture, so as to create a relatively strong collective identity. Hence, it reduces its ability to provide new symbols that would provide flexible guidelines for nation building. Some scholars explain the situation as "the total absence of politicos." The absence of "politicos in the Korean National Assembly may be associated with the Confucian term of Chicho (or virtue)."[9]

It seems that it is not Confucian virtue, but its authoritarian attitude which influences today's Korean ruling class. These elite talk about democracy and modernization at home and in public, but they do not practice what they preach. For instance, there are very few modern ideas expressed about compromise, conciliation, and sharing among leadership groups, including the Christian leaders who are supposed to be more modern than the Confucian-oriented ones. A study shows that Christian representation among political leaders in South Korea has been very significant since 1945.[10] But there is little evidence of their contributions towards modernization and democracy during the past thirty years.[11]

The modern center must provide new, binding symbols of collective identity to overcome the more "particularistic" symbols of the different regions and factions and develop some feeling of a modern community. Modernization is a matter of encounter with foreign forces. Modernization, therefore, requires that the new elite create a national identity from the encounter with these foreign forces.

The internal capacities of the society for reformation may be crucial to adapting to demands of external forces and to success in building new institutional structures to cope with these problems. But the very nature of the modernization process in the Korean society was such that the sources and directions of the cultural transformation were not consistent with modernization. Not only internal transformation is critical but it also requires a new stable structure which is capable of adapting to changing world situations and problems.

Political systems cannot be divorced from the beliefs and values of the people. They must be relevant to what people think is happening in their society. Their beliefs and values might not be based on rationality and scientific data; nevertheless, these are human experiences which cannot be ignored. Unless based on human experiences, modernization can hardly bring benefits to human freedom and life.

9 Economic Aspects of Modernization

Many economists see modernization from the economic point of view exclusively and primarily in terms of man's application of technology to control natural resources to bring about a marked increase in output per head of population. In this sense, Korea is modernized. The gross national product of South Korea increased 15 percent in 1976. It is indeed a remarkable achievement.

All countries desire to better develop themselves and, in fact, this "raising up" process has become almost a mania to some. There are countries today that have more or less lost sight of such economic goals as a better standard of living and reduced unemployment and have blindly concentrated on heavy industry and new military weapons.

Economic development and technological progress go hand-in-hand. With the help of new technology, a resource-poor country can overcome its natural handicaps. However, even though technological progress is the prime mover of economic growth, it is not a miracle drug. It, by itself, is not the answer. Nonetheless, economic development is a significant factor one should not minimize in discussing modernization.

What then is the economic situation in South Korea? Is there an economic "miracle" in South Korea? From the standpoint of the growth, the Korean economy has an extremely high growth rate. Even in 1974, when the Arab oil shock caused worldwide economic stagnation, the growth rate in South Korea was 8.7 percent. The Korean economic situation, unfortunately, cannot be judged under normal conditions. The high growth rate does not indicate the level of modernization one might suspect. The economic growth was achieved by the sacrifice of modernization rather than the accomplishment of it. The reason is that the increase of GNP means an increase of trade, since the Korean economy is basically a trade economy. An increase of trade results in an increase of payment deficits and the sacrifice of the domestic economy for the sake of the trade economy. For instance, in 1976 the combination of national exports and imports represented 78 percent of the total GNP in South Korea. It means, therefore, that the increase of 15 percent in GNP was an increase of national trade. The trade, on the other hand, depends totally on foreign nations, especially Japan. The economic growth of domestic industries has been negligible, and "miracle" means fundamentally the increase of the export-import business. This condition does not support the modernization process. Not only was domestic economic development sacrificed for an export-import oriented economy, but the increase of exports created an increased national debt due to payment deficits. The annual trade deficit has exceeded $1 billion. The deficit, however, reached $2.4 billion in 1974, $2.2 billion in 1975, and in late 1975 and early 1976 the Korean economy was in serious trouble. The Korean economy was barely able to overcome this critical situation when exports to the United States were increased in 1976.

Why did payment deficits occur? Resource-poor Korea must import raw materials from abroad. The price of raw materials went up, but the price of Korean goods did not, for fear of losing customers. Consequently, the more Korea sold, the more money Korea lost. The Korean economy is now trapped in a mechanism whereby growth in exports is inevitably accompanied by an increase in imports. With such a system how long can the Korean economic "miracle" last?

For the sake of modernization, the poor peasants are still exploited. The Confucian virtues of obedience, authority, righteousness, and harmony still are taught. The agricultural population is an important market for a country's industry, but in South Korea, the home market has been bypassed entirely. Can a nation be modernized without farmers getting a fair share? South Korea has failed to carry out this simple act of justice. Agriculture growth is important and a close partner in the general process of economic growth. Its relation to industry cannot be overlooked without serious consequences. The agriculture of advanced countries has contributed to their economic growth. A serious problem in economic modernization is the lack of capital with which to operate. The majority of the capital will have to come from the developing country itself. Since the agricultural sector is the predominant one, most of the capital will have to come from it, at least in the early stages of development. For instance, in Japan, one-half to one-third of the total investment in the late nineteenth and early twentieth centuries was government investment. During that time 50 to 80 percent of the total taxes were drawn from agriculture, so agriculture paid the greatest part of the industrial advancement bill. Unfortunately, these government investments helped to build a few *zaibatsu* monopolists which still dominate Japanese economy today.

How can the leaders of a developing country reach wise decisions as to the mixture between government economic activity and private economic activity that is best for the country? As far as the economic situation in South Korea is concerned, we find several serious problems that are closely related to the decisions made by the Park regime, which is under the influence of the United States government. When the privileged few in the private sector exercise a lot of control over the economy, what results is that the rich get richer and the poor stay poor. Control of the economy is tied up into too few hands. That is the economic situation in South Korea today and the situation is not getting any better. Economic conditions for the Korean people cannot be improved because President Park has serious commitments to foreign investors who influence the present economic policy in South Korea.

We shall now turn our attention to President Park's economic policy which has had full cooperation from the governments of the United States for the past thirty years and more. President Park's present economic policy is not an original one. His economic policy is very similar to the Japanese economic policy during Japan's occupation of Korea from 1910 to 1945. There were three basic Japanese colonial economic policies: (1) agricultural policy; (2) prevention of the accumulation of Korean national capital; (3) trade. These were the fundamental policies of Japan during the thirty-six years of her occupation of Korea. These three basic policies reemerged in South Korea after the 1965 normalization treaty between Japan and South Korea sponsored by the United States.

The Japanese government-general established a "Land Investigation Bureau" immediately following the annexation of Korea, and also organized the Oriental Colonization Company. Through these two government agencies, the Japanese government was able to confiscate much of the Korean farm lands. For instance, in 1930, the highest revenue for the government-general was from farm land—approximately 88 million jungbo (one jungbo equals 2.45 acres), which the government had confiscated from farmers.[1] With few exceptions—those aristocrats and rich Korean landlords who collaborated with the colonial policy—the majority of farmers became the tenants of Japanese landlords. What were the reasons behind this agricultural policy? One reason was to migrate the Japanese to Korea and maintain the semi-feudalistic mode of production in Korea. This goal was rather successfully carried out. Another reason was to supply abundant labor to newly developing Japanese industries in Korea. This policy, too, was successful. Many farmers moved into the cities and waited in line to find a job in Japanese factories. There were always enough laborers, about two million of them, who were ready to be hired by Japanese employers.

Many of them never were hired. About seventy thousand starved to death while waiting in line from 1931 to 1941, according to official reports.

How does President Park's agricultural policy compare with the Japanese colonial policy?

At the time of the national liberation in 1945, the agricultural policy of the American military government was to import American surplus grains to feed the occupied people. The result of importing American surplus grains created serious competition with Korean grains in the market. The troubles for Korean farmers had already begun. It has been recognized that a major portion of the fertile farm land was located in South Korea while the major industries, which were developed by the Japanese, were located in North Korea prior to 1945. In spite of the advantage of having fertile land, South Korea needed to import grains from the U.S. and elsewhere.

For instance, the last years, 1975 and 1976, were good harvest years, but South Korea imported 25 percent of her needed grains from abroad. According to the Ministry of Agriculture and Forestry in Seoul, South Korea paid out $722 million in 1976, $885 million in 1975, and $661 million in 1974 for the grain. It is indeed an ironic situation that an agricultural nation which had been self-sufficient suddenly has to import grain. The money could be better used for new industries.

Why has such a situation developed in South Korea? There seem to be two reasons. One is that the national policy makers are all the city-capitalists who have close relationships with foreign capitalists. Foreign investors are not interested in agricultural development. Second, there is a lack of equilibrium in development between industry and agriculture. To promote city interests, the government has maintained the low-price policy of agricultural products which enables wages to be held down. Korean farmers are confronted with a serious dilemma—to produce or not to produce. Production declined. In 1971, there were about 7,274,000 tons of grain produced in South Korea. The amount was 463,000 tons less than in 1969, and 284,000 tons less than in 1966. In 1966, only 13 percent of the total grain needed was imported, but grain import increased to 30 percent in 1971. South Korea, an agricultural nation, became a nation dependent on foreign countries for grain. Again, President Park sacrificed agricultural development for the sake of an export-oriented industry development, as had happened during the Japanese occupation.

The next most important Japanese colonial economic policy in Korea was concerned with the accumulation of national capital. The Japanese government-general proclaimed "Regulation on Companies in Korea" in December 1910. The major aim of the regulation was to prevent Korean businessmen from accumulating capital. The number of Japanese companies which already engaged in business was more than one hundred with about five million yen investments in Korea at the time of the annexation. There were only twenty-one Korean companies and they were primarily in commerce and agricultural areas. Only one Korean company was engaged in a manufacturing business. There was no serious competition between semi-feudalistic Korean businesses and modernized Japanese businesses. The Japanese government, nevertheless, took no risks and did not allow Korean capitalists to compete with Japanese.

There were three main reasons why the Japanese government did not allow the Koreans to accumulate capital and compete with Japanese businessmen. First of all, the Japanese wanted to eliminate any competition, either from Koreans or non-Koreans in Korea; second, the government wanted to suppress the national consciousness of the Korean people; and third, the government wanted to create a situation where it would have an abundant supply of labor in reserve.

This economic policy was intensified when Japan initiated war against China in 1931. With the "Manchurian Incident," Japanese businessmen expanded the heavy chemical industries in Korea with the support of the government in order to support the Japanese military expansion in China. Such intensification of heavy chemical industries prevented further the growth of Korean capital. For instance, in 1940, 94 percent of the total capital investment in Korea belonged to the Japanese, and only 6 percent belonged to the Koreans. Even that 6 percent disappeared with the Japanese attack on Pearl Harbor in 1941. Korea remained a Japanese market and a supplier of raw materials and labor.

The Japanese capitalists who invested in Korea were protected under a special rule. For instance, the "Control Law of Important Industries" of Japan, which had applied to all Japanese war industries in Japan since 1937, did not apply to Japanese industries in Korea.

How does this compare with President Park's economic policy today?

As pointed out earlier, there is no equilibrium between agricultural and industrial development. Agriculture was sacrificed for the sake of industrial development. For the sake of urban interests, rural interests were suppressed. The price of manufactured goods went up 500 percent between 1955 and 1960 while agricultural prices increased only 20 percent during the same period. Consequently, the required national capital to develop could not be raised from the people, but had to be borrowed from foreign sources. The more borrowed from foreign sources, the less attention paid to farmers. Foreign capitalists' interests lay with immediate profit returns, and a five-year term was most ideal for the lenders.

Foreign capital began to flow into Korea; first from the United States, then from Western European countries, and now mostly from Japan.

Why does major capital flow into Korea from Japan now?[2] Japan began to invest in South Korea with the 1965 treaty between the two countries. Japanese investment was, however, modest. It was the 1969 Nixon-Sato Communique which accelerated Japanese investments into South Korea. It wasn't that Japan had not been interested before in South Korea, but she waited for the proper signal from the United States. The decision was a politico-economic one between Japan and the United States. As pointed out by Dr. Henry Kissinger, the former Secretary of State, in numerous public statements, South Korea was "for the sake of Japan's security," not for Korea's. It became a logical conclusion for Japan and the United States that South Korea was to become a part of Japan's "sphere of influence" since the two governments decided that Japan should play a major role in East Asia and the Pacific to protect American interests there. This situation became more apparent after the 1973 Arab oil embargo.

The true intention of Japan's economic domination of South Korea was exposed in 1973. Japan invested $300 million, or about 95 percent of her entire foreign investments, in South Korea in 1973. She invested another $100 million in 1974. The combination of the loans and investments from Japan amounted to $2 billion at the end of 1975, and the amount has increased speedily since then.

Why has Japan invested such huge amounts in South Korea? It is certainly not for the purpose of the development of Korean industries as the officials of the two governments state occasionally. There is much evidence against such an assumption. Most of the Japanese investments are, so far, in the areas of textiles, electronics, and related labor-intensive industries. The Masan Free Industrial Zone is an example. More than 80 percent of the factories in the zone belong to Japanese and produce

Conditions of Foreign Capital in South Korea
Unit $ Million[3]

Year	Total	Public	Commercial	Foreign Investment	Total	Japan	U.S.	Others
		Types of Loans			Nationalities			
1970	548	115	367	66	65.4	15.8	41.8	7.8
1971	691	303	345	43	50.9	24.7	21.7	4.5
1972	729	324	326	79	113.3	77.6	29.7	6.0
1973	856	369	344	143	314.1	295.2	12.6	6.3

primarily textiles and electronic goods. The wages of the workers are unbelievably low. A high school graduate working twelve hours a day, six days a week, receives about thirty-five dollars a month.

President Park has announced a fourth Five-Year Economic Plan starting in 1977. This plan is to promote heavy chemical industries. So far, 50 percent of the Japanese firms in South Korea are small businessmen exploiting cheap labor. Their investments average $100,000. With the fourth Five-Year Economic Plan, the type of investment and the style of operation will change drastically.

For instance, Japan's Teizin group and Ito-chu group are planning to build a $1 billion oil refinery with a Korean firm—Sunkyung group, which is considered a Lee Hu-Rak/Park Chong-Kyu-dominated group. Lee is a former director of the KCIA and a serious contender as President Park's successor. Another oil refinery in the Yosu district was begun a couple years ago with the Mitsui Zaibatsu group, and will be one of the largest of its kind when finished.

Such major economic movement became more evident after the Ford-Miki Conference in August, 1975. At this conference the leaders decided that Japan would encourage further investments in South Korea, and Japan would also guarantee, if necessary, European loans to the Park regime. To respond to these decisions, President Park proclaimed a "Total Security Attitude," which means more dictatorial government control.

The Japanese economic invasion of South Korea began officially with the 1965 treaty, but intensified after the 1969 Nixon-Sato Communique, and has accelerated since the 1975 Ford-Miki Conference. Japan is dominating not only economic aspects of South Korea but also is expanding its political influence and gradually moving into the military area.

In other words, Korean businessmen are unable to acquire capital while the Japanese and other investors dominate them. Not only have agricultural development and small and medium enterprises failed, but

even large firms which are in a position to borrow cannot maintain
independence from foreign influences. Most of the companies which
borrowed foreign capital are in trouble. Meantime, building national
capital is still far from reality. Major industries are dominated by foreign
capital.

The following list provides only a few samples of foreign capital
representation.

1.	Oil industry	100%
2.	Plate glass	100%
3.	Heavy chemicals	100%
4.	Locomotive wheels	80%
5.	Electricity	80%
6.	Pulps	100%
7.	Automobile	100%
8.	Cement	65%
9.	Refrigeration	57%
10.	Chemical textiles	50%
11.	Electronics	50%
12.	Fertilizers	40%

The third basic economic policy in which President Park has adopted
Japanese colonial policy is trade.

The Japanese monopolized trade in Korea as soon as Japan annexed
Korea in 1910. Japan took Korean raw materials and Korea became a
Japanese market. There was practically no international trade. About 70
percent of Korea's export to Japan consisted of food, and the rest was raw
materials. On the other hand, Korea imported from Japan mostly manufactured goods. As a result, Japan benefitted by such trade while Korea
suffered. Starting in 1910, the trade payment deficit increased ten fold in
the next thirty years. More specifically, as an agricultural country, Korea
sold her products—grains—to Japan at a low price while she paid a high
price for fertilizers and industrial products, which were needed for farming. It was a very cruel method to exploit Korean farmers. This cruel
policy has not been changed since liberation, and it is enforced still today
by the Park regime.

Considering the trade policy of the Park regime, we find the following characteristics: (1) Korean trade is totally dependent on foreign capital
and foreign conditions which are beyond her control; (2) Korea must
import raw material, plants, and other materials which are to be manufac-

tured; (3) manufactured goods must be sold abroad; (4) the result of these three conditions is that Korea's trade is dependent on external conditions.

It has been clearly demonstrated in the past that the South Korean economy is based on international trade which depends totally on Japan and the United States. The importance of international trade is not exaggerated when we consider that 78 percent of the GNP is dominated by trade.

The Korean economy has been experiencing a precarious trading position due to excessive expansion of international trade since 1973. Not only is South Korea incapable of establishing factories without outside aid, but it lacks the raw materials needed to produce goods for export. Imports amount to 40 percent of the total national product. To balance such an overwhelming amount of import, Korea must excel in export trade. The export policy of the Park regime is to concentrate on exports over imports. To promote the export business, the Korean government controls the price of the goods to be exported so as to meet the competition in the international market. For instance, Korea exports fertilizers at $98 per ton and loses $22 per ton since its cost per ton is $120. The more Korea exports, the more money the nation loses. On the other hand, fertilizers have been sold to Korean farmers at $240 per ton or double the amount of the production cost. In other words, farmers are subsidizing the export business. This policy is identical to the one practiced by the Japanese during Japan's occupation of Korea.

Why does the Korean government continue to lose business? Simply, she needs foreign currencies to pay off an ever-increasing national debt as well as the payment deficit of the trade. There are three reasons why the payment deficit continues. First of all, the prices of raw materials have been going up since 1973, and there is no sign of a reversal.

For instance, 22 percent of the total imports in 1976 was of oil. Korea has no oil, and it must be imported. The price of oil is not about to come down. Korea has to pay high prices for oil and raw materials if she wants to maintain an export business. Another reason is the furious competition abroad which forces Korean manufacturers to dump their goods in the market. The United States government is already pressuring the Korean government to restrain Korean goods—shoes, electronic goods, textiles—in the American market. Japan, too, has enforced a similar policy on Korea. The last reason is that as much as Korea is an important ally of both Japan and the United States, they are willing to sacrifice Korea when serious conflicts occur between Korean and Japanese interests, and between Koreans and Americans. For instance, Japanese investors will not try to save their interests in South Korea at the expense of their interests in Japan.

The export-oriented Korean economy is precarious because of external conditions over which it has no control. In 1974, there was a $2.4 billion deficit in the export-import balance of trade. How can the Korean government meet such a problem? As long as the Korean government can borrow from abroad to fill the gap, it can continue almost indefinitely to play this game. Korea borrowed $1 billion in a long-term loan and another $1 billion in a short-term loan from Arab sources to meet the crisis in 1974. To prevent a recurrence of such a crisis, the government succeeded in borrowing $1.4 billion in a long-term loan in 1975, but was still short $700 million. The crisis was overcome only after the economic situation in the U. S. had turned to a favorable condition in the fall of 1975. Korea was able to increase sharply exports to the United States, as shown in the following chart.

Trend of Korean Export and Import[4]

(Export is FOB, Import is CIF prices.)

As indicated in the chart, imports increased steadily in 1975 and moved up sharply in 1976. Meanwhile, foreign loans amounted to $2 billion in 1975 alone. The shortage of capital was, however, still severe during the year.[5]

Korea's imports from Japan have increased each year. For instance, $800 million worth in 1971, $1 billion worth in 1972, and $1.8 billion worth in 1973 were imported from Japan. As a matter of fact, about $5.4 billion flowed back to Japan through trade while Japan invested and loaned to Korea about $2 billion.

Does the trade-oriented Korean economy help the domestic economy? Actually, the needed capital for domestic economic development has been concentrated on export-oriented enterprises, and the domestic economy has suffered. For instance, the price of cotton for domestic consumption increased 45 percent in 1976, while the government stabilized artificially the price of export goods. Consequently, industries for domestic consumption suffer and it is impossible to accumulate national capital.

The following table indicates the trade relationships between South Korea and Japan during 1971–1973, the period before the oil crisis.

South Korea and Japan Trade Relationship[6]
Unit $1,000

Import from Japan

Name of Goods	1971	1972	1973
Machinery	284,691	385,521	675,288
Metals	136,005	181,398	352,766
Textiles	150,344	154,271	340,605
Chemicals	117,432	138,323	202,135
Rice	76,978	—0—	19,316
Other	90,237	120,279	199,004
Total Amount	855,687	979,792	1,789,114

Export to Japan

Name of Goods	1971	1972	1973
Seafoods	40,673	70,594	147,660
Raw silk	39,027	58,558	65,251
Textiles	80,400	119,985	459,262
Machinery	16,240	24,841	85,493
Electronics	14,776	21,615	68,237
Other	83,305	130,398	381,405
Total Amount	274,421	425,991	1,207,308

These figures are based on the customs statistics of Japan. We can see immediately the difference between the total amounts for import and export. In 1971, the Korean payment deficit to Japan was $582 million; in 1972 it was $554 million; in 1973 it was about $600 million. But it jumped to $2 billion in 1974. We also must remember that nine out of ten major trading companies are either owned or controlled by Japanese interests. The table also shows the type of goods Korea imports from Japan. About 69 percent of the total imports from Japan consisted of steel, metals, and heavy chemical products while the major exported goods to Japan consisted of food, raw silk, textile goods, and raw materials. At the present time, 38.5 percent of the total Korean export goods head to Japan while about 41 percent of Korea's total imported goods come from Japan. Thus, Korea's dependency on Japan is clearly evident.[7]

Who controls the importing of raw materials? For instance, consider oil. In South Korea there are three major oil companies—Gulf Oil, Caltex, and Union Oil. President Park is closely associated with Caltex which guarantees 12 percent annual profits on a $2.7 million investment. It has been reported that Gulf Oil's 1976 profit was a 78 percent increase over 1975. Gulf Oil Company contributed $4 million cash to President Park and his political party.

Other raw materials including grain, sugar, and lumber are imported from the United States and Japan. Strangely enough, raw materials are imported from Japan which also has to import raw materials from abroad. Actually, the materials come through Japan to Korea because of long-term contract and credit problems.

Another serious issue is the importing of entire plants. For instance, 28.6 percent of the entire import consisted of factory plants in 1971. The cost amounted to $680 million. What kind of plants were they? It has been revealed in the report to the Japanese Diet that most were outdated plants from Japan, and some were heavy chemical plants which were not allowed to remain in Japan because of environmental conditions. Both raw materials and factory plants were rip-offs before they arrived in Korea.

How about the situation concerning Korean exports? A similarity exists between exports and imports. About 80 percent of exported goods are processed goods. The cost of raw materials is the dominating factor of processed goods. South Korea has to import all the raw materials to process its major exporting goods, including textiles, plywood, rubber, and electronic goods. Why is South Korea engaged in such a risky business? South Korea's abundant cheap labor is the government's reply. Where can a foreign investor find a country where the government supplies cheap labor with one-sixth of its home wages (in the case of Japan) and one-sixteenth (in the case of the United States)? The Korean wage is cheaper than that of Hong Kong or Taiwan.

Again, Korean industries are in a precarious position because of dependence on foreign capital. They can be easily influenced by external conditions. *Chosun Ilbo Daily* reported that 45 percent of textile plants, 60 percent of leather works, and 50 percent of chemical-textile industries were closed in 1974 following the oil embargo.[8] The prices of raw materials for plywood increased between 200 to 300 percent in 1973–1974, but the building industry in the United States was stagnated in that period. There was no demand for Korean plywood and the industry suffered. Of 10,400 medium-sized business firms in South Korea, 40 percent declared bankruptcies in 1974. Meanwhile, big textile companies, including Cheil Textile Company, dominated by Mitsui and Tomei with an $18 million loan, Sunkyung Textile Company owned by Teijin of Tokyo with $40 million, and the Orient Polyester Company, owned by Asai Kasei Company with $34 million, asked the Korean government to allow one-third of their products to be sold in Korea. All of these big companies are already favored by the government. Their taxes are exempted, their customs duties are waived, and strike-free labor laws are enforced to protect them. How can Korean medium-sized companies compete with these giants which are provided special favors by the government?

The last issue concerning South Korea's economic relationships with Japan and other powers is the matter of loans. South Korea owed foreign countries over $10 billion by the end of 1976. There are two types of loans, namely, financial loans and commercial loans. In the beginning the United States monopolized loans, primarily financial loans to the government or the government-managed companies of South Korea, but West Germany, France, and the United Kingdom participated later. The dynamics of the loan, however, began to accelerate with Japan's aggressive economic policy in 1973. The following table indicates the increase of foreign loans in South Korea.

Foreign Loans in South Korea[9]
Unit: $ million

Year	Total Amount	Financial Loan	Commercial Loan	Direct Investment
1959–66	349	141	184	24
1967	238	106	124	8
1968	358	70	269	19
1969	561	139	409	13
1970	548	115	367	66
1971	691	303	345	43
1972	729	324	326	79
1973	855	368	344	143
1974	1,173	317	616	240
1975	1,410	557	848	5

For the purpose of attracting foreign loans and direct investments, the government of South Korea legalized the system through "the law to promote foreign investment" in January, 1960, and added special privileges for foreign investors by expanding the law through "the law of guaranteed payment on foreign loans" in 1962. According to these rules, foreign firms were not limited in the number of shares they could own in Korean companies, unlike the 51–49 ratio system of the past; they were free to send out foreign currencies from South Korea; freedom from taxes for foreign investors was extended; and the government guaranteed payments on all loans.

Commercial loans began to move in 1963, representing 79 percent of the total foreign capital after attractive regulations were offered by the government. The commercial loans, however, did not move as rapidly as the government anticipated. The political atmosphere and economic environment were not inviting foreign capital at this time. This situation changed after the 1965 normalization treaty between Japan and South Korea. Japan began to show her willingness to take leadership by replacing the United States as a major foreign investor in South Korea, especially after the 1969 Nixon-Sato Communique which encouraged Japan to take more initiatives in Korea. The following table indicates Japan's aggressive investments in South Korea since 1969.

Direct Investments of Foreign Countries[10]
Unit: $ million

Year	Japan	U.S.A.	Others	Total
1962–66	—	29.9	0.6	30.5
1967	1.5	18.0	0.6	20.1
1968	4.5	14.6	6.5	25.6
1969	17.7	6.0	6.8	30.5
1970	15.8	41.8	7.8	65.4
1971	24.7	21.7	4.5	50.9
1972	77.6	29.7	6.0	113.3
1973	295.2	12.6	6.3	314.1
1974	94.8	32.2	12.9	139.9
1975	100.0	6.0	89.0	195.0

It has been clearly demonstrated that the Park regime's economic policy since 1969 has been to rely completely on Japan's capital for the development of Korean industries. Following this blueprint, the Park regime announced in December, 1969, another rule to control the labor situation, namely, the "Special law for the labor union and the labor dispute within foreign-invested factories." According to the law, workers are prohibited from engaging in labor organizations and participating in any sort of strike against foreign investors. Thus, the basic rights of workers were stripped away to attract foreign investors. The government of South Korea has been advertising these facts annually each January in the *New York Times*.

This approach by the Park regime was needed to invite direct investment from foreign countries. Loans were difficult to get since the world economic situation was depressed. The Park regime was anxious to attract foreign investment, and Japanese businessmen took advantage of the desperate situation in South Korea. The Park regime succumbed to pressures from Japanese businessmen. In 1970, the Park regime surrendered virtually the right of extraterritoriality to Japan and other foreign nations by declaring the "Free Industrial Zone" of Masan and other parts of the country. Korean workers who are employed by these foreign employers in the "Free Industrial Zone" are practically without legal protection. In other words, they are exploited to the extreme by their foreign employers.

Under such favorable conditions, foreign capital has poured into South Korea. For instance, more than $5.4 billion in foreign capital moved in between 1970–1974. Compared with the previous ten years, 1959–1969, the amount was more than 2.2 times in a five-year period. We also notice a characteristic trend that began with foreign capital coming into South Korea between 1970–1974. Namely, direct foreign investments increased from 5.7 percent during 1959–1969 to 22.8 percent in 1973. The major portion of the foreign capital came as either financial or commercial loans during 1959–1969.

Another characteristic of foreign capital during 1970–1974 was the size of the foreign investment. For instance, less than 10 percent of all the Japanese firms—788 companies in 1974—invested more than 1 million dollars, and more than 50 percent had no more than a $100,000 investment in South Korea. Only a handful, the Zaibaten group, had been involved earlier. The group was led by the Mitsui Trading Company which held about 30 percent of the total Japanese investments with $88 million; followed by Mitsubishi Shyoji, 21 percent or $64 million; Ito Shyoji, 19 percent or $57 million; Toyomen, 11 percent or $34 million; and Marubeni, 2 percent or $6 million in 1970. These five grants occupied 81 percent of total Japanese investment in South Korea. It was the same for trade and loans. The Mitsui Zaibatsu group alone loaned $135 million to twenty major Korean firms while the Mitsubishi group loaned $65 million to ten Korean firms.

For example, Hankook Fertilizer Company built its largest factory with $44 million of Mitsui money in 1970. The company, however, was mismanaged and is now being managed by an officially designated bank.

Some of the situations are worse than this. The amount the companies borrowed from Japan was larger than the company's assets. Taihan Shipping Company is an example. Furthermore, all five plastics companies which were built with Japanese loans declared bankruptcies within a few years. All of these financial scandals have been revealed in the Japanese Diet, but not in Korea. Almost 80 percent of Korean companies which borrowed money from Japan to expand their businesses are considered unhealthy by government evaluations.

The following list consists of major Korean business firms in South Korea.

1. Textile industry: Hanil Hapsun, Tongyang Nylon, Hankook Nylon, Koryu Hapsun, Sunkyung Chemical, Takwang Ind., Junbang, Taihan, Jeil Hapsun
2. Chemical industry: Hankook Fertilizer, Pungnong Fertilizer, Taihan Chemical, Hankook Plastics, Hankook Metanol, Tongyang Chemical, Taihan Hwasung
3. Cement industry: Ssang-Ryong, Tongyang, Hanil, Taihan, Chungpuk
4. Fishery industry: Fishing Development Company
5. Metallic industry: Yunhap Steel, Hankook Aluminum, Samyang
6. Miscellaneous: Kia Ind., Hankook Bearing, Shinjin Motor Company, Taihan Transfer, Hankook Glass, Royal Hotel, Koreana Hotel, Chosun Hotel, Samjung Electronics, Kumsung, Inchun Power, Chungpyong Power

Among these companies there is not one which is clear from foreign loans. All major Korean companies owe considerable sums of money to Japanese, American, or European countries.

Among the Korean business giants which have been growing under the protection of the Park regime are the following:

1. Nakhi (Lucky) group, headed by Chakyung Koo, owns and controls thirty-seven sister companies with more than 36,000 employees. The amount of the combined sales of this group reached about $1.2 billion in 1976. The group controls Nahki Chemical, Honam Oil, Kumsungsa Company, Kumsung Electronics, Bando Trading, and others. It has extended to seventeen different types of businesses, including chemical, electronics, electricity, communications, mining, oil, construction, trading,

insurance, stocks, press, and others. The group is the largest of its kind, similar to the Japanese Zaibatsu in South Korea.

2. Samsung group, headed by Pyung-chul Lee, owns and controls twenty companies and is the second largest group in South Korea. The amount of the combined sales of these twenty companies was close to a billion dollars in 1976. The group controls the Cheil Sugar, Cheil Textile, Samsung Trading, Tongbang Life Insurance, Samsung Electronics, Samsung-Sanyo with Sumitomo, Hankook Fertilizer with Mitsui.

3. Hyundai group, headed by Chu-yong Chung, is the third largest group. It began as a small contractor, but now owns and controls twelve kinds of companies with sales amounting to almost a billion dollars in 1976. The group controls Hyundai Construction, Hyundai Automobile, Hyundai Shipping, Hyundai Cement, and Hyundai Trading Company.

4. Hanjin group, headed by Chung-Hun Cho, a close collaborator of President Park, has a close contact with Osano of Nippon Aircraft Company, which was involved in the Lockheed scandal. Cho was once a "water boy" during the Korean War and became the fourth richest man in South Korea in twenty years. He owns and controls Korea Air Line and Hanjin Company.

5. Dae-Woo group, headed by a young president, Woo-chung Kim, is the fifth largest group. The group is comparatively young and grew rapidly under the Park regime. The group has twenty-two sister companies which employ more than 35,000; the amount of combined sales reached about $500 million in 1976.

6. Ssang-Ryong group, headed by the late Sung-gun Kim's family, closely associated with President Park's political party, owns and controls Ssang-Ryong Cement which was built with Mitsubishi's $38 million, Ssang-Ryong Ind., and Ssang-Ryong Shipping Company.

7. Shinjin group, headed by Chang-won Kim, a notorious political businessman, owns and controls Shinjin Automobile, Hyundae Kia, and G. M. Korea Automobile.

8. Hankook Nylon group, headed by Won-man Lee, owns and controls Hankook Nylon which was built with Mitsui's $15 million, and Hankook Polyester.

9. Sunkyung group—both Lee Hu-Rak and Park Chong-Kyu, who was a chief bodyguard of President Park, are partners in this

group with Chong-gun Choi—owns and controls Sunkyung Textile, as well as New Oil Company, which started with loans from Japan's Sanwa Bank.

10. Samho group, headed by Jaeho Chung, owns and controls Samho Trading, Samho Textile, which is managed by the Commercial Bank of Korea, a fishing industry and others.

Besides these ten groups, there are the International Trading of Jung-mo Yang, the Yo-sung group of Hong-je Cho, the Myon-Ho group of In-Chun Park, and the Hanil of Han-su Kim, which rank with those mentioned above. All of them started their fortunes with the American Military Government and have grown steadily ever since. There is very little chance for a new group to emerge since these groups are well established in business at home and are financed by Japanese, American, and other foreign multi-national corporations. Major characteristics of these groups are their dependence on foreign capital and reliance on international trade. There is not one single company which is free from foreign debt at the present time. One foreign director is able to veto any decision of the Korean members of the board of directors.

The Korean government announced that there was a grand total of $10.3 billion in loans at the end of 1976. Public loans amounted to $4.8 billion, and commercial loans amounted to $5.8 billion. Payment due in 1977 was over $1 billion—$481 million was in interest payments and $530 million was a portion of the principal. The payment in 1978 is expected to be about $1.3 billion, in 1979, $1.5 billion, and in 1981, the payment due will be over $2 billion. Is the Korean economy able to meet these financial obligations? What are the results of the "miracle"?

The economic planners of the Park regime expected to pay these debts by increasing exports. But such expectations did not materialize. The economy of South Korea needed a new economic policy. The United States encouraged Japan to "help" the South Korean economy, and Japan was ready. At the time of the 1965 treaty between Japan and Korea, 93.6 percent, and 82 percent or 784 out of 949 foreign firms in South Korea States. This situation has, however, changed within three years. The economic aid, loans, and investments from the United States were reduced to 44.5 percent in three years. Japan accounted for 65.4 percent of the entire foreign investments while the United States declined to 27.6 percent and 82 percent or 784 out of 949 foreign firms in South Korea belonged to Japan. In the year of 1974, Japan held no less than 95 percent of the total foreign investments.

There has developed another new trend. Major Japanese investments are now concentrating on heavy and chemical industries rather than the light industries as previously pointed out. For instance, 17 percent of Japanese investments were in the tourist business in the past. Japan had hardly any investment in agriculture, forestry, and fishery industries which South Korea needed to develop more than any other areas.

We stated earlier that the more exports South Korea makes, the more money she loses. Now we can say that the more Korea borrows from foreign countries, the more she contributes to the decay of the national economy. According to a government report, the growth of GNP from 1970 to 1974 was as follows: 100 in 1970, 109.1 in 1971, 116.8 in 1972, 136.0 in 1973, and 147.1 in 1974. On the other hand, the repayment of loans has also been increasing steadily. Let us compare the two growths in the following table.

The Trend of GNP and Repayment in South Korea[11]

	1970	1971	1972	1973	1974
GNP growth %	100	109.1	116.8	136.0	147.1
Repayment increase %	100	126.4	185.4	243.5	322.3

As the table indicates, we can see the speedy increase of 100 in 1970 to 322.3 percent in 1974. What does this trend indicate? It means that the Park regime is building an astronomical amount of foreign debt for future generations. The present system will not be rectified but will get worse as the regime obviously intends to accelerate heavy chemical industry development with Japanese capital.

The issue is not simply the failure of agricultural development, the accumulation of national capital, the increase of payment deficits in trade, but also the exploitation of the working class by foreign capitalists under a legalized system. The Labor Bureau reported that 60 percent of the 1.4 million wage earners in South Korea received $80 per month, or about one-half of the minimum required $150 for an average family. Worse yet, 22 percent received less than $40 per month.[12]

How about foreign investors? Gulf Oil Company invested $300 million in South Korea and expected to get its principal back in five years, but succeeded in doing so in four years. Many of us have noted not only the four million dollar contribution to the Park regime but also the royal entertainment of the former prime minister, Kim Chang-pil, by Gulf Oil's officials, including use of its private plane when Kim was visiting the

States prior to the company's investment in South Korea. Not only do these foreign investors make excessive profits, but also the few Koreans who collaborate with them also make fortunes within a few years. For instance, any businessman who has a license to borrow from a foreign country and is able to negotiate a loan with the government's guarantee, can make many times the loan amount the moment he signs the loan contract. The official domestic interest rate is somewhere between 15 to 20 percent in Korea, while the interest rate on a foreign loan is about 6 to 9 percent. There is no wonder, then, that much bribery takes place among businesses and the high officials who control loans. It is generally accepted in the business circle that about 10 percent of the loan amount is automatically deducted for the political fund by President Park's close associates, mainly, the Blue House and the KCIA.

Consequently, the present economic system in South Korea has several unique characteristics. First of all, the South Korean economy is completely dominated by foreign capital. There is not one Korean company which is free from foreign domination. All the major Korean firms are built either with foreign loans or by joint investment with foreign capital. Therefore, the growth of Korean industries depends totally on foreign capital. There has been no opportunity for normal capitalistic competitive growth in the Korean economy as in other advanced capitalist societies.

Secondly, the marriage between the dictatorial Park regime and the growing monopolists in South Korea is another unique feature. The government has absolute power to make or break any company at any time it chooses to do so. Companies such as the Dae-Woo and the Korea Air Line have become economic giants over a short period with President Park's blessings. As a matter of fact, none of these economic giants today could stay prosperous without President Park's personal support. President Park creates these economic giants for his own political purposes, but gradually, these economic giants, which are dominated by foreign capital, have had dominating influences upon the regime.

The third unique feature concerns illicit activities and corruption. The inevitable situation is that economic growth cannot be obtained through a normal competitive system, but through rigid control, conspiracy, and the bribery system. The Tongsun Park bribery scandal is a good example. The present circumstance in South Korea is not conducive for honest businessmen there. Conspiracy and corruption are the way of life among these economic animals and politicians who are closely associated with the Park regime. The regime promotes the development of national industries, the building of national capital, and of political independence, but on the surface only. The economy of South Korea may be a "miracle" in the eyes of the foreign investors, but in reality it is dominated by foreign interests as much as it was under Japanese occupation. The Japanese occupation did not help Korea to be a modern nation. As shown earlier, thirty-six years of Japanese domination left nothing but a stagnated society with starving people. Modernization was for the Japanese, not for Koreans. The past repeats itself in Korea today. There is no escape from the political corruption and economic decay in South Korea as long as the present system continues. Not only has the Korean government failed to give due attention to its modernization policy, neglecting the agricultural sector, but also the United States government has failed to inspire the Korean government toward modernization. Thus, the modernization program has failed in South Korea even though some like to think of South Korea as a "miracle" child of the post-war world.

10 On Unification of the South and the North

The two sections of Korea announced an agreement to end hostilities between Seoul and Pyongyang on July 4, 1972, as a step toward reunification of the nation, divided since the end of World War II in 1945. The historic joint communique was signed by both the Republic of Korea and the Democratic People's Republic of Korea.

The new accord provided for a telephone hot-line between Seoul and Pyongyang to prevent accidental war and a joint political committee to open exchanges in many fields and to promote unification of South and North Korea through peaceful means without outside interference. In an effort to ease tensions and foster mutual trust, the agreement added that the two governments agreed not to slander or defame each other or to undertake armed provocations against each other.

Agreement was reached at meetings in Pyongyang on May 2 through May 5, and in Seoul on May 29 to June 1. Presidents Kim Il-sung of North Korea and Park Chung Hee of South Korea participated in the talks in their respective capitals while Lee Hu-Rak, then director of the South Korean Central Intelligence Agency, went to Pyongyang, and Park Sung-chul, second deputy premier, attended the talks in Seoul. The chief negotiator, Kim Young-joo, director of the North Korean Workers' Party's Organization and Guidance Department, and a younger brother of President Kim Il-sung, remained in Pyongyang.

The communique pointed out three principles for national unification on which the two sides agreed:

First, unification is to be achieved through independent Korean efforts without subjection to external imposition or interference.

153

Second, unification is to be achieved through peaceful means, and not through the use of force.

Third, as a homogeneous people, a great national unity shall be sought transcending differences in ideas, ideologies, and systems.

Prior to this historic announcement, the two Korean governments began efforts toward reconciliation in August, 1971, when Red Cross Societies of the South and North agreed to reunite 10 million families separated by the arbitrary formation of the two governments. The meeting on September 20, 1971, at Panmunjum Truce Village was the first direct contact between North and South Korean government officials since 1945.

The announcement of the July 4 statement and the formation of the North-South Co-ordination Commission opened bright prospects for fifty million Korean people. Peace-loving people all over the world welcomed the news. Both the United States and Japan, both of which have economic and political interests in South Korea, expressed warm support. A statement issued in Washington called the agreement: "A salutary impact on the prospect for peace and stability on the Korean peninsula."[1] At the same time, Washington affirmed continuing military support for South Korea and said there would be no reduction in the current forty-thousand-man U.S. force in South Korea.

The news of accord has nevertheless disturbed Washington policy makers. One State Department expert confessed that, "Considering the degree of distrust and enmity that existed only a couple of years ago between the two Koreas, this announcement's working is unprecedented."[2] The Japanese Foreign Ministry spokesman praised "The courage and leadership of the two Korean governments" and hoped that they would settle their differences.

Background

How did this historic communique come about? The problems of Korea's unification have been politically acute ever since the country's division. The leaders of both the South and the North have repeatedly promised unification. In discussing the problems, one must remember that South and North Koreans are of the same socio-economic-political heritage. They share many aspirations and goals because of this common heritage.

The reunification of Korea might not have been a problem if the United States, the Soviet Union, and the leaders of Korea had reached some sort of an agreement after World War II. The Soviet Union quickly recognized the People's Republic, but the United States refused to deal with it. Instead, the United States attempted to continue the Japanese colonial administration in office. The response to this was so intense that the United States rescinded the order, but not before the People's Republic was disbanded.

In a speech on October 23, 1962, Kim Il-sung stated: "The occupation of South Korea by the United States imperialists and their aggressive policy are the root cause of all the misfortunes and sufferings of the South Korean people, and the main obstacle to the progress of South Korean society and peaceful unification of the country."[3]

Whether one agrees with Kim Il-sung's statement or not, there is not sufficient evidence to indicate that the United States' policy toward the unification of Korea was a positive one. The advocacy of the unification of Korea had been sustained by Kim Il-sung through the post-war years.

The principal policy of South Korea was anti-communism, dating from the time the Republic of Korea was established in 1948 under the auspices of the United Nations, and primarily by the United States. With American encouragement and protection, the South's regime, whether Syngman Rhee or Park Chung Hee was its leader, continued faithfully the anti-communism policy which was an integral part of the universal cold war policy—containment of communism by the United States. The tempo of the cold war has been maintained in South Korea better than anywhere else in the world.

In a major policy statement, President Park Chung Hee of the Republic of Korea said that his administration would continue to foil North Korea's attempt to wage aggression by strengthening the nation's ties with Free World allies. He affirmed that the North Korean communists were engaged in a desperate attempt to translate into action their fundamental goal of unification by military means. The Koreans in the South planned to carry out the second five-year economic plan on schedule and to attain a 10 percent or more economic growth during 1970. By doing so, President Park felt that the Republic of Korea would be able to bolster an independent defense system and succeed in solidifying a national framework designed to attain "self-sufficiency and prosperity." He believed that he could unify the divided nation after demonstrating to North Korea the overpowering national strength of South Korea.

President Park said that the government would push ahead with a flexible diplomatic attitude in the United Nations, hoping to create an atmosphere conducive to achieving national territorial unification. In his presidential inaugural address, President Park expressed his wish to see poverty eliminated and the unification of the fatherland achieved.

Taking the oath of office as the sixth president on July 1, 1967, President Park said, "Our enemies are poverty, corruption, and Communism. I think they are our three great common enemies." As much as he despises communism, President Park does not propose to solve the problem by means of war.

On South Korea's twentieth birthday, President Park issued a special statement in which he stated that the ultimate national goal would be the reunification of the nation.

> Indeed, it is our prime task to achieve a prosperous, democratic and united nation. We do not want the territorial unification by means of war. But the more we wish the unification through a peaceful and democratic formula, the more we have to strengthen our defense posture and complete our self-reliant defense system.[4]

Park believed the building of a prosperous and free society to be as important as having well-trained troops. This prompted the president to suggest a new concept of the "second economy."

His concept of the "second economy" dealt with the spiritual and philosophical aspects of national modernization. It was to be the basic motivation for the development of material, physical, and technological aspects of the economy if the nation was to attain genuine modernization.

Why suddenly at this time does President Park talk about Korea's unification? It has been clearly demonstrated that the people in the South were getting impatient with Park's promised "modernization." Modernization obviously was not emerging even after the second five-year economic plan with its ever-increasing foreign debts. President Park needed to change the political focus from his failure at modernization to the unification issue, which he knows is in every Korean's heart.

The pressure to pursue national unification was not limited to domestic problems in the South. The international situation changed in favor of reunification talks. The big powers system of alliances has changed a great deal since the end of the Vietnam War. President Nixon's visit to Peking and Moscow reduced the intensity of the cold war. The changed situation enhanced the opportunity for small nations to function independently and promote their own interests. Both South and North Korea probably felt that this was the time for them to become less involved in the politics of the big powers if they wanted to change conditions in Korea.

It now also became clear that the big powers would not support an all-out war effort for unification, nor defend one side against the other, as had happened in 1950. The time was ripe for all parties concerned with a peaceful strategy for unification. In other words, the national unification problem in the seventies was entirely different from the setting in the fifties.

In quest of unification, the South Korean government created, at cabinet level, the office of territorial unification. It has three main departments: Planning, Research, Public Information and Education. "From now on, we must engage in a systematic research on our territorial unification," commented Shinn Tai-hwan, the newly appointed minister. His ministry was to pursue flexible measures for territorial reunification adaptable to the realities in Korea.

The South Korean government has kept to the principle that Korea should be reunified only through free elections by the people of South and North Korea under the supervision of the United Nations. Shinn said, "Therefore, the existing unification principle should be evolved in the direction advantageous to us according to the changing international situation." The minister added that he would guarantee freedom of research and discussion on the problems of unification, and recommended to President Park Chung Hee a thirty-six-member advisory committee for unification research including Paik Nak-jun, Yun Tchi-young, Park Sun-chon, Rhee Hyo-sang, Chyung Il-hyung, and Cardinal Kim Su-hwan.[5]

How much serious thought the South Korean regime gave to true territorial unification was still not clear, in spite of the establishment of the cabinet post for that purpose. For instance, Minister Shinn stated that:

> In the foreign policy sector, Korea will adhere to the basic unification policy, under which the government will make efforts to reunify the divided land through the United Nations, during the first half of the 1970s. The government's U.N. strategy will be seasoned . . . invite representatives of the Republic of Korea and North Korea . . . the two-Korea theory might gain force.[6]

The minister revealed official intentions concerning national unification, and no one was surprised at the regime's two-Korea policy at the United Nations later in 1973, which received the support of the United States and Japan. Shinn predicted: "Prospects are that the division of Korea will continue through the second half of the 1970s. . . ."[7]

What did the official position of a "two-Korea policy" indicate? Was this policy a flexible unification policy as the Seoul regime claimed? What else could President Park have done when the U.N. office in Geneva on June 1, 1973, granted observer status to North Korea? Could Park have rejected a *de facto* recognition of the government of North Korea and isolated himself from the world arena? It could have been "senseless competition in the international arena with North Korea," and furthermore, President Park could not alienate his own people who demanded the unification dialogue. Under the circumstances, he suggested the two-Korea policy, which the United Nations rejected overwhelmingly. The Korean people would have done likewise had they been given an opportunity.

Dissolving the United Nations Commission for Unification and Rehabilitation of Korea, which was based in Seoul, the U.N. made its position clear to the world that there must be one Korea without outside interference.

Turning our attention to North Korea, the unification movement has developed somewhat differently from that of the South. First of all, the unification policy of Kim Il-sung is not a recent development. It has been enumerated that President Kim has spoken more than 130 times on the subject of national unification since the liberation in 1945.[8]

It is not the quantity, but quality of Kim's statements that should attract our attention. One of the most publicized statements made by Kim Il-sung in regard to national unification was made during the *Daily Yomiuri*'s interview in Pyongyang. A question was asked: The peaceful reunification of Korea will undoubtedly have much bearing on the security and peace of Asia. What are your determination and concrete plans in this respect?

President Kim replied that the general situation of Korea was developing very favorably for the struggle of the Korean people for an independent, peaceful unification of the country. He said:

> You asked me about our concrete program for the reunification of the country. Our program for national reunification is not different from the previous one. We have invariably maintained that the questions of our country's reunification, an internal affair of our nation, should be solved not by the interference of outside forces but by the efforts of the Korean people themselves, not by means of war, but in a peaceful way.[9]

The significance of the statement is that it includes all the major components of the July 4th Communique which was to follow. Independent, peaceful reunification of the nation without third-party interference was the keystone of the message. The message had also been advanced at a session of the Supreme People's Assembly of the Democratic People's Republic of Korea which was held in April of 1971.

President Kim Il-sung emphasized the importance of the peaceful unification of the country which would in turn enhance peace in Asia as well as in the world. To create a peaceful atmosphere, Kim suggested that the tension in Korea should be reduced. Kim stated, "It is necessary, first of all, to replace the Korean armistice agreement with a peace agreement between the North and South. We hold that a peace agreement should be concluded between the North and South and the armed forces of North and South Korea be cut drastically with the condition that the U.S. imperialist aggressor troops are withdrawn from South Korea."[10]

The issue of the peace agreement between the North and the South was a major issue at a meeting of the North-South co-ordinating committee late in 1972, but South Koreans rejected that proposal. South Koreans feared it would lead to the abolition of the United Nations command in the South and the withdrawal of American military forces.

In addition, North Korea proposed during talks in late 1972 a mutual reduction of troops to the level of 100,000 men, a halt in the introduction of foreign weaponry and making null and void the armistice agreement that ended the Korea War.

In view of increasing American military aid to South Korea, the delivery of a squadron of F-4 Phantoms to the ROK air force at the end of 1969, and intensive militia training of 2 million men, a peaceful proposal to reduce the military force to remove tension in Korea created much confusion to policy makers in the South.[11]

Behind the proposal by North Korea to reduce military forces to remove tension in Korea, there was another serious military matter North Korea probably had in mind. That was the experience of the USS *Pueblo* incident of 1968. The issue had been settled peacefully after eleven months of negotiations.

The USS *Pueblo* was seized by North Korea near Wonsan Harbor, approximately ninety miles north of the DMZ. The *Pueblo* was an American intelligence ship, 179 feet long, 33 feet wide, with a top speed of 12 knots, a crew of eighty-three, armed with three .50 caliber machine guns. It was gathering military data about North Korea. The incident was not the first of its kind by any means. Two American destroyers, the *Maddox* and the *Turner Joy*, in the Tonkin Gulf in 1964 were reported to have been torpedoed by an enemy, and the escalation of war in Vietnam took place. U.S. Senate Foreign Relations Committee Chairman William Fulbright conducted long public hearings which failed to prove whether the vessels had been torpedoed or not. Nevertheless, the Vietnam War was escalated by order of President Johnson.

Why had North Korea seized the *Pueblo*? North Korea claimed that the ship was in its territorial waters, within twelve miles of land. Secretary of Defense Robert McNamara denied North Korea's claims while Secretary of State Dean Rusk was not sure where the ship was really located when seized.

The more important question was not where the ship was located at the time of seizure, but why did the Johnson administration send the intelligence ship into "controversial" areas in a "provocative manner" as Senator Karl E. Mundt put it. The intelligence ship was sent into "controversial" areas in a "provocative manner" in spite of North Korea's warning to stay out of its territorial waters. An American news magazine report stated, "There is evidence of North Korea's intentions about U.S. reconnaissance ships." The report continued:

> On January 9th, the North Korean News Agency warned that the U.S. was "infiltrating boats carrying espionage and subversive elements into the coastal waters of our side." A Japanese freighter captain, who returned to Japan from North Korea January 19th, reported an increase in North Korea's patrol-boat activity.[12]

U.S. authorities had ignored these warnings as General MacArthur had ignored China's warning prior to sending troops to join North Korea's against the Southern forces in 1950. The fact is that the U.S. Navy had sent into hostile waters a ship which was loaded with electronic gear, supposedly so secret that it was to be destroyed by means of explosives if there was danger of its falling into enemy hands. An editorial pointed out:

> The North Koreans were much more circumspect than the Israelis, who mistook the Liberty, another U.S. intelligence ship, for an Egyptian warship and shot her up in the Mediterranean, with heavy loss of life. These incidents are an inevitable accompaniment of our insistence on patrolling the water by land, sea, and air, and making our power felt in every nation, large or small.[13]

It was a time of military frustration caused by the Vietnam War. The superpowers faced a dilemma in Vietnam. The United States had to choose either to get out from Vietnam or escalate its involvement. Another U.S. involvement in Korea at that time was an embarrassment. Senator Mundt seemed to reflect the views of many of his colleagues when he asserted that the Johnson administration took great risks sending a spy ship into "controversial" areas in a "provocative manner." Many Americans felt that the Johnson administration provoked North Korea because of American frustrations in Vietnam. Therefore, the *Pueblo* incident was an outcome of the Vietnam crisis. One magazine editorial commented:

> The North Koreans were known to have patrol boats with speeds up to 40 knots. (The Pueblo's speed was 12 knots.) The *Pueblo* was armed only with a

pair of machine guns. She was a sitting duck for anyone who cared to take her. Although we had any number of fighter aircraft in the vicinity, nothing came to her aid. Even if one takes the position that the mission of the *Pueblo* was a necessary one, it looks like a thoroughly botched job, not on the part of the commander and his men, but as directed by the admirals in charge of all this activity.[14]

Another factor which added questions to the seizure of the *Pueblo* incident was the matter of its settlement. Why did the settlement take eleven months? What was the demand of North Korea for release of the crew? An apology from the U.S. authority was demanded. An apology would indicate that the U.S. was wrong in getting caught in an intelligence ship mission and had to acknowledge this error by publicly apologizing to North Korea. One suggestion was that:

If we can swallow our pride in this situation, such national wisdom might serve to sensitize the national conscience to face the even more difficult task of accepting the fact of our national guilt and folly in the Vietnam crisis.[15]

Moderation in U.S. policy was needed, and it did not come easily. There were some who spoke out more aggressively than the Johnson administration did. For instance, California Governor Ronald Reagan urged a 24-hour ultimatum and then "coming in after it." Secretary Rusk advised both Americans and North Koreans to "cool it." The Johnson-Rusk administration succeeded finally through long negotiations which required twenty-eight secret meetings, and brought the eighty-two American crew-members home safely. Commander Lloyd M. Bucher of the ship said at his first press conference, "I surrendered the ship because there was nothing but a slaughter out there, and I couldn't see allowing any more people to be slaughtered or killed."[16]

The Vietnam War was spreading into Laos, Cambodia, and even Thailand. It could have spread to Korea, Taiwan, and perhaps the Middle East. The Johnson-Rusk policy of containment was at its peak. In view of the time and mood of the policy-makers, the settlement of the *Pueblo* incident was moderate, and indeed, fortunate. One critic of the Johnson-Rusk policy in Asia, Walter Lippmann, said, "Until the miscalculations of our present policy are understood, the formation of a constructive policy in the emerging and awakened Asian continent will not be possible."[17] Lippmann understood the Asian situation better than the Washington policy-makers. The U.S. government took a narrow view of what it considered essential to safeguard America's reputation in the world. "A military promise is not the only form of truth," said Norman Cousins. "The national honor may depend far less on creating respect for our muscle than on maintaining our moral stature. The moral integrity of our purposes and policies cannot be contrived; it can only be demonstrated. Making good our threats may be less vital than keeping faith with our history."[18]

President Johnson, taking advantage of the *Pueblo* incident, called up the reserves on a semipermanent basis to reinforce the 500,000 U.S. servicemen already in Vietnam. The *Pueblo* incident proved to be not a lesson for President Johnson's administration, but an opportunity to escalate the war atmosphere at home. The American people, however, were not in the mood to open another land war in Asia. About this time, Great Britain had announced that she would abandon her role as a military power in South Asia from Suez to Singapore. That left the U.S. in the area without the support of a single large power. The withdrawal of Britain from Asia confirmed the total isolation of the U.S. in Asia. That is why critics like Lippmann and Cousins maintained that the U.S. involvement in Indochina, and certainly sending the *Pueblo* to spy in Asian waters, were miscalculations. It was a strategic mistake for the U.S. to engage the bulk of its military power at any one point, like Vietnam or Korea. The response well could have been a breakout of trouble at other points. Fortunately, the American people in demanding an end to military actions were wiser than their political leaders.

In light of the *Pueblo* and the U.S. Navy's EC-121 reconnaissance plane incidents, it became evident that North Korea was taking a positive attitude toward seeking a peace agreement with South Korea.

It is of great significance that North Korea on September 17, 1971, proposed a confederation of North and South Korea as a transitional step to eventual reunification. A North Korean memorandum, distributed by Pyongyang's official news agency, read:

> If the South Korean authorities, fearful of the communization of the whole of South Korea, still consider it impossible to accept free general elections throughout the North and South, confederation . . . can be established as a transitional step while retaining the existing differing social systems of the North and South as they are.[19]

Political pressures mounted from the North, and President Park Chung Hee had to accept some of the unification approaches. The first positive statement on unification since 1948 by South Korea came on September 17, 1971, when Park suggested cultural and trade exchanges. He coupled the suggestion with a demand that North Korea publicly renounce the policy of "communizing the whole of Korea by force."

It took a long time to arrive at a joint communique, but it arrived nevertheless on July 4, 1972. Both sides agreed that an independent, peaceful unification without outside interference would be the goal for the nation.

President Park declared that "peace, unification and prosperity—these are the imperative tasks imposed upon us in our time and nation." On the occasion of the twenty-seventh anniversary of national liberation on August 15, 1972, he said:

> The recent South-North Joint Communique. means acceptance by the North Koreans of my repeated call for renunciation of force, and signals the opening of a new chapter of national history, as well as signifying a step forward in the great national advance toward peaceful unification.[20]

Regardless of who influenced whom, the July 4th joint communique opened dialogue between the two sides, and merits being labeled an historic event. It was a victory for the national conscience of fifty million Koreans who yearn for a peaceful and independent unification.

Approaches to Possible Unification

Two sides agreeing upon the goal of national unification is one thing, but how to approach it is yet another matter.

If we accept the meaning of unification as an achievement of territorial unification between South and North, and political, economic, social, and cultural integration of two parts of the nation, the term creates unavoidably ambiguous, tautological meanings. Political integration, for instance, closely touches the problem of citizens' loyalties.

Professor Ernst B. Haas comments: "Political integration is a process whereby political actors in several distinct national settings are persuaded to shift their loyalties, expectations, and political activities toward a new center."[21]

In other words, a new center is needed to bring about political integration. Obviously, such an integration process is neither possible nor desirable under the present conditions in Korea. Neither side will allow such a process by government authority.

Unless there is an agreement between the two sectors with regard to a certain degree of commonly shared views on unification, the process cannot be initiated. Views must be shared by the leaders of the two sectors as well as the citizenry. A recent public opinion poll in South Korea indicated an overwhelming desire for unification, but a very small percentage were able to identify any level of the process. For instance, only

14 percent supported visiting privileges between relatives in South and North Korea, while 29 percent favored the immediate exchange of newsmen.[22]

The hesitancy of the majority of the citizens in the South to express more positive views on the political integration process is primarily due to the prevailing anti-communism sentiments of the South.

At the first conference of the Fourth Term of the Supreme People's Council of North Korea on December 16, 1967, Kim Il-sung declared: "We must ideologically and psychologically prepare to mobilize our people to unite to participate in the decisive battle for the unification of the nation when the revolutionary conditions are ripe and the struggle is at a high point."[23]

The basic concept of the revolution has not been changed, but the approach to instigation of revolution in the South has. No longer will North Korea export revolution to the South, for the North now insists upon a peaceful unification. Furthermore, possible federalism of two social systems as they exist should not be threatened in the view of North Korean leaders.

Echoing this official attitude, a recent publication of Pyongyang reveals that whether a citizen is a farmer or a laborer or a writer, he is supposed to be working toward a common political goal—unification of the fatherland.

Under the title "My Working Life of Yesterday and Today," Han Myong-gap writes that "Korea must be unified as soon as possible, so the people of the South can enjoy true happiness in the warm breast of the great father-like leader Premier Kim Il-sung."[24]

A similar statement comes from Ko Tsol-su, an engineer, who claims that he left his native home in the South to join his Northern brothers. He wrote, "If the Southern brothers wish to enjoy true happiness like their Northern brothers under the leadership of a great father-like Premier Kim Il-sung, we must destroy the eternal enemies of our nation—the land-lords, and the capitalists, and must achieve the unification of the fatherland."[25]

Whether writing about agricultural production or one's working conditions at a chemical industry plant or one's gratitude for a state hospital, all the writers express two thoughts in common—the unification of the fatherland and an undisputed loyalty to Kim Il-sung.

These examples illustrate the difficulty of finding political opinions common to both sides. It unquestionably requires a more refreshing and creative political approach to unlatch the closed doors.

Besides political views common to the two sectors, there are other factors which could enhance unification. One of the factors is economic. The unification process would proceed more effectively if the economic situations were more advanced. The necessity for structural adaptation will come about when the politico-economic sector recognizes that adaptation is for its own benefit.

Unless the political actors recognize and favor modernization and urbanization, there will be no structural adaptation. In other words, the more modern the thinking of the actors, the better will be the chance for unification; at least, from an economic point of view.

Professor Haas points out that most conducive to achieving integration are economic and welfare tasks, since these are the most productive in terms of facilitating the transfer of loyalties. The professor comments: "Not merely in economic tasks—but the degree of functional specificity of the economic task is causally related to the intensity of integration. The more specific the task, the more likely important progress will be toward an economic community."[26]

It has been well publicized that President Park's determination to bring about South Korea's industrialization is the cardinal principle of his modernization programs and has been accepted as national policy for the past decade. It is, however, doubtful that Park's regime has actually achieved what he has been claiming. All evidence contradicts his "success story" in South Korea—for instance, agricultural conditions, the living conditions of the workers whose wages are still one-fifth of those of Japanese workers, and the bankruptcy of middle-class merchants. The beneficiaries of Park's economic policy are limited to a handful of rich businessmen and a small group of bureaucrats.

Healthy economic competition between the two sides could contribute to the unification of Korea, but it seems that economic progress is limited to North Korea at the present time. Agriculture in the North has been mechanized, modernized, and produces enough grain to meet domestic consumption, while South Korea, formerly the breadbasket of the country, has to import all sorts of grain—rice, wheat, corn—to support its population. For instance, in 1962, a year after the military coup, the export of agricultural products amounted to $23 million, but dropped to $10 million in 1964, and declined steadily due to lack of government promotion. South Korea in 1973 had to import 80 percent of its corn supplies from abroad, primarily from the United States.

One of the characteristics of the Korean economy is small-scale farming. The average Korean farmer cultivates about 1.5 jungbo or one-fiftieth of his American counterpart. Farming on such a small scale, the average farmer can hardly support his family. This is a perplexing problem. With this situation, one might expect the government to try to improve the farm situation by helping farmers to meet their debts and to improve their lot in general by providing better techniques in household management, production and soil management, and to supply them with fertilizers and introduce modern farm equipment. Enlightened policy is clearly needed if the present chaotic condition of the agricultural economy in South Korea is to change. Park's regime has not provided such a policy. North Korea is self-reliant, while South Korea is still very much dependent on foreign countries, even after thirty years of political independence.

The basic mode of Korean industrial production is as backward in nature as agriculture. The low degree of self-sufficiency in industrial production is evidence of its backwardness. The only industry which supplies local demands in the Korean market is the food industry. Next in line would be the chemical industry, meeting about 70 to 75 percent of demand. The average industry supplies about 72 percent of its domestic needs.

Because the chemical industry has a high ratio of meeting production demands, one must not be misled about its advanced development, since the industry merely produces consumer goods by processing imported materials. The increase of export goods is related to the increase of processed goods using imported raw materials.

Korean industry leans heavily on consumer goods rather than on basic products. Consumer goods including textiles, chemicals, and food products come to more than 72 percent in the number of plants, 80 percent in the number of laborers, and 82 percent in production. In other words, Korean industry is primarily light industry.

The government of Korea has undertaken construction with foreign capital in key basic industries, such as electric power, cement, fertilizer and sheet glass, which constitute basic projects. Korea, like many other underdeveloped nations, is trying to build the basic industries as a matter of national pride as much as to meet national needs. Heavy industry has become a symbol of twentieth century national independence. Economically, however, there is danger in this route. Why did the British government desire to purchase F-111 bombers from the U.S. instead of building them at British aircraft factories? British industry is certainly just as capable of building bombers as American industry. The reason for the British purchase is that it is able to buy F-111 bombers from the U.S.

cheaper than it can build them at home. Should the Korean government build its own fishing boats if it can buy them from Japan at half of the price?

Obviously, not all goods should be purchased from Japan while infant industries at home are crumbling. How should the Korean government then decide to protect and nourish infant industries and what industries should be selected for such treatment? Here, government policy plays an important role.

The Korean economy is too much behind advanced economies of the world. It would be foolish for Korea to try to compete on all levels. Instead, Korea must find those industrial situations where it has an advantage over foreign competition. In this field, we realize the specific character of the medium and small-scale industry of Korea. Generally Korean plants have not converted from tools to automated machinery. They are not modernized. The productive techniques of most industries remain at relatively primitive levels. What Korea needs now is to mechanize its medium and small industries with capital investment by government, rather than having government invest in over-sized heavy industry in efforts to compete with advanced nations or trying to maintain false concepts of national economic independence. This only contributes in many new emerging nations to the halting of economic development.

In 1972, Park's government reported that exports totaled $1.4 billion, an increase of 45.2 percent over the year before. The regime aims for increases each year. The economic growth rate, Park's regime claims, averaged 10 percent annually or the third highest in the world.

Even if we accept these statistics as credible, the meaning of such growth is simply the expansion of exports. It does not help to carry out the development of natural resources; nor does it represent increased industrial skills; nor does it mean an increase in fair employment and further benefits to society. It is only a measure of how workers are exploited by low wages to benefit foreign capitalists. As a result, "The gaining of the foreign currency is not even a match to the minimum of its costs, and it means that South Koreans are exporting their blood to the foreign markets."[27]

The economic growth of South Korea over the past decade has been impressive, but it can hardly be equated with real development, because by and large the size of marginal economic groups has increased and the poverty gap has widened. If this trend continues as it has under present policy, South Korea is headed for a catastrophe. Increases in GNP can be statistically impressive but intrinsically deceptive. Exports of goods can increase while more people are left in greater misery. Given an unjust social framework, increases in the GNP will strengthen the rich and strong and emasculate the weak and poor. This is what is happening in South Korea.

The psychological factor is the third element relevant to the peaceful unification of Korea. In some respects, it is more serious than either political or economic factors in the historical and national sense.

When Premier Willi Stoph of East Germany accepted Chancellor Willy Brandt's offer to meet him in East Germany, and the two leaders discussed the future of the two German sectors, the psychological impact on the people of East and West Germany was tremendous, even though there were no immediate political fruits resulting. In contrast, we find an entirely different situation in Korea. The Korean situation is even more rigid than the Vietnamese situation.

The purpose of the German leaders' meeting was not to talk about reunification. Chancellor Brandt did not propose political and territorial reunification at that time. He sought a limited detente with East Germany, based on mutual renouncing of force. He talked about East Germany as he would with any other government, such as Poland or Czechoslovakia. East Germany, too, opened its doors for talks while presenting a very rigid agenda of its own.

Such communication between the two sections, nevertheless, relaxes tensions and may lead to meaningful dialogue.

Professor Karl Deutsch points out:

> Membership in a people essentially consists in wide complementarity of social communications. It consists in the ability to communicate more effectively, and over a wider range of subjects, with the members of one large group than with outsiders.[28]

Along with the propensity to communicate or share messages, an integrated community will evince a propensity to share commodities and to interchange people as well.

Self-reliance in national defense, based on Kim Il-sung's *Juche* concept, has been the key policy of North Korea.

The policy states that even small communist nations must prepare their own defense rather than rely on the big powers. The Soviet Union's coexistence policy with the United States was considered "revisionistic" by Peking and North Korea, which felt it would indirectly hinder the unification policy of North Korea.

Emphasizing the importance of psychological and ideological warfare, North Korea was exploring four main areas. The first was to encourage anti-government movements in the South. Another approach was aimed against the American presence in Korea. North Korea has been exploiting the theme of "American colonization" in South Korea. One tactic was to parallel American troops stationed in Korea with those in Vietnam. The third area of propaganda was designed to expose the ROK-Japan relationship. The normalization of this relationship has lasted for several years. North Korea looks upon Japanese imperialism as a potential enemy. The fourth area was to unify communist nations under world communism. Therefore, Kim Il-sung advocated military aid to North Vietnam from all communist countries.

The differences between the South and the North in the areas of psychological and ideological matters go beyond the current political attitudes of the two regimes.

Historically the people of the North were penetrated by modern concepts earlier than the people of the South. This was due to the economic structure, strong feudalistic landlordism and fertile land in the South vs. a weak feudalistic system and early Christian influence upon the people of the North, as well as social and cultural heritages which favor the Northerners.

In addition the South has been subjected to ideological orientation of nineteenth-century capitalism as well as misrepresented individualism from the United States' early occupation. As a result South Korea has stagnated under one of the most reactionary political systems anywhere. The first time the concept of modernization was seriously introduced was when the military coup d'etat of May 16, 1961, took place. It is a political irony that a man with a Ph.D. in political science at Princeton under Woodrow Wilson became the bulwark of the reactionary force, only to end his political dream in tragedy. In a practical economic sense, "communistic" North and "capitalistic" South are meaningless labels. The term "communism" is political rather than economic in Korea. More specifically, the term is a politico-psychological one. Communism in North Korea means "have faith in Kim Il-sung" and is almost synonymous with "Kim Il-sung's revolutionary thought" as was the case of "Mao's thought" in China.

Kim Il-sung has commented: "After revolutionary achievement, sharing the good things among us exclusively in the North by closing the door to the South Koreans is the road to suicide." The urgency is psychological.

There are obviously many relevant elements which will affect the unification of divided Korea. The three elements—political, economic, and psychological—dealt with here are seemingly the key factors.

In the absence of some reasonable level of communicative interchange between the two sectors, we might conclude that people in the two sectors are not integrated into a common community. Short of such communication, the transference of individual political loyalties to a newly established political entity cannot take place; therefore, we would not expect to find any significant achievement of unification between two political units.

Professor Deutsch said that mass behavioral patterns are independent of integration, or, in terms of the process, occur prior to the actions or initiatives designed to achieve integration.

There must be relatively significant levels of positive reinforcement before individuals can identify successfully with a new political community. A political community requires the loyalty of its citizens and they must understand how to deal with common social problems through peaceful, nonviolent means.

In other words, a positive approach is to establish a community which must exist prior to the organization of a shared political authority. This would provide the basis for integrating the competing political authorities of the South and the North into a new political system in Korea.

If unification is to be achieved at the national level, there has to be a policy broadly enough constituted to include all political actors and groups. Broadly conceived, the policy of a national organization will be decided by member groups, parties, and organizations that cooperate in common programs.

The security of the community will be established by such integration. Security is the first necessity of modern politics. Individual and national welfare must follow through economic ties. Besides economic security, citizens demand reasonable freedom of movement and thought. Individual dignity and humanistic values should be maintained in an amalgamated community. In short, the new structure should be a modern democratic society. It cannot be overemphasized that only modernized systems and societies can really be unified since only modern society can develop adequate responses to current problems.

Difficult Task Ahead

The achievement of national unification, as we have discussed, is not a simple task. It involves a continuous movement between one's assertions and another's questioning; between thrusting forward and retreating; between being pushed and driven by the forces of the other side. Each section strives to maintain its own advantages, to realize its own goals, and to refuse to change.

Who is delaying the unification process? Who does not want to see Korea unified? Recent developments indicate that President Park's regime has deliberately been blocking the implementation of the July Fourth Joint Communique. He proclaimed martial law in South Korea just a couple of months after the joint communique which promised to bring about an independent, peaceful unification. Park also created an international scandal in having the Korean CIA kidnap Kim Dae-jung, the candidate for president in 1971 of the New Democratic Party.

Two forces that President Park was most afraid of were Kim Dae-jung and the American Congress. So stated Kim Hyung Wook, director of the Korean CIA from 1963 to 1969, testifying on June 22, 1977, before the Subcommittee on International Organizations, chaired by Donald M. Fraser of Minnesota. The former director of the KCIA and a close associate of President Park said that President Park did not hesitate to carry out the unconscionable, tyrannical kidnapping of Kim Dae-jung from Tokyo, and throwing him into prison in Korea.[29]

What justification did he have for ordering martial law in the South? President Park claimed that there was a steadily improving economy and he had opened a political dialogue with the North. One senior U.S. official in Washington commented: "There was simply no justification for it." President Park's declaration of martial law has become a pattern of his political operation. Martial law made clear that foreign reporters would be just as affected by the rule as Koreans. One American reporter, *Newsweek*'s Tokyo bureau chief, Bernard Krismer, commented on his personal experiences with soldiers in Seoul:

> An armed soldier rushed toward me to grab my camera, but I resisted and soon found myself battling three more soldiers who kicked me, yanked at the camera band around my neck and tore at my suit. . . . I was dragged to a corner police box, where I was refused permission to call the U.S. Embassy. After an hour of this, new troops arrived to drag me by the seat of my pants across the street into the occupied New Democratic Party building.[30]

The reporter was trying to photograph the New Democratic Party, an opposition headquarters, as it was occupied by troops. If they handled an American reporter in such a manner, one can imagine how they handled Korean journalists.

It was the third time since President Park seized power in 1961 that he had proclaimed martial law, and he offered another presidential decree as a New Year's Day present to the nation in 1974. This time he made a thorough job of it. Suspending parts of the constitution which he had revised three times, he dissolved the National Assembly (the majority members were hand-picked by Park himself), and he banned all political activities. Press censorship was imposed, and colleges and universities were closed "for an early winter vacation." To make sure the new decrees were carried out, military troops and tanks patrolled the capital and major cities.

President Park revised the constitution which he had drafted earlier to run for a third term as president, and changed it again to allow him to run for two more terms of six years each—which would keep him in power until 1984.

President Park's actions betrayed his own words. Immediately following the July 4th joint communique, he stated at a ceremony marking the twenty-fourth ROK Constitution Day, July 17, 1972:

> As we look back in the footsteps of our constitutional administration, it comes as a conviction to me that from now on application of the democratic system will have to be developed not on the formal level but on the practical level, in a better organized and more competent way. . . .
>
> I am convinced that today this significant function on Constitution Day will become another precious moment for us to pledge ourselves to make further efforts, so that the long-cherished desire of the nation for peaceful unification of the fatherland can be realized proudly within our democratic constitutional order.[31]

With such self-confidence President Park did not need martial law. What changed his mind in two months? On August 15, 1970, President Park had issued his "historical August 15 Declaration." In the statement Park proposed to conduct a competition in good faith to find out which system—that of the South or of the North—would enable people to enjoy a better life. If Park was so sure of his system, why did he need the frequent use of martial law in the South? What kind of a state of emergency was there in the South?

In regard to the matter of security and unification, Kim Yong-sik, the foreign minister of the South, commented:

> To our regret, a certain U.N. member state, under the pretext of creating favorable conditions for the success of the dialogue between the South and the North and for the peaceful reunification of Korea, insists on a debate of the Korean question at the forthcoming session of the General Assembly, calling for the dissolution of UNCURK and the withdrawal of the United Nations Forces in Korea, despite that the presence of UNCURK and the U.N. Forces in Korea have repeatedly been reaffirmed with the support of an overwhelming majority of the member states. It is apparent that the hidden intention behind

this move is . . . to weaken the defense posture of the Republic of Korea, endangering our national security.[32]

Despite the rigid position of the South Korean regime, the United Nation's First Committee at the twenty-eight session in November, 1973, in New York dissolved the "United Nations Commission for the Unification and Rehabilitation of Korea." It was the first victory for North Korea, which challenged the position of the South at the U.N. on its first historic appearance.

At the same time, Li Jonk-mok, the chief delegate of North Korea, proposed the withdrawal of all foreign troops from Korea, the conclusion of a peace agreement between the North and the South to refrain from attack against each other, and the reduction of armed forces of both North and South to 100,000 men or less, in hopes of reducing tensions.[33]

If the South-North dialogue was the most important endeavor by Koreans themselves to put an end to the division of Korea, as South Korean authorities claimed, then, it was not logical to reject the proposal of the North for a peace treaty.

There was a paradox to the unification movement: it proposed change and yet it exhibited a strong resistance to change. It had to be flexible, yet it was rigid. As a psychologist, Maslow, has said, the essential motivating force behind human action is self-realization. This, in essence, is using one's potential for action of all kinds: freely, creatively, and with great personal satisfaction. The individual is in a position to function at the self-realization level if his love and affectional needs are met. On the other hand, he is unable to function, even at the love and affection level, if his self-esteem needs are not met. As long as his needs remain unsatisfied at a given level, his motives and activities will remain at that level. If we accept the concept that self-realization precludes the satisfaction of more fundamental physical and psychological needs as Professor Maslow states, we realize the importance of the achievement and maintenance of self-realization.

In the achievement of nationhood or unification, there are at least two fundamental tasks which must be accomplished. First of all, there must be a socio-psychological adjustment among the people. This demands an early awareness of the needs of the other section of the divided land. Realizing this awareness requires a wide variety of communication skills. Only by interaction with the other section is one able to recognize the feelings, attitudes, and needs of others as well as the messages expressed by them.

Another necessary task to achieve unification or restoration of nationhood may be described as a promotion of tangible teamwork, or cooperative behavior which could result in satisfaction in attaining a common goal. An example could be an interzone mail service, or the exchange of basic commodities. The parties should not aim too high nor go too fast, as they did during the Soviet-American Conferences in 1946.

In the absence of communication, there is no opportunity to develop cooperation. Successful unification can occur when cooperation is optimized and when positive mutual responsives are maximized in a concerted effort towards the ultimate goal. Until such conditions appear, there can be no positive movement for unification. It is hoped that such conditions can be created internally and externally by nations which are concerned about peace and order in Eastern Asia.

Local loyalties take priority before the concept of a stable nation-state. Such attitudes undermine political cohesion. Sharp ideological differences within a society hamper national security, create disorder and civil war. On the whole, the ideological-psychological beliefs of the two sectors in Korea are of vital significance in determining whether the nation will unify to protect its national interests in the international situation, pursue an expansionist course, or engage in a modernization program. Fundamental ideological differences are the principal obstacles between the North and the South. Cooperation between the two sectors can be furthered considerably by muting ideological differences. Neither North nor South has much to gain by stubborn doctrinaire approaches to a solution. They have much to gain nationally as well as regionally if they follow present trends of international conciliation and flexibility as are the major powers. A small nation like Korea has nothing to lose and everything to gain by a moderate and flexible national policy instead of being the slave to an anachronistic national policy of isolationism from world progress.

Difficulties in pursuing a dialogue between the North and the South exist in spite of the July Fourth Joint Communique. Bright prospects for the nation are not at all certain today. It is darker now than six years ago when the joint statement was issued. Under the present circumstances, it is significant to note the five-point program for unification proposed by President Kim Il-sung on June 23, 1973. The statement made the following points:

1. Remove the state of military confrontation and ease tension between the North and the South;

2. Implement many-sided cooperation between the North and South;

3. Convene a national assembly of representatives of all people of all strata, political parties and social organizations in the North, the South and overseas;

4. Institute a North-South Confederation under the name of the Confederal Republic of Koryo;

5. Enter the United Nations under the name of Confederal Republic of Koryo.

This proposal appealed to many Koreans in and out of Korea. The proposal was mild and practical. It omitted ideology entirely and stressed minimum demands on both sides. When compared with the proposal made by Ulbricht of East Germany, Kim's proposal was minimal.

In August of 1956, Ulbricht laid down the prerequisites for the reunification of Germany:

> The national interest of our people and fatherland, the cause of peace and reunification demand: 1. The limitation of armed forces in the two parts of Germany. . . . 2. Removal of all Hitler generals and other revanchists from the state machinery and the armies. . . . 3. The step-by-step withdrawal of foreign troops from Germany. . . . 4. The lifting of the ban on the Communist Party of Germany. A ban on all militarist organization and associations.[34]

If Kim Il-sung made such demands, Park Chung Hee, an ex-officer of the Imperial Japanese Army, would not be eligible to negotiate the matter of unification. Kim Il-sung, in fact, had broadened the ground to include all patriots to participate in the unification movement when he called for a national conference from all walks of life in South and North Korea for the purpose of a well-diversified discussion on the subject of reunification.

The unification process is not just a pleasant series of steps forward. Panmunjom is an indication of that. Every step ahead is taken with certain dangers, risks, and threats. But unification is a genuine wish of the people. The leaders must accept the challenge. With each achievement of every significant task, there are new threats and dangers, as well as new advantages and hopes, with which the nation must cope.

There has to be a balance between the positive forces striving for unification, achievement and positive action on the one hand, and the negative forces demanding security, satisfaction with the status quo, and all other forces that represent threats to one's feeling about oneself if one risks movement ahead.

The whole pattern of the achievement of nationhood is marked by rapid spurts ahead and slower periods of doubt and questioning and consolidation of the resources in preparation for the next movement ahead.

At our present state of knowledge, in which we do not yet have adequate practical theories on unification and on other international issues, we need to learn more. However, we do have general principles of international politics, widely accepted by scholars in the field, which tell us that what we consider international political issues such as unification, political crises, and wars, are simply manifestations of international political interaction which can be understood in terms of causal principles about the behavior of men and of groups, including national groups.

Thus, if we have verified principles stating that any group or tribe or its leadership, when challenged by an action threatening its security, will respond in an aggressive fashion, we can apply this general principle of international politics to the Korean circumstances.

Peaceful unification and restoration of nationhood in Korea is possible when the people and their leaders understand these principles of international politics, and move constructively toward unification on political, economic and psychological levels. At least, there should be a minimum agreement on peaceful unification on a political level, some sort of economic agreement on mutual gains, and increased communications and transactions including limited mail services between two sectors.

Only such positive actions by the leaders of both sections, in view of the presence of a sense of nationhood among the people, will advance the unification movement.

We must admit that even most peaceful people like the Koreans cannot be exempt from the general pattern of human behaviors of competitiveness and aggression. In these days of confrontation and protest, pretending to be free of aggressive feelings is a false and risky attitude.

If Koreans are to be totally free to do as they wish and still be able to live together without destroying one another, they must purge themselves of aggressiveness or find a constructive way to handle aggression.

Koreans are in obvious need of a value system based upon a realistic and pragmatic assessment of man's biological and psychological needs. A humanistic value system could provide maximum freedom and autonomy. It could also provide sufficient controls to keep the people from destroying one another.

The task of defining such a value system presents a critical challenge to all who hope to live in a decent and reasonable society. This task should be first on the agenda for a peaceful unification of divided Korea.

The case for reunification was expressed in an open letter "to parliaments and governments of all countries of the world" by the Supreme People's Assembly, Democratic People's Republic of Korea on April 6, 1973:

> The struggle of the Korean people for peaceful reunification took an epochal turn particularly after Comrade Kim Il-sung, President of the Democratic

People's Republic of Korea, declared in his historic speech on August 6, 1971, that we had a readiness to discuss at any time the question of national reunification with the present ruling party and all the other political parties, all social organizations and individual personages in South Korea.[35]

The idea of the independent and peaceful unification of Korea won almost unanimous support not only of the Korean people but also of world politicians who assembled at the United Nations in 1973.

A letter dated September 10, 1973, came from the representatives of Algeria and thirty-one other nations in regard to a draft to create favorable conditions to accelerate the independent and peaceful reunification of Korea. It stated:

Recognizing that the termination of the interference of foreign countries in the internal affairs of Korea is the key for easing tensions in Korea, turning the armistice into a durable peace, promoting the dialogue between the North and the South smoothly and thereby achieving the independent, peaceful re-unification of the country.

Recognizing that it is in accord with the principles of the Charter of the United Nations . . . with the principles of the North-South Joint Statement and the principle of national self-determination . . . .[36]

With this preamble, the draft proposed the following action to be taken at the U.N. General Assembly:

1. to dissolve the "United Nations Commission for Unification and Rehabilitation of Korea";

2. to abolish the use of the United Nations flag by the foreign troops stationed in South Korea and dissolve the "United Nations Command";

3. to withdraw all foreign troops stationed in South Korea so further steps may be taken in accelerating the independent and peaceful reunification of Korea.

Why was such a draft deemed necessary after thirty-three years of liberation from Japan? Why did South Korea depend so heavily on foreign powers in every aspect of its existence while there had been no foreign soldiers since Chinese troops pulled out twenty-some years ago from the North at the end of the Korean War? Why did United Nations troops remain in South Korea after the armistice in 1953? Many people were puzzled by these questions. Representative Saito of Japan stated his defense of the U.N. troops in South Korea in the following manner:

Should the United Nations Command be dissolved without full consideration of the facts and without regard to the necessity of ensuring the maintenance of peace and security in the area in view of the fact that the present Armistice structure has been playing an indispensable role in the maintenance of international peace and security. . . . Should the United Nation's Command be

dissolved unilaterally, the stability of the Korean peninsula would be
threatened, and this would create conditions which would make it difficult to
continue to dialogue.[37]

Japan has been a strong defender of U.N. troops in South Korea ever
since its capital investment increased there. It was Japan which supported
the two-Korea policy the strongest at the U.N. debate during the 1973
session. For Japan, the security of South Korea is inseparable with the
security of Japanese economic interests in Korea. Is the security of South
Korea really in the hands of the U.N. Command? A different view was
stated during the U.N. debate by Representative Abdulla of the Sudan.
He said:

> It is common knowledge to us that the name and the flag of this organization
> have been used to cover up a blatant foreign intervention. The police action,
> the limited war, the useless war or the travesty of a certain president, or
> whatever might be the phraseology assigned to it by the phrase-makers, was an
> American affair, fought by the United States and its allies.
>
> The United Nations intervention is a United States intervention. General
> MacArthur said: "My relationship with the United Nations was only nomi-
> nal. Everything I did was controlled entirely by the Joint Chiefs of Staff . . .
> even my routine reports had to be censored by the U.S. State and Defense
> Departments. I do not recall getting orders in whatever form from the United
> Nations during the entire war. . . . No, I would not count on the United
> Nations for anything."[38]

Does anyone doubt that the Korean War was the "Truman-
MacArthur War"? If the purpose of the U.N. Command in South Korea
was to bring about the unification of Korea, has it achieved its goal? Or has
the U.N. Command's presence contributed to the reduction of tension in the
country and created two sides to get closer to peace? Does anyone need to
be reminded that South Korea has been under the military dictatorship of
Park Chung Hee since 1961? Who can deny the fact the sole purpose of
U.N. troops in South Korea is to protect the military dictatorship of Park
Chung Hee, just as they had done previously for Syngman Rhee's regime,
which the people of the South overthrew in 1960?

As Baroady of Saudi Arabia pointed out at the U.N. General
Assembly:

> The Korean people are one nation and should never have been divided by the
> two major powers, which were instrumental in the separation of the Korean
> people on ideological and strategic grounds. That sentence bears repetition a
> hundred times.[39]

It is of significance to note that Baroady is a monarchist who spoke in
support of the North Koreans, who are communists. He also said:

Where is our conscience? Are we clients of any of the two powers or are we independent sovereign States which should scrutinize every question on its merits and thereby address ourselves to solutions that are based on justice and not on political arrangements.

It has been general practice for the United States to request its allies not only to take sides politically but to join in the crusade of chastising the communists of the North. It was the United States, with the collaboration of the Soviet Union, that divided Korea, maintained two Koreas, and insists on a two-Korea policy today. Should Koreans rely on the United States and Japan to bring about the unification of Korea? Any sensible plan for unification must come from the Koreans themselves. It would only be wishful thinking to rely on the major powers for unification.

A statement originating in Pyongyang on April 6, 1973 said:

We consider that dialogue and negotiations should be conducted extensively on a democratic basis with the participation of political parties, public organizations and personages of all circles of the north and the south by concerted efforts to achieve the independent, peaceful reunification of the fatherland. . . .

The statement continued:

If the U.S. troops are withdrawn from South Korea and the intervention of outside forces in the internal affairs of our country is brought to an end by the joint struggle of the Korean people and the world people, the danger of war will be dispelled in Korea and the dialogue accelerated, the north-south relations radically improved and the question of the country's reunification smoothly solved in a peaceful way on the principle of national self-determination.[40]

There should be no illusion about the rate of progress toward unification. The delegates of the United States, Japan, West Germany and their allies made very clear their views about the future of Korea in separate speeches at the U.N. General Assembly in 1973. The two-Korea policy is their common aim. It is not an accident that these powers promote the two-Korea policy. The Park regime also promotes the two-Korea policy and has been good to their investments in South Korea.

The historic declaration of the July Fourth Joint Communique has been sabotaged, and the unification of Korea remains a dream of fifty million Koreans. The unification movement failed just as the democratization and the modernization programs have failed in South Korea. Democratization and modernization, as well as unification are left to be achieved by the Korean people themselves.

epilogue

A group of concerned Japanese Christians put a full-page ad in the *New York Times* of May 5, 1974, on behalf of Korean Christians imprisoned by President Park's government. It was an appeal to American Christians which read: "We Japanese Christians are deeply disturbed by the present circumstances in the Republic of Korea, and particularly concerned regarding the plight of Christians in that country who have to endure the religious oppression imposed upon them by the government."[1]

These Japanese, and later American, Canadian, German, and many other Christian leaders and laymen alike expressed their concern over the situation in South Korea.

A group of Christian ministers in the Republic of Korea declared, "Our people have gone through trials and suffering, social chaos, economic deprivation, and especially the tragic Korean war and the resulting political dictatorship. It is the ardent aspiration of our people that a humane community might be restored. However, the hopes of the people for such a restoration have been cruelly crushed by President Park's dictatorship and ruthless political repression."[2]

Thus the underground Christian movement began to challenge Park's regime whose survival depends solely on American military and economic aid.

In view of the serious situation in South Korea, American Christians urged that, "The U.S. government make a strong objection to the denial of human rights by countries which receive U.S. bilateral economic and military aid, and if such objection is ignored, to halt all aid except that which is purely for humanitarian purposes." At the general assembly of the United States Presbyterian Church in Louisville, Kentucky, on June 18–26, 1974, a policy statement and recommendation were adopted which: "Supports the Human Rights Statement of the National Council of Churches of Korea, 1973, and further commends the *Theological Declaration of Korean Christians, 1973*, as a significant example of witness made by Christians in a repressive society."[3] Similar resolutions have been adopted at the National Conference of the United Methodist Churches and the United Churches of Christ in the United States. In other words, major Christian denominations representing many millions of Americans protested the dictatorship of President Park and American support of his repressive regime. Park's dictatorship of Korea is destroying not only the principle of government by law, but has turned the entire community into a jungle. The *Theological Declaration of Korean Christians, 1973* stated that the Park regime "is destroying conscience and freedom of religious belief. There is freedom neither of expression nor of silence."[4] To create such a lawless jungle, President Park's regime uses the mass media extensively. They are controlled by the KCIA and tell the people half-truths and outright lies. The Declaration states that the dictatorship "uses sinister and inhuman and at the same time ruthlessly efficient means to destroy political opponents, intellectual critics, and innocent people."[5]

After sixteen years of dictatorial rule, President Park has wiped out even the vestiges of democracy through the declaration of martial law on October 17, 1972. After scrapping the constitution, which was written under his supervision, dissolving the National Assembly, closing all schools and imposing tight censorship, he forced on the nation a so-called "Revitalization Constitution" that vested unlimited powers in the presidency. On October 12, 1972, the traditional patriotic movement began once again against the dictatorial regime of President Park. The Student Association of Liberal Arts and Science College, Seoul National University, issued a statement: "Today we rise up with deep indignation and in obedience to the mandate of our conscience . . . extreme degree of social injustice, political oppression, and poverty drives our people into a deep pit of terror and despair."[6]

The student protestors risked their lives, liberty, and their future. The students demonstrated with traditional courage and dignity against the barbarous corruption and immorality of the privileged class. The student statement read:

> In this sinister land where there is no trace of freedom we only see the fascist CIA politics of the present regime which has betrayed our people. Their last

attempt to remain in power has driven our people into the jungle of terror. They institutionalized the system of fascist CIA politics, and ruthlessly crushed free democracy which is the aspiration of our people. The government is turned into a fascist system of rule by making the legislative into the servant-maid of the President and by incorporating the judiciary; and they executed the plan to perpetuate their dictatorship by suppressing universities and press.[7]

This was only the beginning of an attempt to end the regime. The students believe that it is their historic task to end the dictatorship. They feel that they must hold the torch for democratic struggle if they are to realize justice, freedom, and truth.

Many overseas Korean groups responded immediately to the students' demonstration. For instance, several Korean organizations united to sponsor a rally in support of the student demonstrations at the United Nations Plaza in New York on October 27, 1973. They issued a statement which declared: "We Koreans, Korean-Americans, and friends of Korea, assembling in the shadow of the United Nations, salute the brave and patriotic youths. Knowing as we do of the brutality and determination of the Park government to crush any opposition to it, we appeal to the statesmen of the world to persuade President Park not to resort to repressive measures but to listen to their requests."[8]

On another occasion, three Korean newspapers, *Free Republic*, *Hanmin Shinbo*, and *Insight*, together with the International Committee to Free Kim Dae-jung sponsored a demonstration in New York on October 20, 1973, and issued a statement which declared, "Social injustice has torn the nation to pieces, political oppression has created a police state, and corrupt economic policy yielded a return to Japanese colonial status."[9] The group demanded that imprisoned students be immediately released, that basic civil liberties be restored, that the notorious Korean CIA be dismantled, that Kim Dae-jung, who had been kidnapped by Korean CIA, be freed.

Starting with Kim Dae-jung's kidnapping in August, 1972, the government has been charging these students and others with being pro-communist. The government's charges have, however, been flatly denied by all those so charged. Kim Dae-jung, presidential candidate of the opposition New Democratic Party in 1971, Yun Posun, former president and an elder of the Presbyterian church, the Reverend Park Hyung-kyu of the First Presbyterian church in Seoul, Bishop Daniel Hak-sun Chi of the Roman Catholic church, Kim Chi-ha, a well-known Catholic poet, and the entire leadership of the Federation of Korean Christian Students—all these noted persons simply could not be identified as pro-communists.

It became obvious that President Park's purpose in oppressing the nation could not be explained by saying it was to defend it from possible communist attack. With a standing armed force of 600,000 and 40,000 American troops, how could anyone conceive that a handful of students would be capable of overthrowing the regime? Even the common people today do not feel an imminent danger from the North. Not only has peace been maintained in the demilitarized zone since 1972, but there has been continuous dialogue between the South and the North. The rationale of Park's repressive policy has nothing to do with defense of national interests as he has claimed. The simple reason for the repressive policy has to do with the selfish ambition of prolonging his tenure. The people felt betrayed. Their opposition to the government was covert but unmistakable. Their long smouldering sense of outrage burst out into the open in the wake of the abduction of Kim Dae-jung.

President Park outlawed not only the students' anti-government activities, but also issued a decree on January 8, 1974, banning any opposition to the present constitution, which gives him absolute power.

Park's "revitalization" constitution, written in November, 1972 under martial law, gives the president vast powers over the other branches of government and restricts the rights of the people. This political tool, however, was not enough for him. He wanted stronger measures to control mushrooming opposition groups. The new decree increased the maximum penalty to death for members of the National Democratic Students Federation and their sympathizers as well as media employers reporting their activities.[10]

In a statement accompanying his decree, Park said, "In view of the rapidly changing international situation, particularly, the turbulent waves caused by the fluctuations of the international economy, and of the various acts of provocation perpetrated by the North Korean communists, I cannot but conclude that our fatherland now faces an extremely harsh reality."[11]

Park warned that anyone violating the decree was subject to arrest without warrant for trial by the military court. There were no precise guidelines of what acts were forbidden. The government wanted to end student demonstrations. With full understanding of the government intention as proclaimed in the presidential decrees, students were compelled to be more covert in their activities.

On April 3, 1974, university students demonstrated against the Park regime by silent marching. Police broke up rallies, beating students and arresting fifty of them. At Seoul National University, five hundred medical students marched with locked arms on the campus and then tried to move onto the streets. Police forced them back and arrested fifteen students. Across the street about one hundred students enrolled in liberal arts and science courses scattered leaflets, shouted antigovernment slogans and brought on police charges. Some of them also were arrested or stomped upon, Richard Halloran reported on his visit to Seoul.[12]

The regime has indicated that 1,024 students were arrested on April 3, and some of them were sentenced to death while others received prison terms from ten to twenty years.

In the same period, six pastors and assistant pastors engaged in evangelistic work in the Urban Industrial Mission were arrested and imprisoned. The project was a Protestant one to evangelize workers and improve working conditions in South Korean factories.[13] What were the reasons for the arrests? Because they were organizing the workers "just like the communists organize the workers," was the government statement, but the KCIA also suspected that these clergymen were supporting the students.

The Urban Industrial Mission in cooperation with a similar group of the Roman Catholic Church denounced violations of human rights of Korean workers on January 21, 1974. A joint statement said: "Korean workers at the Masan Free Export Zone were collectively beaten by their Japanese employers." They also declared: "The president of Kan Yung Textile Company, Mr. Yu Hai-Pung, hired gangsters to kill a worker, Mr. Kim Jin-Su, with a screwdriver on March 28, 1971, and yet no arrest had been made to date. Mr. Chi Dong-Jin, a local union chief at Han Kuk Textile Company, was beaten."[14]

Park's presidential decree was a desperate attempt to destroy all criticism directed at his regime.

In spite of the presidential decree, the students, intellectuals, professors, clergymen, and opposition politicians challenged the regime. According to William Butler, a U.S. lawyer representing Amnesty International, who returned in the middle of July, 1974, from an investigative trip to Seoul, there were about twelve hundred Koreans imprisoned as political prisoners in South Korea. These prisoners were almost exclusively the intellectual elite of South Korea.[15]

Former President Yun Posun, a frail 77-year-old man who walks with the aid of a cane, appeared in the military court accompanied by his wife to face an accusation made by the government. "I gave money because the students are trying to work for democracy. The young people needed the money," the former president stated matter-of-factly. He continued, "Do you think $1,000 is enough to overthrow the government?"[16] It was Yun as president who supported General Park in the early stage of the military coup in 1961, but he finally resigned in protest over the junta rule. He later ran unsuccessfully against Park for the presidency in 1963 and in 1967.

Evidently President Park believed that one sure way to prolong his political power was to invite Japanese capital to industrialize the nation. He commented that Japan was the most reliable ally of Korea.[17] This attitude is understandable since Park is a product of Japan. Professor Edwin O. Reischauer has made the following observation:

> Park and his military henchmen have little faith in democracy or a free society. He and some of the other top leaders were originally products of the Japanese Imperial Army, and all of them have had life-time military careers. To them the techniques of the police state come naturally. They are far removed in their attitudes and ideas from the intellectuals and politicians of Korea.[18]

Under the guise of modernization, President Park's regime has created a corrupt and inefficient administration. The bribery scandal case of Tongsun Park is a good example of corruption. Foreign businessmen were quick to take full advantage of the corruption. Within a year after the declaration of martial law, for example, Japanese investment had increased by more than two and a half times. Furthermore, Japanese investment accelerated during the last two years when South Korea was confronted with national bankruptcy. An advertisement by the government pointed out carefully that "for the first six months of 1973, Japan topped the list of foreign investments approved by the government (Korea) with $159 million for 126 projects."[19] This amount was 99 percent of total foreign investment in South Korea for the period. The United States had only $2 million for four projects for the same period.

The question is not simply the amount of foreign investment, but who is involved in the business projects. The true nature of foreign investment and the astronomical increase of foreign loans in Korea are indications of three basic problems. First of all, the economy of Korea is totally dependent on Japan and the United States. Why is it? Because the Korean economy is based on the export business. Korea imports raw materials, manufactures them, and exports them to the world market, primarily to the United States. Foreign capital is invested entirely, as direct investments as well as through loans, for the purpose of export and industries whose manufactured commodities are sold entirely in foreign markets. The foreign investment has not contributed to the development of the basic industries of Korea. Even the total amount of $800 million which came to Seoul from Japan after the Korea-Japan normalization treaty in 1965 was spent entirely on the export industries.

Due to such excessive investment, South Korea has achieved an average growth rate of 8.3 percent during its first five-year plan (1962–1966) and was able to increase this to 11.4 percent during the second five-year plan (1967–1971), and increased it to 17 percent in 1973, according to the Korean official advertisement.[20] The official announcement in the "Economic White Paper" revealed that Korean exports have increased an average of 38.9 percent per year during the years of 1962–1971. The figures in the following table reveal the results:

Major Economic Statistics
(One Billion Won or about $2.5 Million.)[21]

	1967	1968	1969	1970	1971	1972	1973
GNP	1,853	2,087	2,400	2,589	2,827	3,024	3,534
Percentage in growth	7.8	12.6	15.0	7.9	9.2	7.0	16.9
Agriculture, forestry, fish	635	650	731	725	748	761	801
Mining	334	417	500	591	690	742	1,039
Exports	166	235	310	381	459	643	1,049
Imports	321	468	584	642	774	801	1,142

This chart reveals the inequitable distribution of economic development in Korea as well as the concentration of foreign capital in the export industry. As a result of this erroneous economic policy, the trade balance is increasingly unfavorable to Korea. The more Korean commodities are exported, the more raw materials are needed from abroad. These imported raw materials are paid with newly acquired loans, thus the national debt has been astronomically increased. The following chart depicts that situation.

The Relationship of Exports and Loans[22]
(4 Million)

	1963	1964	1965	1966	1967	1968	1969
Export	87	119	175	250	320	455	622
Import	560	404	463	716	996	1,463	1,824
Balance	−473	−285	−288	−466	−676	−1,007	−1,202
Foreign aid	232	143	136	144	119	126	254
Loans	52	35	31	108	167	300	525

In 1974, the total foreign loans and investments amounted to close to $7 billion. The government has emphasized the increase of exports, and the statistics were impressive. Exports during the ten years of Park's regime rose at an annual average rate of 40 percent and this rate jumped to 80 percent in 1973 after Park declared martial law. The amount of exports today is estimated to be $3 billion. The 1961 base for exports was $41 million.

In spite of this economic "miracle,"[23] as the American sponsors like to call the Korean situation, the economic result to the nation is pitiful.

That brings us to the second characteristic of the Korean modernization economy. The agricultural economy has been sacrificed for the sake of the export economy. The export items, which are primarily of light industrial nature, such as textiles, clothing, wood products, and recently electrical goods, require a labor concentration. The raw materials for these items have to be imported. Therefore, the export economy relies totally on international economic conditions. For instance, the oil crisis of 1973–1974 caused tremendous problems for Korea. The impact on Korea was more severe than on other countries because of the reliance upon Japan, which was confronted with the same problem as Korea. Borrowed sums were invested heavily on new machinery and modern factories in order to compete in the international market of consumer goods. But these consumer goods face stiff competition and the prices on the export items rose 30 percent while the import prices rose at the rate of 50 percent in 1974. Meanwhile, 50 percent of the population are engaged in agriculture and receive no aid from the government. The government initiated a "new village" movement only two years ago after witnessing the agricultural chaos in the nation. During all the years of the modernization process, the government has not built a single factory to improve agricultural tools. Agriculture is still in its primitive stage in South Korea.

The government could force Korean workers to accept low wages, which are about one-fifth of Japanese wages, and prevent them from striking with the labor law. Incidently, the official advertisement of Park's government states: "Other privileges foreign investors in Korea are entitled to include the exemption of income taxes for foreign nationals employed by foreign-invested firms. Foreign firms are also protected from strikes or protracted labor disputes by their Korean employees."[24]

Farmers no longer able to make a living left the farm and moved to the cities looking for jobs. As a result, farm land as well as the farm population declined, forcing South Korea to begin importing food stuff. In 1973, the government imported 30 percent of needed grain to feed the population, and paid with borrowed money. In 1973, the government spent $340 million, while it spent $220 million in 1972 for the purpose of importing rice, wheat, and other grain. The government may claim that the standard of living went up, from $100 to $300 per capita in annual income under the Park regime, but the fact is that living conditions for most of the people became more deplorable.

The last element which needs to be mentioned in relation to economic modernization concerns the small and medium sized enterprises in South Korea. One characteristic of Japanese investment in South Korea is that an overwhelming number of investors are medium size companies whose investments concentrated on light and service industries. For instance, most of the tourist hotels are financed by Japanese. The original agreement of a fifty-fifty investment between Koreans and Japanese no longer is practiced. Most agreements now are on a twenty-eighty ratio. Even the 20 percent reserved for Koreans are sometimes financed privately by Japanese. On top of this, the Korean government opened free industrial zones to the Japanese, such convenient locations as in Masan. Furthermore, the government favors foreign investors, mostly Japanese, by permitting duty-free import of raw materials as well as duty-free exporting of manufactured goods.

Japanese entrepreneurs bring raw materials from Japan, manufacture them with cheap Korean labor, and ship them back to Japan without paying a dime to the Korean government. However, not all goods are shipped to Japan. Some goods find their way to the Korean domestic market and compete with Korean commodities! Most of the Korean goods cannot compete with the Japanese commodities on a fair competitive base. Thus, most of the medium size enterprises are now going bankrupt. In other words, Park's regime favors Japanese investors to Koreans.

President Park promised a GNP of $36.1 billion for 1981, a per capita GNP of $983 and exports of $10.9 billion (up 1,000 percent over 1972). It is obvious now that President Park wants to stay in power to achieve those goals. He believes that anyone against him is against such national achievements. Will such achievements really benefit the people in South Korea?

Professor Sumiya, a Japanese economist at Tokyo University, reports on a scholarly investigation trip to Korea recently:

> The nature of the Korean economy today is bound to rely more on Japanese capital as it tries to develop faster, and she must increase her exports in order to pay her increasing debts, which will bring Korea closer to Japan. She cannot stop now, she will fail if she does. However, such speed of development has nothing to do with the domestic economic situation in Korea, and it is no help to increase the standard of living in Korea. The farm is in poverty. The farm laborers cannot find jobs, so they move to the big cities, create slums under the forest of skyscrapers. . . . More economic growth takes place and more exports increase in Korea, and Korea's economic crisis gets deeper.[25]

As Professor Sumiya points out, equity investments and loans create increasing problems of repayment. As long as the export market booms and the international market demands Korean goods, these obligations can be met, but a slackening of growth and unseen international trade situations could make repayment difficult and can cause severe problems for Korean businesses which operate on borrowed money at steep interest rates.

It becomes obvious now that the "economic miracle" which has been so played up to justify U.S. aid to South Korea over the past three decades has, thus far, had scarcely any significant effect in bringing about either a structural transformation of the Korean economy or an improvement of the living conditions for the majority of the population. Why did this happen? One answer lies in the hands of policy-makers in Washington. Senator James Abourezk of South Dakota said before the United States Senate on June 21, 1974:

> A large part of the problem lies directly within our own State Department. The State Department as well as the entire Nixon administration chooses to pretend that repression, torture, and the abridgement of human rights simply does not exist.[26]

Senator Abourezk then quoted the official denial of the State Department in reply to Senator Kennedy's inquiry on the condition of human rights in South Vietnam. The State Department did not agree with Kennedy's Senate Subcommittee on Refugees' report about civilian prisoners in South Vietnam. To this denial of the State Department, Senator Abourezk commented:

> Time and again, the administration continues to attempt to solve the problems
> of blatant and gross violations of human rights simply by denying that they
> exist.[27]

The State Department asserted that there were no political prisoners in South Vietnam, much less violations of human rights, torture, and mistreatment of prisoners.

The situation in South Korea was no different from the situation in South Vietnam. Only this time, the State Department did recognize the fact of the repressive policy of President Park. Secretary of State Henry Kissinger made clear in his testimony before a Senate committee on July 24, 1974, that Park's regime was a repressive one of which the American government did not approve. What efforts, then, must the American government make to rectify the ill conditions that exist in South Korea?

A high official from the Department of State testified before the House Foreign Affairs Subcommittee on International Organizations and Movements and Asian and Pacific Affairs on July 30, 1974. The official said: "In our view, the prevention of war on the Korean peninsula is the first and most important step toward the maintenance of human liberties."[28]

If the Department of State considers "the prevention of war" as "the first and most important step toward the maintenance of human liberties" in Korea, then, why doesn't it react to the proposal from North Korea on "Peace Agreement with United States"? Congressman Michael Harrington said, "Very significantly, amid the latest development in Korea, a letter from the North Korean Supreme People's Assembly addressed to the U.S. Congress was broadcast from North Korea in English. The letter has not received much notice in the United States, but it is nevertheless important because it signals a dramatic change in the North's position on peace talks. It formally proposes direct negotiations with the United States for a peace agreement."[29]

What was the American official reply to this proposal? President Ford made an official trip to Seoul to encourage Park's regime on November 22–23, 1974.

The American government has not learned a lesson from either the Vietnam war or the recent Greek experience in which a civilian government replaced a military dictatorship. As an editorial of the *New York Post* pointed out:

> Secretary of State Kissinger, in testimony before a Senate committee, reiter-
> ated the futile policy that it can be in our "strategic" interest to protect

dictatorships. He was speaking about South Korea, explaining why the United
States should not cut off aid to the authoritarian regime of President Park
Chung Hee despite its brutal suppression of dissent.[30]

Why does Washington have to support Park's regime? Why does a
free society have to support dictatorships anyway? Secretary Kissinger
said that the Ford administration decided to authorize aid to Park's regime
"even when we would not recommend the actions of the government of
South Korea." What an irony of policy for a free society! When are we
going to realize that it will never preserve American interests anywhere by
preserving dictatorships? "Will we have to wait for a disaster in Korea
similar to the one in Cypress (or in Vietnam) before the inherent moral
and political weakness of this position is acknowledged?" editorially asked
the *New York Post*.

When the United States abstains from its moral duty to work against
forces of repression in conduct of its foreign policy, it cannot defend itself
against injustice at home. The Watergate incident was not an accident, but
a clear reflection of the Vietnam war. Can a free society like America's
survive when the nation loses its morality in the policy-making process?
The delicate international balance of East Asia, particularly in Korea,
cannot be achieved by its attempt to repress all political and social dissent.
A popular uprising which brought the end to the Rhee regime should be a
lesson to Washington policy-makers. Compare today's chaos in South
Korea under Park's regime with Rhee's regime. The possibilities for chaos
today are manifold. To avoid another Vietnam tragedy in Korea, the
policy-makers in Washington must solve the Korean issue peacefully and
promptly.

Bishop Daniel Haksun Chi, a Roman Catholic Church leader in
Korea, who has been sentenced to fifteen years in prison for aiding
students who demonstrated against Park's dictatorship, made the following statement from his prison cell:

> The so-called emergency decrees Number 1 and Number 4 which they have
> indicted me for having offended, are the cruelest violations of national law in
> our long history. These prohibit any petition for reform or even the communi-
> cation of the fact that there was such a petition and any complaint or expres-
> sion of opposition is made under the penalty of life imprisonment or even
> death.[31]

The courageous bishop continued to defy the government even while
under arrest. He publicly said that he would never submit voluntarily to
judgment by court-martial. Before he was arrested, the bishop charged
that the military court-martial, which has sentenced fourteen persons to

death and many others to life imprisonment or long prison terms, is "only a puppet which cannot by law or conscience judge independently." Don Oberdorfer reported from Seoul on the bishop's statement as he witnessed the respected friend of slum dwellers speak with dignity.[32]

Koreans were as concerned about the security of their country and its freedom as Secretary of State Kissinger was concerned for American interests in Korea. Right now, however, the security of South Korea is threatened by the internal dictatorship of Park's regime, rather than by an invasion from North Korea. Koreans believe that their security lies with a democratic government. They also believe that a democratic government is not a dream, but a possibility, in spite of the long dictatorial governments of Rhee and Park, supported by the untiring aid of the American government. The Korean people were able to overthrow Rhee's dictatorship, only to face Park's dictatorship which came into power, and stays on, again with military and economic aid from the United States.

If only the United States were sincere about its commitment as enunciated by Secretary of State Dean Acheson in 1950:

> United States aid, both military and economic, to the Republic of Korea has been predicated upon the existence and growth of democratic institutions within the Republic.[33]

The American government and the people must seek this goal. That is the only possible way to achieve peace and security in Korea and Asia, and therefore in the world.

chapter notes

1 Introduction

[1] Ralph N. Clough, *Deterrence and Defense in Korea: The Role of U.S. Forces* (Washington: The Brookings Institution, 1976).

[2] Dean Acheson, *Present at the Creation: My Years in the State Department* (New York: W. W. Norton and Co., 1969). Acheson said: "We have direct responsibility in Japan. . . . The same thing to a lesser degree is true in Korea." See details in the chapter on the Korean War.

[3] Sam Jameson, *Los Angeles Times*, May 27, 1977. "South Korea in 1977 possesses a formidable army, in contrast to the virtually unarmed constabulary it had in 1950. The ground troop [U.S.] withdrawal is not unacceptably risky."

[4] A statement issued after President Carter talked to the Foreign Minister of South Korea, Park Tong-jin, in Washington. The statement said: "Our ground force withdrawals would be carefully carried out after consultation with the Korean government. . . . This would be accomplished in a manner which would not upset the military balance or contribute to instability on the Korean peninsula." Reported by the *Associated Press*, March 11, 1977.

[5] "Our commitments in Asia," Hearing before the Subcommittee of East Asia and Pacific Affairs of the House Committee on Foreign Affairs, 93:2, Government Printing Office, 1977.

[6] *Korea Week*, Washington, D.C., April 6, 1977.

[7] *Columbia Tribune*, Columbia, Mo., June 30, 1977.

[8] Barry Blechman and Steven Kaplan: Their report was the product of two years of research on a $180,000 contract of the Pentagon's Advanced Research Projects Agency. The latest incident covered in the report was the navy and marine task force sent in connection with the rescue of the U.S. merchant ship *Mayaguez* from Cambodian waters in May 1975.

[9] *Korea Week*, April 27, 1977.

[10] *New York Times*, July 25, 1974.

[11] Glenn D. Paige, *The Korean Decision* (New York: The Free Press, 1968), p. 128. At the time of the Korean War, General Omar Bradley maintained that Korea was not of strate-

gic importance to the United States. Professor Paige quoted from the general's testimony, *Hearings*, part IV, pp. 1110f.

[12] William Butler, Chairman of the Committee on International Human Rights of the New York City Bar Association, visited Seoul. I have discussed the human rights issue in South Korea with him in New York City.

[13] Professor Gregory Henderson and Rev. Newton Thurber coordinated the project, and the statement was issued on July 15, 1974, in the City of New York.

[14] Donald G. Tewksbury, ed., *Source Materials on Korean Politics and Ideologies* (Institute of Pacific Relations, 1950), p. 145.

[15] Gregory Henderson, "Political Repression in South Korea," issued on July 19, 1974, in New York City. It stated that "The excuse for Korea is essentially transparent. South Korea's armed forces remain 50 to 75 percent greater than those of North Korea; they have combat experience in Vietnam whereas North Korea's armed forces have had none for over twenty years . . . armed incidents have, since 1971, fallen to an almost infinitesimal percentage of what they were between 1967–1969, at which time martial law was not declared in South Korea. . . ."

[16] See also U.S. Public Law 94-329, sec. 502B, which states that "no security assistance may be provided to any country the government of which engages in a consistent pattern of gross violations of internationally recognized human rights."

[17] During the Korean war, General Douglas MacArthur advocated the unification of Korea by force while Lieutenant General Samuel T. Williams advocated the bombing of dikes and dams.

[18] Hans Morgenthau, "Death in the Nuclear Age," in *Commentary*, September 1961.

[19] Kim Sun-il, "Chosen mondai-ni okeru hasso-no tenkan," in *Sekai*, September 1976, p. 85. In this article, Mr. Kim states that: "America calmly repeats statements, truly humiliating for us [Koreans], that for Japan's sake South Korea must be placed under its control. Even now, thirty years after liberation, the independence and prosperity of this people are treated with the contempt that such a way of thinking implies."

[20] For details on this subject, see Hakwon Harold Sunoo, *Repressive State and Resisting Church: The Politics of KCIA*, New York and Fayette, Mo.: Korean-American Cultural Association, 1976.

2 Korea Under Japan's Domination

[1] For details, see Tyler Dennett, *Americans in Eastern Asia* (New York: Barnes & Noble, 1941), ch. 15 and 16, and by the same author, *Roosevelt and the Russo-Japanese War* (2nd ed.) (New York: Doubleday, 1925).

[2] For details, see Harold Hakwon Sunoo, *Korea: A Political History in Modern Times* (Seoul: Kunkuk University Press, 1970).

[3] Compiled from the Government-General of Korea's *Chosen-no Nogyo* (*Agriculture of Korea*), Seoul, 1924, 1932 editions. In Chong-sik, *Chosen-no Nogyo Kiko* (*The Agricultural Structure of Korea*) (Tokyo: Hakuyosa Co., 1940).

[4] There were ten Korean landlords who had more than one thousand jungbo in all of Korea.

[5] Ki-jun Cho, "Transformation and Problems in the Study of Korean Social Science," *Korea Journal*, Seoul, June, 1971, p. 5.

[°] Kyoji Asada, *Nihon Teikoku-shugito Kyushokuminchi Jinushi Sei* (*Japanese Imperialism and Old Colonial Landlord System*), (Tokyo: Ochano mizyu shoten, 1968), p. 69.

[7] Matsuro Kato, *Kankoku Nogyo-ron* (*A Study of Korean Agriculture*) (Tokyo: Shyokato Co., 1904), p. 258.

[8] *Chosen Shakai Keijaishi Kenkyu* (*A Study of Korean Social Economic History*) (Seoul: Imperial University Press, 1933), p. 43.

[9] Sunoo, op. cit., p. 256.

[10] *Chosen Keijai-no Kenkyu*, (*A Study of Korean Economy*) (Seoul: Imperial University Press, 1929), p. 159.

[11] Tokuichi Fujihara *The Old Tales of Japanese in Korea* (Tokyo: Shokato, 1930), p. 190.

[12] Yong-hyop Yi, *Hankuk Kuntae Toji Chedosa Yonku* (*A Study of Korean Land System in Modern Times*) (Seoul: Pomunkak, 1968).

[13] See detailed story in Sunoo, op. cit., ch. 13.

[14] The Government-General of Korea (Bureau of Agriculture and Forestry), *Chosen-ni okeru Gosakuni kansuru Sanko jiko Tekiyo (References on the Farm Tenants in Korea)* (Seoul: Bureau of Agriculture and Forestry, 1932), p. 24.

[15] Shigeru Kobayashi, *Kinsei Noson Keizai-no Kenkyu* (*A Study of Modern Agricultural Economy*) (Tokyo: Miraisha, 1968), p. 98.

[16] *Hwajunmin* means the people living in the fire-field. The landless peasants cultivate land in the hillside or mountain side by burning the trees down. It was, of course, an illegal action. *Hwajunmin* numbered about 340,000 households and more than 12 million people on about 400,000 jungbo in Korea in 1930.

3   Korea Against Japanese Imperialism

[1] Carton Waldo Kendall, *The Truth about Korea* (San Francisco: The Korean National Association, 1919), p. 49.

[2] Ibid.

[3] Ibid.

[4] Ibid.

[5] International Review of Mission, Vol. 11, New York, p. 343.

[6] *Los Angeles Times*, April 6, 1919.

[7] The poem, "The German Fatherland," contains a strong Germanic feeling.

[8] Kendall, op. cit.

[9] *Tong-A Ilbo* or *Tong-A Daily News*, Seoul, Oct. 28, 1928.

[10] The Government-General of Korea, *General Reference on the Farm-tenant in Korea* (Seoul), p. 74.

[11] Ibid., p. 105.

[12] The Government-General of Korea, *Chosun-e Sojak Kwansup* (*The Tenancy Custom in Korea*) (Seoul, 1933), p. 58.

[13] Hoon-ku Lee, *Chosun Nongupron* (*A Discourse on Korean Agriculture*) (Seoul: Ulgusa Co., 1935), p. 326.

4   Liberation and After

[1] U.S. Department of State, *Bulletin*, Washington, D.C., 1945, p. 1004.

[2] Molotov's three points were: (1.) The establishment of a provisional Korean democratic government with broad participation of Korean democratic parties and social organizations; restoration of Korea as a democratic and independent state; and development of its national economy and culture. (2.) The establishment of democratic bodies of power throughout Korea by free elections on the basis of general and equal suffrage. (3.) Aid to

Korea to expedite political and economic unity as a self-governed state independent of foreign interference, which fact would eliminate the division of the country into two zones.

[3] The statement said: "From political common sense there is no reason for the Worker's Party and its leaders to have been involved in such a brazen act as the currency fraud. The Worker's Party most bravely fought against Japanese imperialism for Korea's liberation and is now faithfully fighting for the establishment of Korean self-government and democracy. All its leaders have sacrificed and given their lives for the Korean people."

[4] Statements are based on information sheets distributed by the union during the disturbances.

[5] Based on an interview of a former medical student in Taigu city during the author's visit in the summer of 1961.

[6] *International News Service*, Washington, D.C., Oct. 4, 1946.

5   The Cold War Begins

[1] Harry S. Truman, *Years of Trial and Hope* (Garden City, N.Y.: Doubleday, 1956), p. 326.

[2] *Jayu Shinmoon*, Seoul, May 11, 1948.

[3] Ibid.

[4] *Kyunghyang Shinmoon*, Seoul, May 11, 1948.

[5] Ibid.

[6] *Noryokja*, Seoul, Jan. 1, 1949.

[7] *Minju Ilbo*, Seoul, Nov. 21, 1948.

[8] President Park Chung Hee of South Korea was a commanding officer of the company which led the rebellious forces at Sunchun on Oct. 20, 1948. He was sentenced to death but later pardoned. His life was spared in return for a list of names of the leaders. For details, see *Kyunghyang Shinmoon*, Feb. 17, 1949; *Seoul Shinmoon*, Feb. 18, 1949; see also *Dong-A Ilbo*, Oct. 14, 1963, and *Kyunghyang Shinmoon*, Oct. 8, 1963.

[9] *Tass*, Nov. 6, 1948.

[10] *Noryokja*, Jan. 1, 1949.

[11] Ibid.

[12] *Minju Chosun*, Seoul, Feb. 3, 1949.

[13] Ibid.

[14] Based on interviews by the author of several army officers who had participated in such activities. These officers are still holding important positions in the ROK army.

[15] *Minju Chosun*, op. cit.

6   The Korean War: An Interpretation

[1] *Associated Press*, March 1, 1946.

[2] Franz Michael and George Taylor, *The Far East in the Modern World* (New York: Holt, Rinehart and Winston, 1964), p. 770.

[3] *The Voice of Korea*, Jan. 27, 1950, Vol. 7, No. 143, Washington, D.C.

[4] Clause (b) of Section 3, Korea Aid Bill, quoted in *The Voice of Korea*, March 1, 1950, Vol. 7, No. 144.

[5] Glenn D. Paige, *The Korea Decision* (New York: Macmillan, 1968), p. 35.

[6] Robert Leckie, *The Wars of America*, vol. 2 (New York: Harper Row, 1968), p. 360.

[7] *China Digest*, Hong Kong, April 20, 1948, p. 6.

[8] Louis J. Halle, *Civilization and Foreign Policy*, (New York: Greenwood, 1955), p. 243.

[9] Soon Sung Cho, *Korea in World Politics: 1945-1950* (Berkeley: University of California Press, 1970), p. 263.

[10] Harry S. Truman, *Years of Trial and Hope* (New York: Doubleday, 1955), p. 334.

[11] Military Situation in the Far East: Hearings before the Senate Armed Services and Foreign Relations Committee, 82nd Congress, 1st session, Washington, 1951, part 5, p. 3369.

[12] *Time*, July 3, 1950, p. 7.

[13] "War and Peace in the Far East," in the *New York Times*, July 16, 1950.

[14] Truman, *Years of Trial and Hope*, pp. 334–35.

[15] Ibid., p. 332–33.

[16] Congressional Record, vol. 96, part 7, June 28, 1950, pp. 9319–9327. See also Paige, *The Korea Decision*, p. 217.

[17] Paige, *The Korea Decision*, p. 165.

[18] Roy Macartney, "How War Came to Korea," in Norman Bartlet, *With the Australians in Korea* (Canberra: Australian War Memorial, 1954), p. 171.

[19] Paige, *The Korean Decision*, p. 246.

[20] McGeorge Bundy, *The Pattern of Responsibility* (Boston: Harvard University Press, 1952), p. 266.

[21] Truman, *Years of Trial and Hope*, p. 352.

[22] John W. Spanier, *American Foreign Policy since World War II* (New York: Praeger, 1973), p. 87.

[23] K. M. Panikkar, *In Two Chinas* (London: Free Press, 1955), p. 110. Also see Edward Friedman's "Problems in Dealing with an Irrational Power: America Declares War on China," in *America's Asia*, edited by Edward Friedman and Mark Selden (New York: Random House, 1971), p. 231.

[24] Allen S. Whiting, *China Crosses the Yalu* (Stanford: Stanford University Press, 1960), p. 109.

[25] Carl K. Spaatz, General, USAF, retired, was quoted as saying he believed that the Chinese would not commit their forces in major strength in a Korean war. *Newsweek*, Nov. 13, 1950, p. 35.

[26] Robert Leckie, *Conflict: History of Korean War* (New York: Random House, 1962), p. 165.

[27] Ibid., p. 159.

[28] Robert T. Oliver, *Syngman Rhee: The Man Behind the Myth* (New York: Dodd Mead, 1954), p. 307.

[29] Spanier, *American Foreign Policy*, p. 85.

[30] Carl K. Spaatz, General, "Enter the Chinese Communists," in *Newsweek*, Nov. 13, 1950, p. 35.

[31] Leckie, *Conflict*, p. 165.

[32] Francis T. Miller, *War in Korea and the History of World War II*, (Philadelphia: Arms Service Memorial, 1955), p. 20.

[33] Ibid., p. 33.

[34] Truman, *Years of Trial and Hope*, p. 450.

[35] Miller, *War in Korea*, p. k-33.

[36] Ibid., p. k-39.

[37] Walter G. Hermes, *Truce Tent and Fighting Front* (Office of the Chief of Military History, U.S. Army, 1966), p. 31.

[38] Richard P. Stebbins, *The United States in World Affairs* (New York: S. and S. Co., 1968), p. 219.

[39] "Key to Conflict," *Newsweek*, Nov. 13, 1950, p. 36.

[40] "Why the Main War Will Be Fought in Asia—Not Europe," *U.S. News and World Report*, Jan. 19, 1951, p. 34.

[41] Dean Rusk, "Security Problems: Far East Area," U.S. Department of State *Bulletin*, Dec. 4, 1950, p. 892.

[42] Ibid.

[43] Trumbull Higgins, *Korea and the Fall of MacArthur* (New York: Oxford University Press, 1960), p. 77.

[44] Leckie, *Conflict*, p. 158.

[45] Whiting, *China Crosses the Yalu*, p. 169.

[40] S. L. A. Marshall, *The River and the Gauntlet* (New York: Greenwood, 1953), p. 14.

7   Syngman Rhee

[1] *The Voices of the People*, a monthly publication by Channing Liem, New Paltz, N.Y., vol. 4, no. 7, July, 1975.

[2] Ibid.

[3] *New York Herald Tribune*, Nov. 1, 1949.

[4] *New York Times*, Mar. 2, 1950.

[5] *The Voice of Korea*, Washington, D.C., vol. 9, no. 172, June 20, 1952.

[6] Four national assemblymen were arrested on May 26, 1952. Others escaped the crackdown. A government spokesman declared on May 27 that communists were sending secret funds across the border into South Korea to create disorder.

[7] Dr. Rhee not only ignored the assembly's protests against martial law, but personally directed the Korean military police to arrest nine opposition members of the National Assembly. In addition, five assemblymen were sought and a dozen more were afraid to come out of hiding to attend assembly sessions for fear they would be arrested. Dr. Rhee declared: "I am sure there will be more arrests." Report of Keyes Beech in *San Francisco Chronicle*, May 29, 1952.

[8] *Associated Press* dispatch from Pusan, Korea, May 29, 1952.

[9] Dr. Chang, who resigned on grounds of ill health on April 21, was in the U.S. Army hospital, and his close associate, Chong-won Sunoo, was arrested on the charge of engaging in a "communist conspiracy."

[10] Contrary to his strong dictatorial attitude toward his own people, Dr. Rhee was totally dependent on American friends for his survival. He was more than willing to give up his presidential power as the commanding chief of military forces to General Douglas MacArthur. On July 15, 1950, President Rhee wrote a letter to General MacArthur: "I am happy to assign to you command authority over all land, sea, and air forces of the Republic of Korea during the period of the continuation of the present state of hostilities; such command to be exercised either by you personally or by such military commander or commanders to whom you may delegate the exercise of this authority within Korea or in adjacent seas." The letter clearly indicated how much President Rhee was willing to accept the leadership of a foreign general to govern his nation. See *MacArthur: His Rendezvous with History* by Courtney Whitney (New York: Knopf, 1965), p. 338.

[11] *San Francisco Chronicle*, June 18, 1952.

[12] *Chicago Daily News*, May 29, 1952.

[13] *Associated Press*, June 4, 1952.

[14] Ibid., June 5, 1952.

[15] *United Press*, June 5, 1952.

[16] *Associated Press*, June 7, 1952.

[17] Ibid.

[18] *New York Herald Tribune*, May 6, 1956.

[19] Syngman Rhee, "Why I Stood Alone," *This Week Magazine*, August 16, 1953.

8 Modernization and Traditional Value Systems

[1] Bernard Lewis, *The Emergence of Modern Turkey* (New York: Oxford University Press, 1961).

[2] David E. Apter, *The Politics of Modernization* (Chicago: University of Chicago Press, 1965).

[3] William Letwin, "Four Fallacies about Economic Development," *Daedalus*, Summer, 1963, p. 396–414.

[4] Neil J. Smelser, in *Modernization*, Weiner, Myron, ed. (New York: Basic Books, Inc., 1966), p. 121.

[5] Marion J. Levy, *Modernization and the Structure of Societies* (Princeton, N.J.: Princeton University Press, 1966), pp. 10–11.

[6] Samuel P. Huntington, "Modernization and Corruption," in *Political Order in Changing Societies* (New Haven, Conn.: Yale University Press, 1968), p. 59.

[7] Lucian W. Pye, "Political Development: The Concept of Political Development," in *Politics in Transitional Societies*, H. G. Kebschull, ed. (New York: Appleton-Century-Crofts, 1973), p. 285.

[8] Harold W. Sunoo, *Korea: A Political History in Modern Times* (Seoul: Kunkook University Press, 1970).

[9] Kim Chong-Lim, *Political Representation in the Korean National Assembly* (Iowa City: University of Iowa Press, 1971), p. 23.

[10] Of all political leaders 32.5% identified themselves as members of Christian churches, mostly Protestant, while the Christian population is no more than 2.4% of the total population in South Korea, according to the *Korean Statistical Almanac*, 1962.

[11] Bae-ho Hahn and Kyu-taik Kim, "Korean Political Leaders: 1952–1962, Their Social Origins and Skills," *Asian Survey*, vol. 3, no. 7, July, 1963.

9 Economic Aspects of Modernization

[1] Harold W. Sunoo, *Korea: A Political History in Modern Times*, Chapter 13, "Japanese Agriculture Policy in Korea" (Seoul: Kunkook University Press, 1970).

[2] Harold Hakwon Sunoo, *Repressive State and Resisting Church: The Politics of KCIA in South Korea*, Chapter 10, "Why the Flow of Foreign Capital into South Korea?" (New York and Fayette, Mo.: Korean-American Cultural Assn., 1976).

[3] Institute of Asian Economic Research, *A Yearbook of Asian Trends* (Tokyo, 1975).

[4] *Monthly Economic Statistics*, Bank of Korea, Seoul, Dec. 1976.

[5] *Tong-A-Ilbo Daily*, Seoul, June 16, 1975.

[6] Customs Bureau of Japan, *The Statistics of the Custom* (Tokyo, 1976).

[7] Mikio Sumiya, "Kankoku Keijai-no Kiken-to Sentaku" ("The Danger and Choice of Korean Economy") *Sekai*, Tokyo, April, 1977.

[8] *Chosun Ilbo Daily*, Seoul, July 11, 1974.

[9] Economic Planning Board, *Major Statistics of Korean Economy* (Seoul, 1975).

[10] Ibid.

¹¹ Kim Kyung-Jim, "Oeja-wa Hankook Kyungje" ("Foreign Capital and Korean Economy") *Hanyang*, Tokyo, March, 1977.

¹² Ibid.

10   On Unification of the South and the North

¹ *Denver Post*, July 4, 1972.

² Ibid.

³ *Minju Chosun*, Pyongyang, July 24, 1962.

⁴ *Korea Herald*, Seoul, August 16, 1968.

⁵ *Kyunghyang Shinmoon*, May 24, 1969. A year later, Kim Yong-sun, the successor of Shinn Tai-hwan, suggested further that a new policy, replacing the proposed nationwide election under U.N. supervision, might be adopted in view of the changing international situation. In addition, Kim also stated that a new educational policy based on the unification spirit was needed, rather than maintaining the old anticommunist policy in South Korea. See *Hankook Ilbo*, Sept. 3, 1971.

⁶ Shinn Tai-hwan, "Prospect for Territorial Unification 11," in *DRP Bulletin*, Seoul, March, 1970.

⁷ Ibid.

⁸ *Dung-dae (Lighthouse)*, Pyongyang, No. 175, 1973, p. 23.

⁹ *The Daily Yomiuri*, Tokyo, Jan. 21, 1972.

¹⁰ Ibid. President Park Chung Hee proposed for the first time a nonaggression pact with North Korea on Jan. 18, 1974. Pyongyang had made a similar bid several times in the past. See the *New York Times*, Jan. 19, 1974.

¹¹ Kim Sung-eun, Minister of National Defense for six years prior to his appointment as special assistant to President Park early in 1968, praised highly the newly organized militia force, armed with U.S. M-I rifles and carbines which had been shipped from the United States. See the *Los Angeles Times*, August 8, 1969.

¹² *Newsweek*, Feb. 5, 1968, p. 9.

¹³ *The Nation*, Feb. 5, 1968, p. 162.

¹⁴ Ibid.

¹⁵ *Christian Century*, Feb. 7, 1968.

¹⁶ *Associated Press*, Dec. 23, 1969.

¹⁷ Walter Lippmann, *Newsweek*, Feb. 12, 1968.

¹⁸ Norman Cousins, "In the Wake of the Pueblo," *Saturday Review*, Feb. 17, 1968, p. 24.

¹⁹ *Associated Press*, Sept. 17, 1971.

²⁰ *Japan Times*, August 15, 1972.

²¹ Ernst B. Haas, *The Uniting of Europe* (Stanford: Stanford University Press, 1964), p. 16.

²² *Hankook Ilbo*, Seoul, Feb. 20, 1970.

²³ *Nodong Shinmoon*, Pyongyang, Dec. 17, 1967.

²⁴ Han Myong-gap, "My Working Life of Yesterday and Today," in *The Heart of the Fatherland* (Pyongyang, 1969).

²⁵ Ko Tsul-su, *The Heart of the Fatherland*.

²⁶ Haas, *The Uniting of Europe*, p. 101.

²⁷ The Research Institute of Korea Society, "Prospects of Korean Economy" in *The Series of Social Research*, vol. 1, p. 75 (Seoul, 1965).

28 Karl W. Deutsch et al., *Political Community and the North Atlantic Area: International Organization in the Light of Historical Experience* (Greenwood, N.Y.: 1957), p. 97.

29 For details on the story of the Kim Dae-jung kidnapping, see Harold Hak-won Sunoo, *Repressive State and Resisting Church: The Politics of KCIA* (New York and Fayette, Mo., Korean-American Cultural Association, 1976).

30 *Newsweek*, Oct. 30, 1972, p. 55.

31 *Korea Herald*, Seoul, July 17, 1972.

32 *Japan Times*, August 15, 1972.

33 *United Nations General Assembly*, A/C, I/PV, 1957, Nov. 14, 1973, p. 37.

34 Walter Ulbricht, *Whither Germany*, Helga Kargus and Harry Kohler, ed. (Berlin: n.p., 1960), pp. 187–88.

35 "Letter to Parliaments and governments of all countries of the world; Letter to the Congress of the United States," Pyongyang, April 6, 1973.

36 *United Nations General Assembly*, A/9145, Sept. 10, 1973, p. 5.

37 *United Nations General Assembly*, A/C, 1/PV, 1958, Nov. 14, 1973, p. 37.

38 Ibid., p. 52.

39 Ibid.

40 "Letter to Parliaments," p. 5.

Epilogue

1 *New York Times*, May 5, 1974.

2 Ibid.

3 United Presbyterian Church in the U.S.A., "Christian Social Witness in Repressive Societies and United States Responsibility," Louisville, Ky., June 26, 1974.

4 *New York Times*, May 5, 1974.

5 Ibid.

6 Translated from a handbill distributed to the students.

7 Ibid.

8 Quoted from a copy of a handbill distributed to the public on October 27, 1973, New York City.

9 Quoted from material distributed to the public on October 20, 1973, New York City.

10 *Washington Post*, April 4, 1974.

11 *Associated Press*, January 8, 1974.

12 *New York Times*, April 4, 1974.

13 Elizabeth Pond, *Christian Science Monitor*, Boston, April 3, 1974.

14 *Dong-A-Ilbo*, Seoul, January 21, 1974.

15 Butler testified at Congressional Hearings on Human Rights in South Korea, House Foreign Affairs Subcommittees on International Organizations and Movements and Asian and Pacific Affairs, Washington, D.C., July 30, 1974. A similar figure is provided by the Department of State, Bureau of Public Affairs, *Special Report: Human Rights in the Republic of Korea* (Washington, D.C., Sept. 1974), p. 3.

16 *New York Times*, July 14, 17, 18, 1974.

17 Harold Sunoo, *Japanese Militarism* (Chicago: Nelson-Hall, 1975), p. 142.

18 Edwin O. Reischauer, "The Korean Connection," *New York Times Magazine*, Sept. 22, 1974.

19 *New York Times*, Nov. 4, 1973.

20 *New York Times*, Nov. 3, 1974.

[21] *Major Statistics in Charts*, Economic Planning Board, Seoul, 1974; see also Sumiya Mikio, "Kiki Fukamaru Kan koku Keijai" ("Crisis of Korean Economy"), *Sekai*, Tokyo, no. 347, October, 1974.

[22] Ibid.

[23] Arthur W. Hummel, Jr. Acting Assistant Secretary of State for East-Asian and Pacific Affairs stated: "Korea's economic progress over the past decade has been little short of miraculous." Dept. of State, p. 2.

[24] *New York Times*, Nov. 4, 1973.

[25] Sumiya, "Crisis of Korean Economy."

[26] *Congressional Record*, 93rd Congress, 2nd Session, Vol. 120, No. 91.

[27] Ibid.

[28] Bureau of Public Affairs, Department of State Office of Media Services, *Special Report: Human Rights in the Republic of Korea*, No. 5 (Washington, D.C., September, 1974).

[29] *Congressional Record*, 93rd Congress, 2nd Session, Vol. 120, No. 51, April 9, 1974.

[30] *New York Post*, July 26, 1974.

[31] Translated from his "Statement of Conscience," July 23, 1974.

[32] *Washington Post*, July 24, 1974.

[33] Tewksbury, op. cit.

bibliography

Books on United States Foreign Policy

Acheson, Dean. *Present at the Creation: My Years in the State Department*. New York: Norton, 1969.

Beard, Charles A. *A Foreign Policy for America*. New York: Alfred A. Knopf, 1940.

Bohlen, Charles E. *The Transformation of American Foreign Policy*. New York: Norton, 1970.

Brzenzinski, Zbigniew. *The Soviet Bloc: Unity and Conflict*. Cambridge: Harvard University Press, 1960.

Deutsch, Karl W. *The Analysis of International Relations*. Englewood Cliffs, N.J.: Prentice-Hall, 1968.

Falk, Richard A. *Legal Order in a Violent World*. Princeton, N.J.: Princeton University Press, 1968.

Fulbright, J. William. *The Arrogance of Power*. New York: Random House, 1967.

Hartmann, Frederick H. *The New Age of American Foreign Policy*. New York: McGraw-Hill, 1968.

Kennan, George F. *American Diplomacy: 1900–1950*. Chicago: University of Chicago Press, 1951.

Kissinger, Henry A. *American Foreign Policy: Three Essays*. New York: Norton, 1968.

Lippmann, Walter. *The Cold War*. New York: Harper and Bros., 1947.

Mason, Edward S. *Foreign Aid and Foreign Policy*. New York: Harper and Row, 1964.

Morgenthau, Hans J. *Politics Among the Nations: The Struggle for Power and Peace*. 5th ed. New York: Alfred A. Knopf, 1973.

Niebuhr, Reinhold. *The Irony of American History*. New York: Charles Scribner's Sons, 1962.

Reitzel, William; Kaplan, Morton A.; and Coblenz, Constance G. *United States Foreign Policy: 1945–1955*. Washington, D.C.: Brookings Institution, 1957.

Rostow, W. W. *The United States in the World Arena: An Essay in Recent History*. New York: Harper and Bros., 1960.

Thompson, Kenneth W. *Christian Ethics and the Dilemma of Foreign Policy*. Durham, N.C.: Duke University Press, 1959.

Truman, Harry S. *Memoirs*, Garden City, N.J.: Doubleday and Co., 1956.

Books on Nuclear Weapons, War, and Peace

Aron, Raymond. *The Century of Total War*. New York: Doubleday, 1954.

Aron, Raymond. *Peace and War: A Theory of International Relations*. New York: Doubleday, 1966.

Bennett, John C., ed. *Nuclear Weapons and the Conflict of Conscience*. New York: Charles Scribner's Sons, 1962.

Boulding, Kenneth E. *Conflict and Defense: A General Theory*. New York: Harper and Row, 1962.

Janowitz, Morris. *The Military in the Political Development of New Nations: An Essay in Comparative Analysis*. Chicago: University of Chicago Press, 1964.

Kissinger, Henry A. *Nuclear Weapons and Foreign Policy*. New York: Harper and Bros., 1957.

Osgood, Robert E. *Limited War*. Chicago: University of Chicago Press, 1957.

Thayer, Charles W. *Guerrilla*. New York: Harper and Row, 1963.

Wright, Quincy. *Study of War*. 2nd ed. Chicago: University of Chicago Press, 1965.

Books on U.S. Policy in Asia

Badgley, John. *Asian Development: Problems and Prognosis*. New York: Free Press, 1971.

Ball, W. M. *Nationalism and Communism in East Asia*. Melbourne: n.p., 1952.

Barnett, A. Doak. *A New U.S. Policy Toward China*. Washington, D.C.: Brookings Institution, 1971.

Barnett, A. Doak, and Reischauer, Edwin O., eds. *The United States and China: The Next Decade*. New York: Praeger, 1970.

Fairbank, John K. *The United States and China*. Cambridge: Harvard University Press, 1958.

Fall, Bernard. *Vietnam Witness: 1953–1966*. New York: Praeger, 1966.

Griswold, A. Whitney. *The Far Eastern Policy of the United States*. New Haven: Yale University Press, 1964.

Hinton, Harold C. *Communist China in World Politics*. Boston: Houghton Mifflin, 1966.

Mehert, Klaus. *Peking and Moscow*. New York: Putnam, 1963.

Paige, Glenn. *The Korean Decision, June 24–30, 1950*. New York: Free Press, 1968.

Reischauer, Edwin O. *Beyond Vietnam: The United States and Asia*. New York: Alfred A. Knopf, 1968.

Books on Pre-Liberation in Korea

Chung, Henry. *The Case of Korea*. New York: Revell, 1921.

Conroy, Hilary. *The Japanese Seizure of Korea*. Philadelphia: University of Pennsylvania Press, 1961.

Cynn, Hing H. *The Rebirth of Korea*. New York: Abingdon Press, 1920.

Dennett, Tyler. *Roosevelt and the Russo-Japanese War*. New York: Doubleday, 1925.

Gales, J. S. *The History of Korean People*. Seoul: Royal Asian Society, 1935.

Gradanzev, Andrew J. *Modern Korea*. New York: Institute of Pacific Relations, 1944.

Hahm, Pyomg-chon. *The Korean Political Tradition and Law*. Seoul: Hollym Co., 1967.

Harrington, Fred. *God, Mammon and the Japanese*. Madison: University of Wisconsin Press, 1944.

Hubert, Homer B. *The History of Korea*. 2 vols. Seoul: Royal Asia Society, 1905.

Kendall, C. W. *The Truth about Korea*. San Francisco: Korean National Association, 1919.

Kim, C. I. Eugene, and Kim, Han-kyo. *Korea and the Politics of Imperialism, 1876–1910*. Berkeley: University of California Press, 1967.

Lee, Chong-sik, *The Politics of Korean Nationalism*. Berkeley: University of California Press, 1963.

Lee, Hahn-Been. *Korea: Time, Change, and Administration*. Honolulu: East-West Center, 1967.

McCune, George M. *Korea Today*. Cambridge, Mass.: Harvard University Press, 1950.

Osgood, Cornelius. *The Koreans and Their Culture*. New York: Ronald Press, 1951.

Sunoo, Harold W. *Korea: A Political History in Modern Times*. Seoul: Kunkook University Press, 1970.

Books on the Syngman Rhee Regime and Korea War

Berger, Carl. *The Korea Knot: A Military Political History*. Philadelphia: University of Pennsylvania Press, 1967.

Cho Soon-Sung. *Korea in World Politics*. Berkeley: University of California Press, 1970.

Clark, Mark W. *From the Danube to the Yalu*. New York: Harper and Bros., 1954.

Henderson, Gregory. *Korea: The Politics of Vortex*. Cambridge, Mass.: Harvard University Press, 1968.

Lyons, Gene M. *Military Policy and Economic Aid: The Korean Case, 1950–1953*. Columbus: Ohio State University Press, 1954.

McCune, Shannon. *Korea: The Land of Broken Calm*. New York: Van Nostrand, 1966.

Oh, John K. C. *Korea: Democracy on Trial*. Ithaca: Cornell University Press, 1968.

Oliver, Robert T. *Syngman Rhee: The Man Behind the Myth*. New York: Dodd, Mead, 1954.

Sawyer, Robert. *Military Advisors in Korea: KMAG in Peace and War*. Washington, D.C.: Office of the Chief of Military History, 1962.

Spanier, John W. *The Truman-MacArthur Controversy and the Korean War*. Cambridge, Mass.: Harvard University Press, 1959.

Books on the Park Chung Hee Regime, Modernization, and Economic Development

Cole, D. C., and Lyman, P. N. *Korean Development: The Interplay of Politics and Economics*. Cambridge, Mass.: Harvard University Press, 1971.

Documents on the Struggle for Democracy in Korea. Tokyo: National Christian Council of Japan, 1975.

Kim, Kwang-Bong. *The Korea-Japan Treaty Crisis and the Instability of the Korean System*. New York: Praeger, 1971.

Kim, Se-Jin. *The Politics of Military Revolution in Korea*. Chapel Hill: University of North Carolina Press, 1971.

Kim, Se-Jin, and Cho, Chang hyun. *Government and Politics of Korea*. Silver Springs, Mo.: The Research Institute on Korean Affairs, 1972.

Letters from South Korea. Translated by David L. Swain. Tokyo: Iwanami Shoten, 1975.

Park, Chung Hee. *Our Nation's Path: Ideology of Social Reconstruction*. Seoul: Dong-A, 1962.

Sunoo, Harold Hakwon. *Repressive State and Resisting Church: The Politics of the CIA in South Korea*. Fayette, Mo.: Korean American Cultural Association, 1976.

Books on North Korea

Baik Bong. *Kim Il-song: Biography*. 3 vols. Tokyo: Miraisha, 1970.

Byong-sik, Kim. *Modern Korea*. New York: International Pub., 1970.

Chung, Joseph Sang hoon. *North Korea Economy: Structure and Development*. Stanford: Stanford University Press. 1972.

Il-sung, Kim. *For the Independent Peaceful Reunification of Korea*. New York: Guardian Associates, 1976.

Il-sung, Kim. *Revolution and Socialistic Construction in Korea*. New York: International Pub., 1971.

Kim, Il-Pyong. J. *Communist Politics in North Korea*. New York: Praeger, 1975.

Koh, Byung-chul. *The Foreign Policy of North Korea*. New York: Praeger, 1969.

Paige, Glenn D. *The Korean People's Democratic Republic*. Palo Alto: Hoover Institute, 1968.

Scalapino, Robert A., ed. *North Korea Today*. New York: Praeger, 1963.

Scalapino, Robert, and Chong-sik, Lee. *Communism in Korea*. 2 vols. Berkeley: University of California Press, 1972.

Suh, Dae-Suk. *Documents of Korean Communism*. Princeton, N. J.: Princeton University Press, 1971

Suh, Dae-Suk. *The Korean Communist Movement, 1918-1948*. Princeton, N.J.: Princeton University Press, 1968.

index